KEY TEXT
REFERENCE

Alternative Risk Transfer

Wiley Finance Series

Alternative Risk Transfer

Integrated Risk Management through Insurance, Reinsurance,
and the Capital Markets

Erik Banks

John Wiley & Sons, Ltd

Other Wiley Editorial Offices

John Wiley & Sons Inc., 111 River Street, Hoboken, NJ 07030, USA

Jossey-Bass, 989 Market Street, San Francisco, CA 94103-1741, USA

Wiley-VCH Verlag GmbH, Boschstr. 12, D-69469 Weinheim, Germany

John Wiley & Sons Australia Ltd, 33 Park Road, Milton, Queensland 4064, Australia

John Wiley & Sons (Asia) Pte Ltd, 2 Clementi Loop #02-01, Jin Xing Distripark, Singapore 129809

John Wiley & Sons Canada Ltd, 22 Worcester Road, Etobicoke, Ontario, Canada M9W 1L1

Wiley also publishes its books in a variety of electronic formats. Some content that appears
in print may not be available in electronic books.

Library of Congress Cataloging-in-Publication Data
Banks, Erik.
   Alternative risk transfer : integrated risk management through insurance, reinsurance, and the capital
   markets / Erik Banks.
      p.   cm. — (Wiley finance series)
   Includes bibliographical references and index.
   ISBN 0-470-85745-5 (Cloth : alk. paper)
   1. Finance.   2. Risk management.   3. Capital market.   4. Risk (Insurance)   5. Reinsurance.
   I. Title.   II. Series.
HG173 .B336 2004
658.15′5—dc22   2003025310

British Library Cataloguing in Publication Data

A catalogue record for this book is available from the British Library

ISBN 0-470-85745-5

Typeset in 10/12pt Times by TechBooks, New Delhi, India
Printed and bound in Great Britain by The Cromwell Press, Trowbridge, Wiltshire
This book is printed on acid-free paper responsibly manufactured from sustainable forestry
in which at least two trees are planted for each one used for paper production.

Contents

Acknowledgements

I would like to express my gratitude to various individuals for their help in making this project come to fruition. Specifically, great thanks are due to Samantha Whittaker, publishing editor at John Wiley & Sons, for her support on this, and various other, writing projects. Thanks go also to Patricia Morrison, publishing editor, and Carole Millett, editorial assistant, for help along the way. Thanks also go to Samantha Hartley, production editor, for her help in coordinating production of the book.

I would also like to acknowledge the valuable assistance provided by numerous individuals from various organizations, including the Insurance Services Office, Insurance Information Institute, XL Capital, and Merrill Lynch. They provided important input and information as the project developed.

And, most of all, my thanks to Milena.

E. Banks
Redding, CT
2003

Biography

Erik Banks has held senior risk management positions at several global financial institutions, including Partner and Chief Risk Officer of Bermuda reinsurer XL Capital's energy and weather derivatives subsidiary, and Managing Director of Corporate Risk Management at Merrill Lynch, where he spent 13 years managing credit risk, market risk and risk analytics/technology teams in Tokyo, Hong Kong, London and, latterly, New York. He received early bank training at Citibank and Manufacturers Hanover in New York. He is the author of a dozen books on risk management, emerging markets, derivatives, governance, and merchant banking.

Part I
Risk and the ART Market

1
Overview of Risk Management

Risk management is a dynamic and well-established discipline practiced by many companies around the world. Traditional forms of risk management – loss control, loss financing and risk reduction, arranged through mechanisms such as insurance and derivatives – have been actively used by companies for many decades, and are an essential element of most corporate strategies. But newer forms of risk protection – including those from the **alternative risk transfer**[1] (ART) market, the *combined risk management marketplace for innovative insurance and capital market solutions* – often surface as viable, flexible and cost-efficient options. In fact, some firms already use ART mechanisms to supplement their traditional risk management strategies; many others, however, have yet to take advantage of the benefits offered by the marketplace. Regardless of a firm's specific approach to risk management, it should always consider ART-related solutions so that it has complete knowledge of all available options and can make the best, most informed, decisions possible.

Our discussion in this book is on the ART market, its function, participants and products, its advantages and disadvantages, and its future prospects. Before considering the specifics of the marketplace, however, we review some of the essential concepts of risk and risk management; this helps to provide a proper framework for the material that follows. In the remainder of this chapter we explore issues related to risk and return, general risk management processes and techniques, and fundamental risk concepts and measures.

1.1 RISK AND RETURN

Risk is a broad, complex and vitally important topic that touches on virtually all aspects of modern corporate operation. Although we shall consider matters in greater detail as we progress through the text, we begin by defining **risk,** in its most general form, as *uncertainty associated with a future outcome or event*. To apply this more specifically to corporate activities, we can say that risk is the *expected variance in profits, losses, or cash flows* arising from an uncertain event. Other terms commonly associated with risk – such as peril and hazard – are often encountered in the risk management industry (indeed, we shall also use them throughout the text); they are, however, distinct. A **peril**, for instance, is a cause of loss, while a **hazard** is an event that creates, or increases, peril. While both have a bearing on risk, risk itself is a broader concept. Companies are exposed to a wide range of risks that might, at any time, include such things as business interruption, catastrophic and non-catastrophic property damage, product recall/liability, directors and officers liability, credit default/loss, workers compensation, environmental liability, and so on. These risks must be managed if the market value of the company is to be increased – or, at a minimum, if the probability of financial distress is be lowered. Some of the risks can be retained as part of core business operations, while others are best transferred elsewhere – but only when it is cost-effective to do so.

---

[1] Emboldened items are listed in the glossary.

We shall consider risks in more detail later, but we begin by classifying them broadly as operating risks and financial risks:

- **Operating risk**   The risk of loss arising from the daily physical (non-financial) operating activities of a firm.
- **Financial risk**   The risk of loss arising from the financial activities of a firm.

Operating and financial risks can be decomposed further. For example, within the general category of operating risks we can consider subclasses such as personal liability and commercial property/casualty liability. Within commercial property/casualty (P&C) liability we might differentiate between losses related to commercial property (direct/indirect), machinery, transportation (inland/marine), crime, commercial liability, commercial auto, workers compensation, and employers' liability. Similar decomposition is possible within the category of financial risks, where we might first divide exposures into credit risk, market risk, liquidity risk, and model risk. A category such as market risk might then be segregated into directional risk, volatility risk, time decay risk, curve risk, basis risk, spread risk, correlation risk, and so on.

We can also categorize financial and operating risks as being pure or speculative.

- **Pure risk**   A risk that only has the prospect of downside, i.e., loss.
- **Speculative risk**   A risk that has the possibility of upside or downside, i.e., gain or loss.

Regardless of the taxonomy, the central point is that risk comes in many forms, a factor that becomes apparent and important in the risk management process.

A company creates goods and services that it sells to clients in order to generate returns. These returns are used to expand business (e.g., internal funding via retained earnings) and compensate equity investors who have supplied the equity risk capital needed to fund productive assets (e.g., factories, machinery, intellectual property). Investors must be compensated for supplying risk capital. Generally speaking, they require returns related to the inherent riskiness of the company: the riskier the company, the greater the return (or **risk premium**) the investors demand. Whether a company is risky or not, however, investors will always seek the maximum possible return. This means a key corporate goal is the maximization of **enterprise value** (EV), which we define as the sum of a firm's expected future net cash flows (NCFs), discounted back to the present at an appropriate discount rate (e.g., risk-free rate plus relevant risk premium). We summarize this as:

$$EV = \sum_{t=1}^{n} \frac{NCF_t}{(1 + r)^t},$$

where NCF(t) is the expected net cash flow at time t, and r is the discount rate, comprising a risk-free rate $r(f)$ and a risk premium $r(p)$.

We shall explore this in more detail in Chapter 2, but note for the moment that expected NCFs can be impacted by the expected size, timing, and variability of cash flows. Risk can also change all three dimensions, meaning that it can alter the value of the firm. In fact, unexpected changes in NCF can be quite damaging to enterprise value, and protecting against such changes surfaces as one of the primary motivations for active risk management.

1.2   ACTIVE RISK MANAGEMENT

Companies need to control their exposure to risk in the normal course of business. While speculative risks can bring gains or losses, pure risks generate only losses. In either case, failure to focus on the potential downside through active risk management means that firms face financial uncertainty – to the possible detriment of shareholders, creditors, and other stakeholders who might be economically impacted if a firm becomes insolvent. Risk management is an important discipline because, unlike the world presented through pure corporate finance theory,[2] shareholders cannot effectively manage a firm's risks by themselves. Investors face information asymmetries, lack access to the same risk transfer mechanisms as a corporate entity (which faces lower friction costs), and cannot influence or control corporate investment policy. Accordingly, active risk management is not only desirable, but also necessary, if corporate value is to be maximized in practice.

There are, of course, many reasons why a company should actively, rather than passively, manage its risks. An active approach to risk management – centered on control, retention, transfer and/or hedging – can help to:

- provide funds when they are most needed, helping to ensure a liquid position and minimizing the possibility of **financial distress** – a state of financial weakness that might include a higher cost of capital, poorer supplier terms, lower liquidity, and departure of key personnel;
- lower cash flow volatility and minimize the disruption of investment plans;
- reduce the possibility of **underinvestment**, or the process of directing capital toward projects with lower returns and risks (to the benefit of creditors rather than equity investors);
- stabilize revenue streams and thus benefit from specific tax treatment (e.g., asymmetrical tax structures where firms with more volatile revenue and profit performance pay greater taxes);
- create more stable earnings, which often helps to generate higher stock price valuations.

It is increasingly common in the corporate world of the twenty-first century for companies to implement a risk management process to control risks. It is important to stress at the outset that the exercise relates to *controlling* risks, not *eliminating* them. This is an important distinction because risk is not inherently bad, and is not a variable that must be removed from corporate operations at any cost. As we shall see in subsequent chapters, there are times when it makes sense for a company to retain, and even increase, its risk exposure, as this helps to increase the value of the firm to shareholders. Instead, the focus is on controlling – that is, understanding and closely managing – risk exposures, so that stakeholders are fully aware of how the firm might be impacted. The essential element of controlling risks is ensuring that no surprises arise. Losses are acceptable if the possibility that they may occur is understood by stakeholders, and if the appropriate economic evaluation occurs. Indeed, risk is a game of chance: speculative risks will produce favorable outcomes and losses, pure risk events only losses. The risk-taking firm must expect both, and if it is controlling its exposures properly it is helping to increase its value. Unexpected losses that occur when the company and its stakeholders have no idea that the firm is exposed to particular types, or amounts, of risk, must be regarded as unacceptable; this essentially means that risk is not being controlled. The development and use of a formalized risk management process must therefore be a central part of overall corporate operations and governance.

---

[2] For instance, in a Modigliani and Miller framework.

1.2.1 Risk management processes

The standard **risk management process** can be seen as a four-stage process centered on identification, quantification, management, and reporting. Each element is a vital link in the chain and must be implemented correctly in order to be effective.

- **Risk identification**   The identification process centers on defining and identifying all of the firm's actual, perceived, or anticipated risks. In a large firm, this might encompass dozens of financial and operating risk drivers, implying a significant degree of complexity. In some cases risks are readily identifiable, at other times they are more difficult to discern. For instance, a firm that produces goods in the US for dollars and sells them in Japan for yen is exposed to changes in the $/¥ foreign exchange rate, and identifying this risk is relatively simple. Likewise, a company that has a factory located in the path of hurricanes can easily identify potential exposure to catastrophic damage. Alternatively, a firm that has to purchase power in the spot electricity market when temperatures rise above 95 °F is actually exposed to the absolute level of, and correlation between, electricity prices and temperature; in this case the different dimensions of exposure are somewhat more difficult to identify. This stage of the process is vital, of course, as failure to properly identify all financial or operating risks impacting the firm may lead to surprise losses (e.g., those coming from an 'unknown' source).

- **Risk quantification**   The quantification process determines the financial impact that risks can have on corporate operations. This is typically done through various quantitative tools. Returning to the $/¥ example, a company with a foreign exchange exposure will be interested in knowing, as precisely as possible, the impact of the risk on its profit and loss (P&L) account (e.g., a 5% decline in the value of the yen might produce a $5m loss). The company with a factory in the hurricane path may need to quantify a number of different types of scenarios, including smaller losses from temporary business interruption (e.g., if a hurricane causes damage that forces it to suspend operations for 2 months) to larger losses from total destruction (e.g., the hurricane destroys the facility beyond repair). Specific techniques for measuring the financial impact of risks vary widely, and depend largely on the nature of the underlying exposures. Some, such as credit and market risks, can be measured through financial mathematics based on analytic computation, closed-form pricing models, and simulation methods. Others, such as high-frequency insurance-related risks, can often be estimated by using actuarial techniques; certain low-frequency insurance exposures, such as catastrophic risks, may be modeled through simulation.

- **Risk management**   After risks have been identified and quantified, they must be managed. Through the core process of active decision-making, a firm must decide whether it will control, retain, eliminate or expand its exposures. For instance, a firm may decide that it is comfortable retaining a potential loss (or gain) of $10m on its $/¥ foreign exchange exposure and will constrain it at that level; alternatively, if it wants to face zero chance of loss, it might eliminate the risk entirely (for a price). Similarly, the potential cost of sustaining partial or complete destruction as a result of a powerful hurricane may be too great for the firm, so it might decide to transfer the exposure entirely. Risk management decisions ultimately depend on several variables, including the financial resources of the firm, the operating philosophy of management, the expectations of shareholders, and the costs and benefits of various risk strategies. We consider these points in the section below.

- **Risk monitoring**   Once the firm has decided how it wants to manage its risk profile, it must actively monitor its exposures. This means regularly tracking and reporting both risks

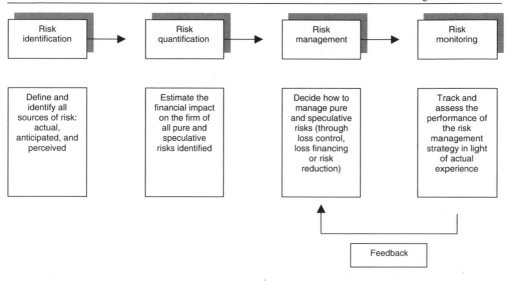

Figure 1.1 The generic risk management process

and risk decision experience, and communicating information internally and externally so that interested parties (e.g., executive management, board directors, regulators, creditors and investors) are aware of any possible upside or downside. Good monitoring is especially important for internal decision-makers, who require feedback in order to assess, and even adjust, their decisions. Thus, the $/¥ exposure that the firm has chosen to retain must be measured and reported regularly (e.g., daily, weekly) so that managers are aware of its size and potential impact as the market moves and the risk position changes. The catastrophic hurricane exposure, which is unlikely to change very often (unless the firm expands or contracts the size of its factories), must still be monitored and reported, but less frequently. An important by-product of the risk-monitoring process is the ability to change how risks are managed; without such visibility, a firm's risk strategies remain static. Monitoring thus feeds back into management.

We shall revisit aspects of this generic risk process (summarized in Figure 1.1) at greater length in the next few chapters, but for the moment let us expand on the third stage of the process below by considering specific management alternatives available to a company with financial or operating risks.

1.2.2 Risk management techniques

A company with any degree of risk exposure is wise to develop a philosophy that explicitly indicates its approach to risk and the resources it is willing to allocate (and potentially lose) in its endeavors. Best practice governance calls for a firm's board of directors to clearly express risk tolerance (or appetite) by relating exposures to overall corporate goals, stakeholder expectations, and financial/technical resources. Firms that are in business primarily to take risks, and have the financial resources to support potentially large losses, might choose to take a large amount of financial and operating risk. For instance, a bank might assume a considerable amount of credit and market risk as the core of its operation; given sufficient financial resources per controls, it should be able to actively retain and manage such exposures. Those that are in business primarily to produce goods or services that are not based on active risk-taking, or those that lack sufficient financial resources to absorb large losses, are unlikely to favor significant risk exposure. For instance, a company that produces automobiles might be exposed to a series of input risks, such as steel and rubber; these form part of the core business and the board might wish to manage them by retaining them or hedging a portion of them. However, in order not to be distracted from its primary operations, it may not want to assume any risks related to non-core business activities, such as foreign exchange risk from sourcing raw materials or selling completed automobiles in other countries; these might not only be a distraction, but they might fall outside the firm's technical expertise. Assuming that the costs of doing so are consistent with its risk/return goals, the company may eliminate non-core risks.

It is common to consider three broad approaches to the management of risks, including loss control, loss financing, and risk reduction.

- **Loss control** Under this process (sometimes also referred to as loss prevention) a firm takes necessary *precautions* in order to reduce the threat of a particular risk. For instance, to diminish the likelihood of financial damage arising from a fire within a factory, a company might install a sprinkler system. Alternatively, a company dealing with hazardous material might reduce the chance of worker injury by introducing a comprehensive safety program. Loss control techniques vary by form of risk and potential threat, but typically involve an upfront investment and/or ongoing cost (e.g., paying for the sprinkler system, training personnel in safety procedures). As we shall see, the costs and benefits must be weighed in order to arrive at an appropriate decision.
- **Loss financing** This broad category of risk techniques, which involves the *transfer*, *retention*, or *hedging* of exposures, is primarily concerned with ensuring the availability of funds in the event of a loss. For instance, rather than installing a sprinkler system, a firm may choose to protect against potential fire damage by transferring risk through the purchase of an insurance policy that provides compensation if a fire occurs. Alternatively, the company exposed to $/¥ foreign exchange risk might purchase a currency option as a hedge. Or, if a company feels that its risk exposures are particularly 'well-behaved' – reasonable in size and predictable with some degree of certainty – it may retain a portion. There are special instances where a company might choose to bundle together various techniques to produce a hybrid, or customized, solution. For instance, it might want to retain a portion of its $/¥ risk and transfer the balance through a hedge, or it might wish to combine disparate risks – such as its property exposure from fire risk and its $/¥ risk – into a single transfer mechanism. In fact, the hybrid management of risk is a cornerstone of the ART market, as well shall discover in later chapters. Regardless of the specific technique used, the relative costs of retention, transfer, hedging, or some hybrid must be weighed against possible benefits before a decision can be made.
- **Risk reduction** In some instances the risks may be too idiosyncratic or misaligned for a company to consider loss control or loss-financing methods. Accordingly, it might employ *risk reduction* techniques that involve partial or complete *withdrawal* from a business with particular characteristics or the *diversification* of exposures through a pooling or portfolio concept. Either can lead to a reduction in risk levels. Again, the risk reduction process has an associated cost and must therefore be considered in the cost/benefit framework before a decision is taken.

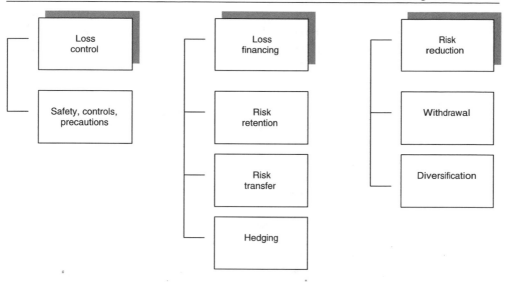

Figure 1.2   Risk management techniques

Risk exposures that are not eliminated must be managed through retention, transfer or financing (while loss control measures may be beneficial, they are generally applied to risks that are retained, e.g., loss control measures are more likely to be dependent on retention levels rather than vice versa). In fact, the general category of loss financing is a major focus of active risk management. Loss-financing techniques – including use of retained earnings, self-insurance, captives, contingent capital, and so on – can be managed from an internal or external perspective and may be funded or unfunded prior to a loss. We shall discuss a number of these techniques in subsequent chapters, as they form an essential part of the ART market. Figure 1.2 summarizes some common **risk management techniques**.

In practice, financial and non-financial corporations can turn to a range of instruments to execute active risk management strategies. Firms often use a combination of tools and may even bundle them together in order to produce a more efficient and cost-effective solution. For instance, an insurance company, which is in the business of underwriting risks, must manage its own risk profile actively and continuously, and may do so by:

- retaining some amount of risk, after having assessed the likelihood of loss and charged an appropriate premium (that covers expected losses and provides a fair return);
- identifying risks where it feels it must raise premiums in order to compensate for increased risks;
- ceasing to underwrite risks where it does not feel it is earning a proper return;
- creating additional reserves to cover unexpected losses;
- diversifying its portfolio further by expanding its underwriting efforts into new, uncorrelated, and profitable markets;
- purchasing reinsurance cover for portions of its portfolio from a reinsurer;
- issuing an insurance-linked security or structuring a contingent capital facility to provide additional funded or unfunded cover.

There are obviously many possibilities to consider that are applicable to both industrial and financial corporations, and most sectors enjoy access to multiple risk management solutions.

Each scheme has specific costs and benefits, but many can be applied in the structuring of an appropriate risk management program. In many cases it takes time to reshape the risk characteristics of a portfolio of businesses, and although some solutions can be enacted quickly, processes such as increasing premium rates, diversifying a portfolio or issuing an insurance-linked security might take several months (or longer). Therefore, companies must always be aware of the time dimension of the risk management process.

A convenient "rule of thumb" related to risk management techniques suggests that core risks – those that are central to a firm's daily business – should be retained, while non-core risks – those that are a byproduct of daily business – should be transferred or hedged. The premise is that a company has information and expertise regarding its core risks and, therefore, greater ability to manage its exposures intelligently (e.g., safely, efficiently, and cost-effectively). Exposure to risks where it lacks knowledge or competitive advantage can be more dangerous and costly. The generalization is interesting, but is complex and often nebulous. For instance, should an aircraft manufacturer view the price of steel, one of its key inputs, as a core or non-core risk? If it is a core risk should it actively retain and manage the exposure by dedicating resources and time to the effort? Should it transfer, hedge or eliminate a core risk if there is a remote possibility of an excessively large loss? If it is a non-core risk should the firm ignore the price of steel by simply locking in a price for future steel delivery, or should it be more dynamic about its hedging? Many other issues can obviously influence the decision, so the rule of thumb may be seen as somewhat simplistic.

In fact, while the core/non-core distinction may be applicable in some instances, it may not necessarily result in the best decision for every company in every scenario. The risk management decision process is complicated and must generally be considered through a rigorous analytical framework, such as a cost/benefit analysis. This can help a company to determine how it should manage its individual and aggregate risk exposures in order to max-imize value (which, as we shall note in Chapter 2, is a general corporate goal). The cost/benefit tradeoff, characteristic of every risk-related decision a firm must make, is straight-forward:

• Pay a cost and gain a benefit by eliminating or reducing NCF uncertainty.
• Pay nothing but accept the NCF uncertainty and remain exposed to potential cash flow volatility.

Since every risk has a theoretical price, it is possible to create a risk-free company by paying all the costs associated with eliminating every aspect of risk (e.g., through premiums, safety measures, diversification, withdrawal from businesses, and so on); the uncertainty associated with expected NCFs will then be eliminated. This, as we shall note later, is likely to be prohibitively expensive and impractical, and will almost certainly not result in a maximization of enterprise value. Accordingly, risk management solutions, consistent with the firm's appetite and philosophy, must focus on the tradeoffs between costs and benefits; only when this is thoroughly understood can a solution that leads toward enterprise value maximization be developed.

1.2.3 General risk management considerations

Risk management is concerned with the best and most efficient way of coping with financial and operating uncertainties. When crafting a risk strategy, firms often consider the process in two different stages: pre-loss management and post-loss management. **Pre-loss management** prepares a firm for possible losses in a way that maximizes corporate value and covers legal and contractual obligations. **Post-loss management** ensures that a firm operates as a "going concern" with stable earnings and a minimal possibility of financial distress. The techniques we discuss in this book can be categorized as pre-loss or post-loss risk management tools.

The corporate governance process demands that a company, in fulfilling its responsibilities to shareholders, consider and define its tolerance for operating and financial risks. Directors must ensure that executives and independent control functions monitor, manage, and control exposures on an ongoing basis. In addition, shareholders must be made aware of the risks the company is retaining, eliminating, or transferring.

As noted earlier, a key element of the process is the firm's definition of a **risk philosophy**, a statement that reflects the firm's objectives related to the management of risk. Ideally, this should correlate with the specific type and amount of exposure the firm intends to take, retain, transfer, or reduce. For instance, in a pre-loss state a company might want to implement a risk management strategy that allows it to reduce the possibility of financial catastrophe, meet regulatory requirements, and operate more efficiently. In a post-loss state a company may want to ensure that its strategy allows it to operate as a going concern, and to continue expanding revenues and stabilize earnings.

We shall see throughout the course of the text that there are many ways of considering and managing risks, and the construction of a standard 'template' to fit every situation is simply not feasible. All companies are different. They engage in a wide range of businesses, have unique financial profiles and mandates, and are subject to unique internal and external pressures – meaning that there is no universal paradigm when it comes to creating a risk management program. We can therefore propose only general approaches to the management of risks for a generic 'risk averse' company. In particular, we note that it is often advantageous from a cost/benefit perspective for a firm exposed to low-frequency risks (i.e., those that are highly improbable) and low-severity risks (i.e., those with a small financial impact) to simply retain the exposures and fund them as losses occur (or fund them in advance through a self-insurance fund). Low-frequency but high-severity risks (i.e., infrequent, but with a large financial impact) are often good candidates for some type of loss financing (e.g., insurance, hedging). High-frequency but low-severity risks (i.e., those that are highly probable but not especially damaging) can often be accommodated via loss prevention and/or loss retention programs. High frequency and high severity risks (i.e., highly likely and highly damaging risks that can lead a company into financial distress) must typically be avoided. Although these are simple generalizations, they will help to focus our discussion at various points in the text. Table 1.1 and Figure 1.3 summarize these guidelines.

Table 1.1   Generalized risk management guidelines

Frequency	Severity	Guideline
Low	Low	Retention
Low	High	Loss financing (insure, hedge)
High	Low	Prevention, retention
High	High	Avoidance

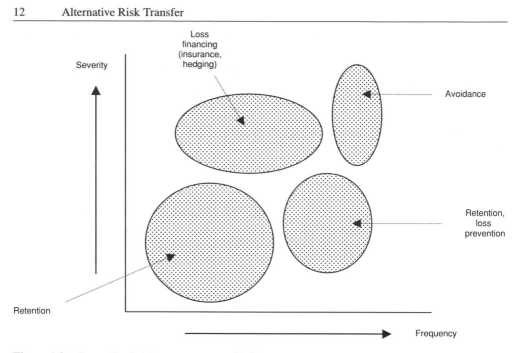

Figure 1.3   Generalized risk management guidelines

1.3   RISK CONCEPTS

To further frame aspects of our discussion we introduce several fundamental risk concepts in this section. This will assist in the chapters that follow when we consider the specific benefits provided by a variety of risk management instruments and techniques. Risk concepts can quickly become highly technical (with a great deal of intricate mathematics and statistics) but we have chosen to focus our discussion on basic ideas; readers interested in a detailed, technical treatment of these topics may wish to consult the references listed at the end of the book.

1.3.1   Expected value and variance

We begin with the concept of a **random variable**, which is simply a variable with an uncertain outcome. The variable can be discrete (appearing at specified time intervals) or continuous (appearing at any time), and may carry a defined value or any value at all; the result of a fair coin toss is thus a random variable with one of two possible values. By drawing many samples of random variables we can create a distribution that identifies all possible outcomes and their probability of occurrence. Distributions can take different shapes, but we shall concentrate primarily on the normal distribution, with its traditional bell shape. All the information regarding a random variable is summarized in the statistical distribution, which then becomes a useful tool when trying to estimate, *ex-ante*, the possibility of some event occurring. For instance, we can use statistical properties to obtain information about the likelihood that a particular event (e.g., a loss) will occur and the magnitude of the event that occurs.

Expected value (EV), the value that is obtained given a certain probability of occurrence, is a central element of statistics and of considerable use in risk evaluation. EV is determined

Probability

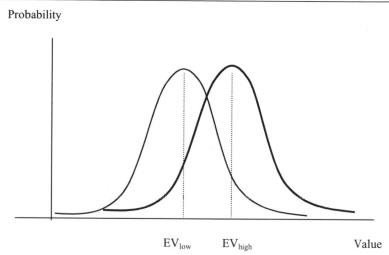

EV_{low} EV_{high} Value

Figure 1.4   Distributions and expected values

by multiplying the probability of occurrence by the outcome of an event; in risk management terms this is often summarized as frequency (probability) times severity (outcome). More formally, we can say

$$EV = (\text{Probability} \times \text{Outcome}) + ((1 - \text{Probability}) \times \text{Outcome})$$

or

$$EV = \sum_{i=1}^{N} x_i \, p_i$$

where x_i is the outcome and p_i is the probability.

Thus, a payoff of \$80 occurring with 20% probability, and a payoff of \$100 occurring with 80% probability generates an EV of \$96. The EV of a probability distribution provides information of average outcomes. A distribution with a higher EV will have a higher outcome, on average, than one with a lower EV; this relationship, for a normal distribution, is depicted in Figure 1.4.

From a pure risk perspective we can create a probability distribution that focuses strictly on losses; the EV of the loss distribution is equivalent to the **expected loss**. Creating a loss distribution can be done through historical loss experience (this is possible for insurance companies and other financial intermediaries with a long history of risk management data) but still demands considerable geographic depth and breadth. Alternatively, certain simulation techniques or non-statistical estimates (e.g., those that might be found via technical or economic studies) can be used.

Next we introduce the **variance** (or standard deviation, which is equal to the square root of the variance); this is a measure of the magnitude by which an outcome differs from the EV and is given as:

$$Var = \text{Probability} \times (\text{Outcome} - EV)^2$$

or

$$\text{Var} = \sum_{i=1}^{N} p_i (x_i - \mu)^2$$

where μ is the expected value and all other terms are as defined above.

Standard deviation is simply:

$$\text{SD} = \sqrt{\text{Var}}$$

When variance is low, the actual outcome is likely to be close to the EV, and when it is high it may be quite far away and difficult to predict. Not surprisingly, since variance is a measure of the difference between actual and expected outcomes, it serves as an important measure of risk – indeed, it reflects variability against expectations, which is the essence of risk. Standard deviation is useful when we are trying to consider the likelihood that an observation will lie within a particular range of values. Using the normal distribution, an observation falling within ±1 standard deviation is expected to occur 68% of the time; ±1.96 standard deviations includes 95% of observations, and so on. With this information we can construct a loss distribution to determine possible losses arising from risky activities, adjusted to a specified statistical confidence level (e.g., 90%, 95%, 99%). It is also possible to compute the **probability of ruin**, or the chance that the distribution of average losses will exceed a solvency benchmark value (e.g., some minimum surplus or tangible net worth amount); this, again, is an important measure in risk management.

Since representation of an entire population of observations is not realistic, we need to rely on smaller samples; accordingly, we use the sample mean (μ) and sample standard deviation (σ) as appropriate representations. Assuming that the correct sampling techniques are used, then the greater the sample size the narrower the range of error at particular statistical confidence intervals. Figure 1.5 summarizes the normal distribution, expected value, and standard deviation parameters.

Statistical loss forecasting, which is an important dimension of risk management, can be accomplished through probability analysis, regression analysis, loss distribution analysis, and other techniques. For instance, probability analysis focuses on the number of events that could give rise to risk exposure and considers the dependence/independence characteristics associated with each. We shall consider this at greater length in the risk-pooling example below. Regression analysis makes use of historical data to determine how a dependent variable is impacted by a series of independent variables (e.g., damage to a fleet of automobiles (dependent variable) based on the number of inches of snow or rain (independent variable)).

1.3.2   Risk aversion

Risk aversion is characteristic of a company that prefers less, rather than more, risk, and is willing to pay a price for protection (via reduction, transfer, hedging). The existence of risk aversion can be demonstrated by the demand for insurance and other risk mitigants: individuals and institutions are willing to pay for risk management because they are averse, to varying degrees, to the risk of loss. If risk aversion did not exist, there would be no willingness to pay for mitigation; individuals and firms would simply bear the risk of loss to which they were exposed.

Probability

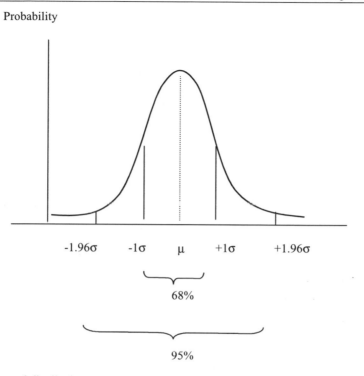

-1.96σ   -1σ   μ   +1σ   +1.96σ

68%

95%

Figure 1.5   Normal distribution

We know that the greater the variability in potential outcomes, the greater the risk; this stems primarily from lack of *ex-ante* knowledge about the outcome that will occur. In the absence of risk, decision-making is simple: outcomes that generate the highest value are preferred and the rational firm will select the outcome that yields the greatest EV. Relating EV to the economic concept of **expected utility**, or the weighted average utility value (e.g., satisfaction from income or wealth) derived from some activity, we can consider the law of diminishing marginal utility, which indicates that the utility derived from an incremental (or marginal) unit of wealth begins to diminish at some point. The risk averse firm faces a concave utility function, such as depicted in Figure 1.6, and will attempt to protect against risk of loss if the **risk premium**, or protection payment, it must pay is less than or equal to the EV of the loss. The expected utility of not protecting appears as a point below the utility function; if the risk premium is no greater than the EV of the loss, then acquiring protection will move the expected utility point of the risk averse firm up to the frontier of the curve. As a result of the concave utility function, parties that are risk averse demonstrate a willingness to pay to avoid risk that would jeopardize wealth. They may choose to do so through any of the risk management techniques summarized above, including loss control, loss financing, and risk reduction. Knowing this, it should be clear that the risk-seeking firm faces a convex utility function, as the marginal utility of wealth increases as wealth increases.

While utility functions can be interesting to consider in a theoretical sense, they are seldom used in practical corporate risk management applications as constructing a meaningful utility function is challenging, if not impossible. However, the notion of the risk averse firm is fundamental to the working of the risk management markets.

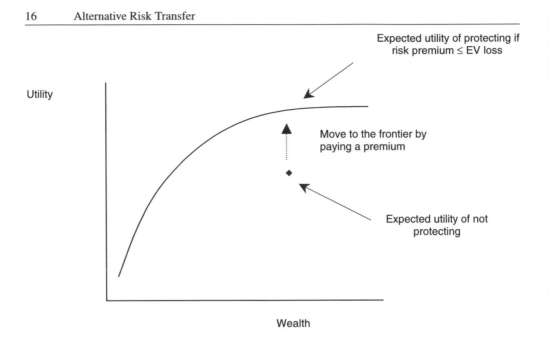

Figure 1.6   Risk premium and utility of a risk averse firm

1.3.3   Risk transfer and the insurance mechanism

The insurance market is premised on two fundamental characteristics: the transfer of exposure from a single party to a broad group, and the sharing of losses by all those in the group. **Risk transfer**, as the name suggests, occurs when one party pays a second party a small, certain cost (e.g., a risk premium) in exchange for coverage of uncertain losses; this is equal to a shifting of exposures. The risk averse firm, in creating its risk philosophy, may decide to shed an exposure by transferring it through one of several different mechanisms, including insurance/reinsurance, derivatives or hybrid structures. The amount of risk that a firm transfers is a function of overall tolerance (i.e., its level of risk aversion), the specific benefits it hopes to derive, and the total cost; this is often determined in a cost/benefit analysis framework.

An insurer can generally predict, within fairly tight ranges, the amount of losses that will occur for a given type of risk exposure. A large sample improves the estimate of the underlying probability of occurrence. Thus, when an insurer has a very large portfolio of relatively homogeneous policies, its ability to estimate losses improves. The process works on the basis of two statistical principles: the **Law of Large Numbers**, which indicates that as the number of participants (N) gets very large, the average outcome approaches the EV; and the **Central Limit Theorem**, which indicates that the distribution of the average outcome approaches the normal distribution as N gets very large.[3]

An **insurance contract** is an agreement between two parties (the insurer, as protection provider, and the **cedant** (also known as insured, beneficiary), as protection purchaser) that exchanges an *ex-ante* premium for an *ex-post* claim, with no ability to readjust the claim amount once it has been agreed. Insurance contracts are governed by the principle of **indemnity**,

---

[3] With mean μ and standard deviation $\sigma / \sqrt{N}$.

which indicates that the cedant cannot profit from its insurance activities; that is, insurance exists to cover a loss, not to generate a speculative profit. Coverage can be created through an **indemnity contract** (covering actual losses sustained) or a **valued contract** (covering a specific amount agreed upfront). A contract covering actual fire damage is an example of an indemnity contract, while a life insurance policy paying out a stated amount on death of the cedant is a valued contract. In order for a contract to qualify as insurance, the cedant must generally demonstrate an **insurable interest** – that is, it must prove that it has suffered an economic loss once the defined event occurs. Insurable interest exists to reduce or prevent gambling and moral hazard (as discussed below). An insurer, as cedant, may seek protection through a **reinsurance contract**; likewise, a reinsurer can obtain protection from another reinsurer through a **retrocession contract**.

A company may opt for **full insurance** (complete coverage of a risk exposure in exchange for a higher risk premium), or **partial insurance** (fractional coverage of risk for a lower risk premium). A cedant can create partial insurance by including a **deductible** (a 'first loss' amount paid by the cedant before the insurer makes a payment), a **coinsurance** feature (a 'shared loss' component between cedant and insurer), and/or a **policy cap** (a maximum amount payable by the insurer). We shall consider these, and associated technical details, in Chapter 4.

If it is economically sensible for the firm to pay the larger risk premium to secure full insurance (and consistent with its risk philosophy), it will do so. Alternatively, it may select from one of the partial insurance options. When a firm can clearly identify an optimal EV loss scenario that is preferable, the choice of protection becomes relatively straightforward. However, it is possible to create a range of full and partial insurance options with EV loss rankings; in such cases a firm needs to examine its utility function to determine whether one option dominates. In practice, since it is difficult for a company facing a complex set of businesses with varying priorities and goals to know the slope of its utility function, it must turn to alternative techniques (e.g., a cost/benefit review, a mean-variance analysis that takes specific account of variance/standard deviation and does not require *ex-ante* identification of a utility function, and similar "practical" measures).

1.3.4 Diversification and risk pooling

Diversification – a spreading or diffusion of risk exposures – is a common technique of risk management that seeks to lower risk by combining exposures that are not related (correlated) to one another. Much of this work has its foundation in Markowtiz' 1952 work related to capital markets portfolio theory, which demonstrates how diversification permits the risk averse investor to create portfolios that optimize various levels of risk and return. The intent is to create a portfolio on the **efficient frontier**, or the boundary that provides the maximum possible return for a given level of risk. Any portfolio that is below the efficient frontier fails to maximize value for a given level of risk, and can be enhanced through diversification (note also that superior portfolios of risk/return, along the "capital markets line" can be obtained by borrowing and lending at the risk-free rate).[4]

---

[4] From a pure investment perspective, an investor must look at the individual μ and σ of each security, as well as the correlation between the two, to determine how to construct an optional portfolio that minimizes risk and maximizes return. When all possible combinations of weighted portfolios have been found, the efficient frontier can be created. Portfolios on the efficient frontier represent the best possible tradeoffs between risk and return; those below the frontier are suboptimal (e.g., too much risk for a given return). Borrowing or lending an unlimited amount at some risk-free rate $r(f)$ means the investor can invest in both risky and non-risky securities and create leveraged portfolios that are better than those on the efficient frontier, regardless of the level of risk aversion; the "capital markets line" depicts these. Thus, investors that are risk averse can do better holding part of their capital in X and lending at $r(f)$.

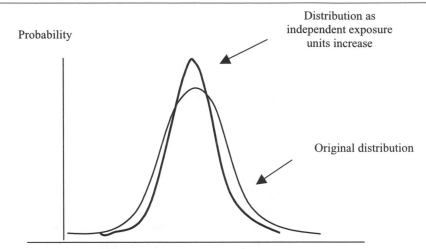

Probability

Distribution as
independent exposure
units increase

Original distribution

Figure 1.7   Distribution changes with independent exposure units

Risk pooling – a practical implementation of diversification and a fundamental mechanism of the risk management markets – is based on the idea that independent risks can be combined to reduce the overall level of risk. In addition to the Law of Large Numbers and CLT cited above, pooling relies on correlation to measure how random variables – i.e., individual risk exposure units, such as insurance policies – relate to one another. Correlation between two random variables, formally defined as the covariance of the two variables divided by the standard deviation of each one,[5] is measured on a scale of $+1$ to -1, where $+1$ implies perfect positive correlation and -1 perfect negative correlation; a correlation of 0 implies no relationship, indicating that the variables are independent. Thus, if two random variables have a correlation of $+0.7$, a movement of $+1$ in one leads to a movement of $+0.7$ in the other. Risk pooling reduces risks if expected losses are uncorrelated; when this occurs there is no change in the expected loss (or cost) but there is a reduction in the standard deviation. Consider the following simple example:

An automobile driver (A) has a 20% probability of being in an accident that will cost $2500. By the equations introduced earlier, the EV is $500 (e.g., $(80\% \times \$0) + (20\% \times \$2500)$) and the standard deviation is $1000 (e.g., $80\% \times (0 - 500)^2 + 20\% \times (2500 - 500)^2$). Assume

Those who are more aggressive can borrow at $r(f)$ and invest in X. Accordingly, all investors choose the same portfolio, but vary the level of financing.

Let us assume that an insurance company has individual units of risk exposure (e.g., individual policies) that are independently exposed to the risk of loss; thus, if a loss occurs on one policy, it need not necessarily occur on others. Each unit of risk exposure has some probability of loss, and the sum of all units represents the insurance company's total liability. The statistical distribution of the entire group of independent risk units depends on the distribution of each individual unit (which might take any specific form); however, if they are truly independent, then the distribution of the average loss (e.g., all units of exposure) approaches the normal distribution. This means that we can draw some conclusions about the expected loss and variance of loss. In particular, as the number of units increases to some large number N, the actual loss experience approaches the expected loss experience, and the variance around the expected loss declines, as illustrated in Figure 1.7. This means that if an insurer can diversify its risks sufficiently (i.e., if it can create enough independent risk units), it can reduce the riskiness of its operations. In practice, the degree of independence is measured through correlation and is implemented through pooling techniques. Pooling is applicable to a broad range of risk classes; while it is commonly associated with risks arising from automobile accidents, worker safety, or health claims, it is equally applicable to financial risks, such as credit risks generated by corporate loans (indeed, insurers have become key players in the credit risk transfer market through their application of these techniques). The properties of a portfolio of risk exposure units are different from the sum of the individual units, so a focus on portfolio characteristics is important. If a firm has only a small number of units the portfolio risk profile will not change markedly, and the number of risk units is therefore a key driver in diversification. However, some benefit will still accrue if N is not particularly large, as long as the units are not perfectly correlated.

[5] More formally, $\rho(x, y) = \mathrm{Cov}(x, y)/(\sigma(x)\sigma(y))$, where $\mathrm{Cov}(x, y)$ is $\Sigma p((x - \mu(x)) \times (y - \mu(y)))$.

Table 1.2   Accident scenarios

Accident claim	Cost ($)	Cost per driver ($)	Probability (%)
0	0	0	$80 \times 80 = 64$
1 (A)	2500	1250	$20 \times 80 = 16$
1 (B)	2500	1250	$20 \times 80 = 16$
2 (A and B)	5000	2500	$20 \times 20 = 4$

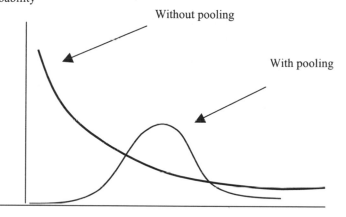

Figure 1.8   Pooling and costs

that another driver (B) faces the same accident parameters, and that driving events/behavior are uncorrelated (i.e., an accident by A will not lead to an accident by B, and vice versa). Under a pooling concept, both drivers agree to share the costs of an accident equally. Thus, if A has an accident he will only pay $1250 (B will pay the balance), and vice versa. We can now summarize various accident scenarios and costs in Table 1.2.

Through pooling, the probability distribution of costs for each participant has changed and the standard deviation, as a proxy of risk, has declined. For instance, a loss of $2500 now occurs 4% instead of 20% of the time, since two accidents, rather than just one, must happen. It is easy to extend the logic and demonstrate that the more participants in the pool, the lower the risk – as long as the exposures of the participants are not correlated. In addition, the probability of extreme outcomes declines. Risk pooling is not a risk transfer mechanism, but a risk reduction method, as long as the events are uncorrelated. If exposures are positively correlated to some degree, risk reduction is still possible, although it will not be as great (i.e., diversification helps but the beneficial effects are limited); when they are strongly positive, little (or no) benefit can be obtained. When exposures are negatively correlated they will not reduce risk to the same degree as independent exposures, but they can be used as 'counter cyclic covers' (and thus have favorable risk reduction characteristics). Summarizing, then, we note that when losses are uncorrelated, the risk in the pool (as measured by standard deviation) approaches zero as the number of pool participants increases; when losses are perfectly correlated risk remains unchanged. Figure 1.8 illustrates the effects of costs borne by each party with and without pooling.

It is worth noting that while risk transfer and pooling are often considered jointly when discussing insurance techniques, they are not synonymous or, indeed, mutually dependent. That is, in transferring risk, pooling can occur, but may not be necessary. For instance, there are times when an insurance company will accept a risk that it does not pool with others. Risk transfer, in contrast, must occur; that is the essence of the insurance mechanism.

1.3.5 Hedging

Insurance is generally associated with the transfer of an insurable risk and can result in a reduction of exposure. **Hedging**, in contrast, is generally associated with risks that are uninsurable through a standard contractual insurance framework, and typically result in transfer rather than reduction. Through hedging a firm transfers named risks to another party (via standard agreements rather than the more complex contracts that characterize insurance dealings). **Derivatives**, or financial transactions that derive their value from a market reference, are commonly used to hedge financial risks. They may be traded on a standardized basis through an exchange (as a listed contract) or in customized form through the over-the-counter (OTC) market. Unlike insurance contracts, derivatives represent an optionable, rather than an insurable, interest, meaning that a party to a contract does not need to be exposed to risk of loss. This suggests that derivatives can generate profits, and can be used to speculate rather than hedge. Derivatives are available in the form of:

- **Futures**   Standardized exchange contracts that enable participants to buy or sell an underlying asset at a predetermined forward price.
- **Forwards**   Customized off-exchange contracts that permit participants to buy or sell an underlying asset at a predetermined forward price.
- **Swaps**   Customized off-exchange contracts that enable participants to exchange periodic flows based on an underlying reference.
- **Options**   Standardized exchange or customized off-exchange contracts that grant the buyer the right, but not the obligation, to buy or sell an underlying asset at a predetermined strike price.

Insurance and derivatives have different features that can make one or the other more suitable in a given situation. For instance:

- Derivative contracts are linked to specific market references (or indexes) and are not limited by a cap or subject to the indemnity principle. Since derivatives are generally related to an index rather than a specific loss exposure, they are subject to **basis risk**, or the risk of loss arising from an imperfect match between the loss-making exposure and the compensatory hedge payment (as we discuss at greater length below). Derivatives are typically valued (e.g., marked-to-market) on a periodic basis and can often be traded/transferred between counterparties; in some instances credit exposures arising between two derivative parties are secured by collateral.
- Insurance contracts are based on specific losses or agreed amounts and are generally capped at an upper limit. Cedants must disclose all relevant information in "utmost good faith" through insurance documents and prove an insurable interest in order to make the contract valid and enforceable. Since most insurance contracts are related to specific risks, they

feature no basis risk (but there are some exceptions, as we shall note later). Insurance is not traded or marked-to-market, and credit exposures (i.e., those where the cedant is exposed to the credit of the insurer) are not generally secured.

Given these differences, derivatives are often more suitable when information about risk is well known, or where a company's exposure can be well correlated with a reference index (i.e., basis risk is not a concern). Insurance might be more suitable when the insured has private information about a particular risk exposure and the loss cannot easily be correlated to an external index. Ultimately, however, the relative costs and benefits (e.g., fees, premiums, bid-offer spreads, tax benefits, post-loss financial benefits) are likely to be the most decisive factors.

1.3.6   Moral hazard, adverse selection and basis risk

We now consider several additional concepts that are prevalent in the risk management markets, including moral hazard, adverse selection and basis risk. In its simplest form **moral hazard** can be regarded as a change in behavior arising from the presence of insurance or other forms of risk protection.[6] Theory and practice suggest that the availability of a compensatory payment in the event of loss removes a firm's incentive to behave prudently. For instance, a firm might be exposed to the risk of fire in its operations; if fire strikes its factory and destroys its equipment, it will be unable to produce its goods and thus suffer a loss of sales revenue. Accordingly, it may purchase a policy that covers losses attributable to fire damage. Once in possession of the policy, however, it may behave more carelessly – perhaps leaving flammable material on the factory floor, not upgrading its fire extinguishers and sprinklers when they become outdated, and so on. It will do so because it knows that it is protected: the insurance policy will cover any fire-related losses, so it no longer needs to be too careful. The same behavior can be found in many other types of risk exposure/risk protection schemes and is often a key concern of intermediaries providing alternative forms of risk protection. To combat moral hazard, insurance firms and other financial institutions providing protection modify the terms of their coverage to ensure that the firm bears some of the economic loss. This can occur through use of deductibles (e.g., the cedant bears the first losses, either per event or in aggregate), co-payments/coinsurance (e.g., the cedant and insurer share losses on some pre-arranged basis) or policy caps (e.g., the insurer limits the amount of cover granted to the cedant). Moral hazard may also be explicitly or implicitly priced into the premium, becoming a cost of risk borne by the company and its shareholders.

Adverse selection is defined as the mispricing of risk as a result of information asymmetries, and occurs when a protection provider cannot clearly distinguish between different classes of risk. The end result is that the protection provider supplies too much or too little risk cover at a given price, leading ultimately to an excess of losses or dearth of business. For instance, if an insurer is unable to distinguish between the risk characteristics of two groups of cedants – a high-risk group and a low-risk group – one of two scenarios will emerge: it will price all risk at the low-loss level, meaning that the high-loss group will purchase large quantities of

---

[6] Moral hazard is generally associated with *ex-ante* behavior, and might be considered *ex-ante* moral hazard (e.g., failing to take actions to prevent losses knowing that insurance coverage exists). There is also a form of *ex-post* moral hazard that can arise from the presence of reinsurance; under this concept, an insurer might relax its loss settlement/claims adjustment procedures in the aftermath of a loss, knowing that it has reinsurance coverage. This can lead to an accumulation of claims/fraud.

cover and generate excessive losses for the insurer; or, it will price all risk at the high-loss level and write no cover for the low-loss group, thus losing business. Risks, in either case, are said to be 'adversely selected', which will have a detrimental effect on the insurer. To protect against adverse selection the insurer must thoroughly understand the nature of its portfolio; this typically means devoting proper resources to identifying, classifying, and tracking the loss experience of each of the parties it is protecting, enabling it to properly stratify and, then price, the protection it is offering.

As indicated above, basis risk is the risk that arises between an exposure and a risk transfer/hedge mechanism that is imperfectly correlated with the exposure. Basis risk arises in derivative and insurance contracts when a company attempts to protect a particular exposure with a proxy that is not precisely matched with the potential loss. An indemnity-based insurance contract, which provides a payment that matches precisely the losses sustained by the insured, features no basis risk. A derivative contract that provides a payment to a hedger based on a proxy has basis risk; the degree of risk depends on the correlation between the exposure and the hedge, and how that correlation performs over time. Of course, not all derivative contracts carry basis risk (e.g., it is possible for a corporate hedger to find a market reference that covers an exposure precisely) and not all insurance contracts are free from basis risk (e.g., a reinsurance contract that provides loss coverage based on an index or parametric trigger, rather than a specific indemnity, has basis risk). All else being equal, a contract that has basis risk is cheaper than one that provides a perfect match; this is logical as the hedger is bearing an incremental amount of risk and the protection provider is not including any premium for moral hazard.

1.3.7   Non-insurance transfers

In addition to some of the risk management mechanism we have summarized above, there are other ways of transferring pure risks, including hold-harmless agreements, indemnity agreements, and leases. In fact, these can allow coverage of risks that might not normally be insurable through standard mechanisms, and they may be a cost-effective way of protecting business. However, coverage can be ambiguous and the level of credit risk the company assumes necessarily rises. While these are certainly valid risk transfer mechanisms, we shall not discuss them in detail in this book.

1.4   OUTLINE OF THE BOOK

With this brief overview of basic risk management issues, we are now prepared to consider how and why the ART market exists and the specific products, vehicles, and solutions that are available to those who actively manage their risks. The balance of the book is structured as follows:

- In Chapters 2 and 3, we discuss important theoretical market drivers that promote growth and innovation in the ART market, the scope, development, and evolution of the marketplace, the nature of convergence, and the role that key participants play in promoting activity.
- In Part II (Chapters 4, 5, and 6) we turn our attention to specific insurance/reinsurance-based ART products and vehicles, including risk transfer and risk financing contracts, captives, and multi-risk (multiple peril and trigger) products.

- In Part III (Chapters 7, 8, and 9) we consider the capital markets dimension of the marketplace, with a particular focus on insurance-based securitization, contingent capital structures and derivatives.
- In Part IV (Chapters 10 and 11) we focus on the future of ART by reviewing the nascent, but increasingly important, field of enterprise risk management (based on integrated risk products and corporate solutions) and conclude with thoughts on future growth prospects.

2
Risk Management Drivers: Theoretical
Motivations, Benefits, and Costs

The ART market, as we shall note in detail throughout the book, is an innovative sector comprising intermediaries, capacity suppliers, services, products, and solutions, that helps institutions manage their financial and operating risks efficiently. The ART market supports the loss control, loss financing, and risk reduction techniques we have summarized in Chapter 1, and has gradually become a complete and holistic marketplace.

The market did not, of course, simply commence operations at a particular point in time. It has evolved over a period of several decades through a number of exogenous forces, including those allowing companies to:

- maximize enterprise value in order to meet the demands of shareholders;
- cope with market cycles that can influence the supply (and thus pricing) of risk capacity;
- access new sources of risk capacity;
- diversify credit exposure to risk intermediaries;
- manage enterprise risks intelligently;
- reduce taxes and costs;
- overcome regulatory barriers;
- capitalize on deregulation.

We shall consider each of these points, summarized in Figure 2.1, at greater length below. This will help us to understand why specific ART mechanisms have developed over time, and the growth prospects each faces over the coming years.

2.1 MAXIMIZING ENTERPRISE VALUE

A corporation is accountable and responsible to a variety of stakeholders, particularly its equity investors.[1] Investors who supply equity risk capital demand an appropriate return on their capital, and directors and managers, as their agents, must strive to provide the greatest possible return within the mandate of the firm's business. A company's share price, which we consider to be a reflection of the discounted value of future risky cash flows of the firm, is one measure of value. Maximizing enterprise value in order to provide investors with the highest possible share price often becomes an overarching corporate goal. Naturally, different claimholders have different values at stake and different attitudes toward risk; value maximization accounts for the risk costs imposed on all corporate claimholders, not just shareholders.

In attempting to maximize enterprise value a firm pursues projects in which the rate of return is greater than the firm's cost of capital. From a practical perspective, management will seek to maximize the discounted future net cash flows of the firm (as we have noted in Chapter 1). Maximizing net cash flows generally infers minimizing expected losses – a key

---

[1] In practice, a firm has various direct and indirect stakeholders, including employees, creditors, clients, suppliers, regulators and communities. Legally, however, directors and officers are fiduciaries of the investors.

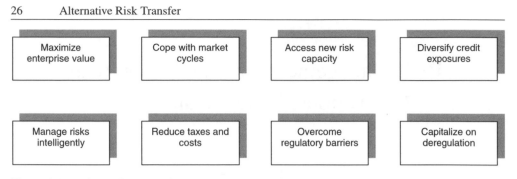

Figure 2.1   Drivers of ART market growth and innovation

goal of corporate risk management programs; in fact, firms seek to minimize losses to protect the capitalized value of future earnings. In effect, the process involves a decision by a firm to commit current resources to generate future value. It also involves minimizing the volatility of expected losses, as less volatile earnings can lead to a lower cost of capital. Indeed, many academic studies strongly support the benefits of using risk management products to boost cash flows and lower expected loss volatility. Although value maximization is the ideal goal, a firm strives, at a minimum, to avoid financial distress and the costs associated with a weakened financial position; it must understand loss events that can damage its financial performance and creditworthiness, and – within the confines of rational cost/benefit behavior (e.g., there may be little point in spending for risk protection in an amount that greatly exceeds the value of expected loss) – it must do what is possible to mitigate against such events.

Value creation centers on the actual returns that can be obtained from corporate assets, less the cost of capital needed to support those assets. Value is created when the net return is positive, and the focus is on what assets earn, how much it costs to fund them, and the amount of leverage involved. For instance, an insurance company creates value when the net return from underwriting and investment activities (the two primary sources of income for a typical insurer) is greater than the cost of capital. Actions that are taken to lower the cost of capital can create even more value. Through diversification and reinsurance an insurer can lower the volatility of underwriting results and the cost of capital, and raise enterprise value – assuming that the cost of diversification and reinsurance are not so great that they offset the gains generated from lower volatility of underwriting results.

We have noted in Chapter 1 that a company can be exposed to a range of financial and operating risks. These risks can impact enterprise value by affecting expected NCFs through size, timing and variability. We have further noted that the risk management process allows a firm to implement a variety of techniques – loss control, loss financing, risk reduction and variations on the theme – in order to reduce the likelihood of unexpected changes in expected NCFs. These, of course, are only achievable at a cost, and therefore impact enterprise value. Fundamentally, a firm must consider the **cost of risk** – the implicit or explicit price paid to manage risk exposures – when it is creating a risk management strategy, since the cost of risk directly affects enterprise value. The cost of risk comprises various theoretical components, including:

- expected cost of direct and indirect losses arising from retained risks
- expected cost of loss control activities
- expected cost of loss financing activities
- expected cost of risk reduction activities.

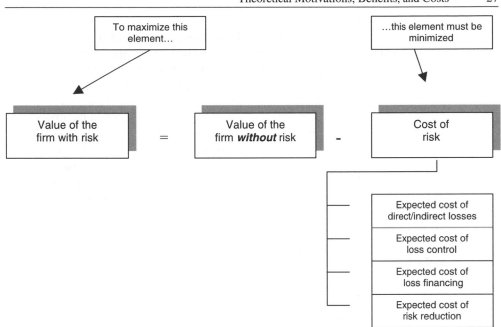

Figure 2.2   Value maximization relationship

The ultimate goal of any value-maximizing firm must be minimization of the cost of risk. This, as we shall see, is not necessarily the same as minimizing risk. Figure 2.2 summarizes this elemental relationship.

The more a company spends on its cost of risk, the more variability it eliminates from expected NCFs, but the more it reduces its operating income. All other things being equal, a firm with lower expected NCFs reduces its probability of insolvency (which carries costs of its own). However, at some point the marginal cost of loss control, loss financing and risk reduction will be greater than the reduction in expected losses; when this occurs the firm's risk elimination, diversification and control techniques no longer serve to maximize enterprise value. This brings us back to our earlier point: it is possible to create a completely risk-free company, but the endeavor is unlikely to yield an enterprise with maximized value.

Let us consider a simple framework to illustrate several key points of the concept. To begin, we assume that maximizing enterprise value means maximizing the present value of expected NCFs. Thus, if a firm has a 90% probability of earning NCFs of $100 (outcome 1) and 10% probability of earning $70 in one year (outcome 2), the expected NCF one year from now is $97. Discounting back at a 5% rate yields a present value (PV) of expected NCFs of $92.38; this is the enterprise value today, before the firm undertakes any risk management activities. One year from now the expected value of the firm will be 5% more than it is today (e.g., $92.38), but the actual value will depend on the occurrence of outcomes 1 or 2. The return will either be 8.25% (outcome 1) or −24.23% (outcome 2) – not surprisingly, this is equal to 5%, e.g., 90% × 8.25% + 10% ×−24.23%.

Let us now inspect aspects of this example. In the first instance we have used 5% as a discount rate. This is effectively the firm's cost of capital, or the rate needed to attract capital to fund operations, and comprises two elements, a risk-free benchmark rate $r(f)$ and a risk premium $r(p)$. The rate $r(f)$ is compensation to the investor for the time value of money, while $r(p)$ is compensation for the riskiness of the investment. If expected NCFs are riskier (i.e., more variable), the $r(p)$ demanded by investors will be higher; this means that the total cost of capital, r, will also be higher. Second, if the firm can undertake some cost-effective risk management activity to reduce the probability of generating $70 to 5% or even 0% (thus increasing the $100 scenario to 95% or 100% and also increasing expected NCFs), then it must consider taking that action. Although the cost of risk rises, the value of the firm should also rise if NCF variability (i.e., the $70 scenario) has been lowered. In fact, if a company can lower the variability of its expected NCFs it reflects less volatility and less risk, and requires less return to attract investors. This lowers its cost of capital by decreasing the $r(p)$ component of r. A tradeoff exists: the variability of NCFs can be reduced at a cost, and the $r(p)$ element can ultimately be reduced if the variability of NCFs declines; one is a cost, the other a benefit. Accordingly, a firm must consider whether it should employ one of the risk management alternatives summarized in Chapter 1: loss control (e.g., safety), loss financing (e.g., insurance, self-insurance or derivatives hedging) or risk reduction (e.g., withdrawal or diversification). In all cases the decision hinges on a cost/benefit determination:

• If the expected cost of risk management techniques is *greater* than the benefit obtained from a reduction in the cost of capital, then hedging, diversifying or otherwise protecting expected NCFs may not increase enterprise value.
• If the expected cost of risk management techniques is *less* than the benefit obtained from a reduction in the cost of capital, then hedging, diversifying or otherwise protecting expected NCFs may increase enterprise value.

For instance, a company might wish to purchase insurance to reduce NCF variability (e.g., in the example above it might pay some premium to receive $30 if the $70 scenario occurs). If the expected cost of the loss-financing protection is less than the estimated future NCF, then it is sensible to acquire the protection and eliminate the uncertainty. However, if the company believes that the cost of insurance is too high, it may proceed 'unprotected' by retaining the uncertainty. If it has sufficient cash on hand to cover any losses arising from a future event it must then decide whether to use internal funds to cover the loss when it occurs, or borrow against expected future cash flows and use funds on hand to invest in an alternative project. The cost/benefit tradeoff decision surfaces once again: if the project has a positive NPV and outweighs securities issuance or bank-borrowing fees, it may be optimal from an enterprise value perspective to borrow to fund the loss. A company that does not have sufficient funds on hand and lacks loss-financing protection is in a slightly different position: it can borrow against future cash flows in order to cover today's losses, or it can declare bankruptcy.

A firm might also consider a diversification strategy. Theoretically, if a company is able to diversify away risk, investors should demand a lower $r(p)$. The question is whether a company can do this diversification efficiently. Risk can be divided into two components: diversifiable risk (often known as idiosyncratic risk) and non-diversifiable risk (systematic risk). **Diversifiable risk** is company-specific, and can be reduced by holding a portfolio with a large number of obligations/exposures. **Non-diversifiable risk**, which is common to all companies, cannot be eliminated. While it seems that a company lowering its risk through diversification should receive a lower $r(p)$ (and thus r), the actual savings might be negligible, as investors can often diversify more efficiently than individual companies; this depends largely on the nature of the company and its businesses. Figure 2.3 highlights these relationships.

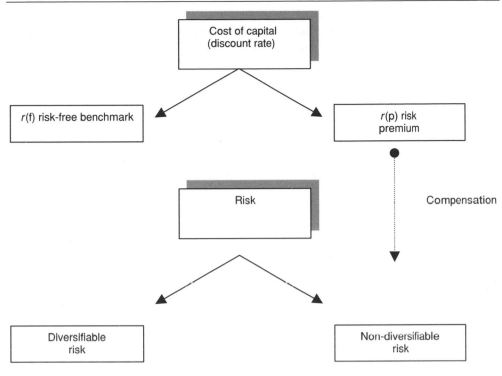

Figure 2.3 Cost of capital and risk

The main point to stress is that a company must make decisions regarding management of risks and how they will impact enterprise value. These can be determined in the quantification stage of the risk management process through a technique such as cost/benefit analysis; if a particular technique is shown to create greater value by lowering expected NCF variability, it may be optimal.

2.2 THE DECISION FRAMEWORK

A firm engaged in active risk management faces a series of financial decisions that must be resolved in the ongoing course of its operations. These can be categorized broadly as investment decisions and financing decisions. For instance, if a firm decides to invest in loss control measures as part of its risk strategy, then it must decide how to finance the program; if it opts not to employ any loss control, then no financing is necessary. Likewise, if a firm decides to abandon a project that has been impacted by physical damage, then it requires no financing. However, if it decides on post-loss reinvestment (replacement) it must then decide whether to arrange financing on a pre-loss or post-loss basis. Each of these will have explicit cost/benefit tradeoffs that must be considered.

More formally, we can define **pre-loss financing** as anticipatory financing that is arranged in advance of any loss situation; this can include vehicles such as insurance, derivatives or contingent capital. Each form of pre-loss financing has an *ex-ante* cost associated with it, such as a premium payment, arrangement fee or bid–offer spread. **Post-loss financing** is funding arranged in response to a loss event; it may come from cash/reserves, short- or long-term debt or equity, each with its own *ex-post* cost (i.e., foregone investment income, interest expense or dividend expense). Though we shall not consider specific post-loss financing vehicles in further detail, we note in summary that common mechanisms include balance sheet cash/liquid securities, lines of credit (generally as a form of bridge, rather than permanent, financing), term loans, bonds (with long-term securities being a form of semi-permanent financing), and equity (a permanent form of funding that results in dilution). The common debt and equity tradeoff presents itself in any of these situations: while debt is less risky than equity for the investor (and cheaper for the company to issue), it results in greater leverage and thus increases the possibility of financial distress. Naturally, the lower the average cost of capital, the greater the discounted value of the firm's earnings – and the greater the enterprise value. Equity, though more expensive than debt, lowers leverage and can be beneficial in reducing the likelihood of encountering financial distress.

It is important to note that post-loss financing does not imply a lack of risk management planning, but simply that a company, in analyzing the costs/benefits and the likelihood of experiencing losses of a particular magnitude, opts not to bear an *ex-ante* cost for an uncertain event. However, it is possible that arranging financing in the aftermath of a loss event might be more expensive. If the loss is especially large the company might be susceptible to financial distress, and therefore unable to negotiate satisfactory financing terms. Financing of any type will, of course, lead to market scrutiny, and the size of the financing relative to losses sustained will be embedded in relative borrowing costs or issuance price. The general categories of investment and financing decisions are summarized in Figure 2.4.

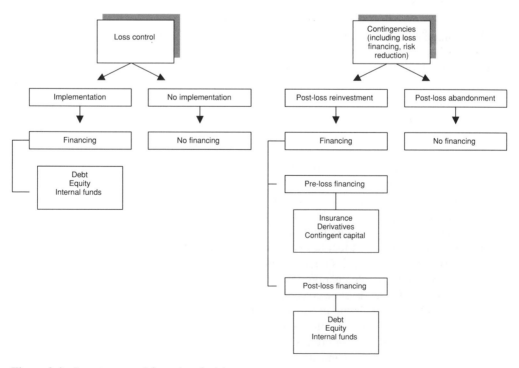

Figure 2.4   Investment and financing decisions

2.2.1 Replacement and abandonment

A firm engages in risk management activities in order to preserve the value of its earning assets. If the assets are damaged or destroyed, the earnings power of the firm is temporarily or permanently reduced, and its enterprise value declines. If a firm can immediately replace lost assets without any transaction costs it will do so, and return to its pre-loss state of production.

Assuming that there are no transaction costs, the prudent firm will always select replacement when the return is greater than the cost of capital. However, if the assets that have been damaged or destroyed yield a marginal return that is less than the cost of capital (i.e., a negative NPV scenario), investment is suboptimal and assets should not be replaced; indeed, if they can be abandoned without transaction costs, it is better to do so as enterprise value will increase. If the immediate sale value is greater than the discounted future cash flows from the asset, pre-loss abandonment may be advisable; if the sale value is less than the discounted future cash flows which, in turn, are less than the cost of investment, the assets should not be abandoned, but should not be replaced post-loss (e.g., the insured firm will benefit from an infusion of cash that can be used for more productive purposes).[2] Of course, if the cost of investment is less than the discounted future cash flows, then assets should never be abandoned, even post-loss. The replacement versus abandonment decision is central to any risk management consideration involving productive assets.

2.2.2 Costs and benefits of loss control

Loss control is the sum total of all physical activities and protections taken to reduce the EV of aggregate losses, where the specific benefit can be considered to be a lower amount of losses. The process generally involves an upfront investment in safety measures/infrastructure that generate benefits over time. Accordingly, costs/benefits can be considered through a standard NPV framework. The safety measures are often physical (e.g., sprinklers, hazmat storage, alarms) but may also be procedural or educational (e.g., safety training). In either case, they require upfront funding before they can begin to generate direct/indirect gains. Gains must be measured on a net basis as the loss control scheme might involve periodic maintenance costs. (These, however, are likely to be minor compared with the initial investment.) In a standard NPV/capital budgeting framework we note that

$$\text{NPV} = \sum_{i=1}^{t} \frac{\text{CF}_i}{(1 + r)^i} - I_0$$

where CF_i is the net periodic benefit achieved through the loss control measures and I_0 is the initial cost of investment.

Since effective loss control measures can preserve financial resources that can be used for other wealth-enhancing activities, they should be evaluated in a reinvestment framework (e.g., reinvestment of CF_i). Given that loss control is a multi-year process, it must be viewed over the entire time horizon, rather than the typical one-year insurance horizon.

---

[2] Insurers might fear some instance of moral hazard in these situations.

2.2.3 Costs and benefits of loss financing

Loss-financing techniques are the centerpiece of the risk management process for many firms and demand considerable analysis since many variables and alternatives are involved. While loss control is certainly important, it can be viewed as a fairly static process that is directly influenced by risk retention levels (e.g., after the initial loss control measures are implemented, they only require periodic review). Likewise, when a firm opts for risk reduction by eliminating its risks, it no longer needs to worry about them (the diversification process is, of course, more dynamic and demanding).

In contrast, when determining an approach to loss financing, a company must weigh the relative costs and benefits of retention, transfer and hedging. We have noted in the previous chapter that some companies might choose a strategy based on retaining core risks and transferring or hedging non-core risks. While this is convenient, it may not yield the best results, and only a rigorous review can determine if enterprise value is actually being maximized through such a process.

Risk retention

Risk retention (sometimes referred to as self-insurance) is based on preserving a certain amount of risk exposure. Retention may occur passively (through failure to recognize the presence of a particular risk) or actively (through a specific decision to preserve a particular risk). Passive retention can be the result of a failed or flawed governance process, which causes a firm to improperly identify or quantify its exposures. Active risk retention, in contrast, arises when a firm properly identifies its risks and consciously decides to preserve some portion. It might do so if the costs of insuring or transferring are too great, if losses are reasonably predictable, if worst case scenarios are financially manageable, or if risks are uninsurable. If a loss occurs a firm finances the loss internally or externally (as noted below), or abandons the project/asset that has been damaged.

Risk retention can be viewed as a self-funding technique, since a firm often establishes an internal account to cover losses from its operations. In general, exposures that are "well behaved" – that is, they are large in number but small in size, and appear with reasonable predictability – are candidates for retention. The high level of predictability and reasonable size mean that they can be budgeted into, and absorbed by, corporate cash flows. For instance, retention is quite common in workers' compensation and employee health plans (indeed, risk retention groups that preserve and pool such risks are popular). Risk retention has several theoretical benefits: lower expenses, greater motivation to enact loss control mechanisms, and greater flexibility/use of internal cash balances. In addition, no separate organizational structure is needed for risk retention (as would be needed for risk transfer to a captive, for instance). It also has certain disadvantages, however, including excess losses if risks are not as predictable as estimated and greater tax liability (i.e., instances where losses can only be deducted when they occur, and payments that are not deductible if they are not considered premiums). Once again, costs and benefits must be weighed to determine whether a risk retention approach boosts enterprise value.

In considering appropriate retention levels, a firm might choose to set them equal to the maximum amount of economic loss that it can sustain without seriously impacting earnings (and hence enterprise value), or it might create a threshold equal to some percentage of working capital, liquid assets or equity. Alternatively, it might synchronize retention levels to financial goals and the overall corporate mandate. As discussed earlier, funding of retained risks can be arranged before losses occur (in the form of pre-loss financing), or after they occur (in the form of post-loss financing). Facilities may be funded or unfunded, and can be internal or external. For instance, internally unfunded arrangements might call for post-loss use of retained earnings, while externally unfunded arrangements might draw on post-loss capital markets issuance or bank borrowing. Internally funded arrangements are often associated with pre-loss self-insurance/captives and finite programs, while externally funded arrangements might center on pre-loss contingent capital and securitizations. Each of these structures (which we consider in subsequent chapters) has economic costs and benefits. A funded arrangement reflects greater certainty, which is available at an *ex-ante* price; an unfunded arrangement suggests more uncertainty and might involve a significant *ex-post* price (e.g., not only the cost of a financing arrangement in the aftermath of a loss, but the potential cost of financial distress if the loss is large and insufficient financing is available). Risk retention funds, which can be accumulated gradually to cover future losses, are a popular way of managing the cash flows associated with this process.[3] In all cases the specific source of funds must again be considered from a cost/benefit perspective. For instance, if investment yields are greater than a company's cost of capital, and a company can access external capital freely, it may be better to finance the retention fund through external, rather than internal, sources.[4]

Risk transfer and hedging

Generally speaking, risk transfer and hedging occur through the insurance and derivative markets; although we consider specific products and techniques at greater length later in the book, we briefly introduce concepts related to the costs/benefits of using insurance and derivatives in this section. Fundamentally, the risk transfer/hedging markets can increase the available pools of unsystematic risk and promote greater financial stability by diffusing exposures; there is sufficient evidence to suggest that such mechanisms are quite resilient in the face of dislocation.

The insurance mechanism transfers the cost of post-loss financing for reinvestment from the cedant to the insurer in exchange for the payment of a premium. This provides funding as well as earnings stability, both of which are essential in the quest for value maximization. The practical and economic benefits of transfer via insurance are various: indemnification in the event of loss, reduced NCF uncertainty, loss control benefits and tax deductibility of premium payments. There are, of course, practical and economic costs, including the payment of premium, negotiations and delays in the claims settlement process and the pricing of moral hazard. Certain limitations also exist: if insurance does not fully cover post-loss transaction costs, the complete restoration of equity value may not be possible. Equally, if business interruption losses are not covered, then a reduction in equity value may result. A full insurance policy, which covers the cost of repair/replacement,[5] business interruption,[6] liability settlement and legal costs, is an option for any company. However, because the scope of coverage is broad

---

[3] Reserves that are established for self-insurance or retention are often specifically earmarked so that creditors and investors can easily refer to the existence of such protection.

[4] In other words, the decision should focus on the relationship between the risk-adjusted return on the fund's assets and the risk-adjusted cost of the fund; if returns are greater than costs, value is being generated.

[5] In some instances a firm must consider whether insurance coverage should extend to 'redundant' assets – i.e., those that have value but are unlikely to be replaced if they are destroyed. Though they generate cash that can be used for investment, the decision on whether they should be specifically insured is not always clear and must be analyzed as a separate cost/benefit issue.

[6] In practice, quantifying *ex-ante* (and *ex-post*) the losses associated with business interruption is very difficult. The process relies heavily on subjective assumptions about production, inventory levels, supply/demand for goods and services, market conditions, capacity, competitive barriers, and so forth.

and the dollar amount of any restitution is potentially large (as a result of a small deductible and a high policy cap), it can be expensive and may only be suitable for particular types of risk. For instance, small losses that can be estimated with a reasonable degree of accuracy can be budgeted into the corporate process and may be funded internally at a lower cost than full insurance. Alternatively, the costs associated with partial insurance may be reasonable in light of the benefits that can be obtained. As noted earlier, some firms prefer to transfer risks that are difficult to estimate, such as low-frequency/high-severity exposures. Although this clearly involves a premium cost, two benefits arise: costs savings from not having to precisely quantify the potential impact of a 'disaster' (a difficult and sometimes imprecise exercise) and *ex-ante* post-loss funding that is secured in the aftermath of what might be a significant loss event. By generating an inflow of cash in the event of a claim, a firm is also positioned to reduce the possibility of financial distress. Financial distress carries with it specific costs; short of bankruptcy, a company in distress faces higher borrowing costs, poorer supplier terms, and so forth. Since these are actual expenses for a firm in a weakened financial position, they must form part of the cost/benefit analysis. As a general rule, if an insurance premium is less than, or equal to, the expected loss, a company will purchase insurance. If the premium is a constant multiple of the expected loss, the company might choose to retain some portion of the exposure (e.g., partial insurance through deductible/coinsurance features).

The hedging process can be viewed in a similar light. The theoretical benefits that can accrue are very similar to those noted immediately above – i.e., a compensatory payment, reduced NCF uncertainty, and lower probability of financial distress; if the derivative qualifies as a hedge, it may also have certain tax deductibility features. (It is worth stressing again that derivative contracts are optionable instruments and proof of loss need not be established.) The cost of hedging a risk through a derivative contract comes in the form of an option premium (which is, of course, distinct from an insurance premium) or a bid–offer spread on a swap or forward contract. If hedging is executed through the exchange-traded market (e.g., listed futures and options), the cost comes in the form of contract fees and posting of collateral.

Risk management in a loss-financing framework is often based on incremental decisions. In a standard process a corporate risk manager reviews a potential risk exposure, considers the cost of insurance premium or derivative hedge fee against the EV loss and potential benefits, and makes a decision. Since the consideration is discrete, and is often done in isolation from other portfolio risks, a decision to proceed with coverage (particularly for pure risks) might lead to instances of **oversinsurance** or **overhedging** – that is, an excess of protection that might not actually be required when taking account of broader portfolio exposures with "beneficial" correlations that produce natural offsets. Overinsurance/overhedging is redundant and represents an excess cost that detracts from enterprise value: paying unnecessary premiums for a degree of risk protection that is unnecessary can never lead to value maximization. A framework that permits risk managers to review incremental exposures in the context of broader firmwide risk exposures can reduce the chances of overinsurance and overhedging. Multi-risk products and enterprise risk management solutions that have gained popularity among corporate end-users in recent years permit just such a portfolio review and can lead to more efficient use of risk management resources. Examining risks on an aggregate basis gives a company the opportunity to optimize its risk coverage; by doing so it is almost certainly able to improve its enterprise value. As we shall note later in the book, the proper enterprise risk management program examines risks from a wide variety of sources (e.g., financial, operational, insurable, uninsurable), in order to create the most efficient and cost beneficial structure.

2.2.4 Costs and benefits of risk reduction

Risk reduction can be achieved by withdrawing from a business activity that gives rise to unwanted risks (preservation of which cannot be economically justified through a cost/benefit framework or a company's own business priorities and strategies). Alternatively, it can occur through the diversification techniques discussed in the previous chapter (i.e., the creation of portfolios of uncorrelated risks). The relative costs associated with withdrawing from the market can be quantified through an abandonment or sale scenario; the ensuing benefits relate to reduced variability of cash flows from operations once impacted by an unwanted peril, as well as the cost savings associated with no longer having to protect against that exposure. If risks are simply reduced through a portfolio diversification scheme, then the cost/benefit analysis focuses on the incremental costs required to achieve a particular portfolio balance. This, not surprisingly, will depend on the specific risks involved (e.g., speculative, pure), the nature of the diversification process (e.g., purchase of uncorrelated risk assets, use of synthetic baskets, portfolio mechanisms, and so on), and the amount of risk that is actually reduced. Benefits, once again, center on reduced cash flow variability.

Regardless of the risk management technique employed, the cost/benefit framework (or some similar objective metric that can crystallize inflows and outflows) is an essential element in decision-making and the determination of enterprise value.

2.3 COPING WITH MARKET CYCLES

2.3.1 Insurance pricing

In this section we consider supply and demand cycles impacting the market for insurance coverage. We focus specifically on forces within the insurance sector because these tend to dictate pricing imbalances that can drive companies to seek other risk management solutions (including derivatives, capital markets securities, and so forth). In fact, there is no particular evidence to suggest that the reverse is true; that is, when swap spreads are wide or option premiums and quoted volatilities are high as a result of low-risk appetite among derivative dealers, corporate risk managers do not then turn to the insurance market to obtain more competitive pricing.

We begin with a brief review of insurance pricing. Even as a corporate risk manager wants to pay the lowest possible cost for a risk transfer mechanism, an insurer needs to earn the best possible return. If it cannot, it will lack the financial incentives and resources to participate in the marketplace. In a theoretical sense insurance premiums must be sufficient to cover expected claims (simply EV loss) and operating and administrative costs, and to provide a fair return to suppliers of risk capital. This might be regarded as a **fair premium** (also known as the gross rate) and becomes a forward looking estimate of expected future claims (losses),[7] costs and profit margins. The cost charged to the cedant is generally referred to as the **rate on line**, and is simply the premium paid divided by the amount of coverage (or limit) provided. Thus a premium of $1m for $10m line of coverage is equal to a 10% rate on line. The price of coverage is often determined by dividing the rate on line by the actuarial probability of loss (minus 1); when the price is zero, coverage is said to be 'actuarially fair.' In fact, premiums must be at least large enough to cover expected losses and costs because, if they are not, the insurer

---

[7] Insurers establish and fund **loss reserves**, which include an estimated amount for claims reported and adjusted but not yet paid, claims reported and filed but not yet adjusted, and claims incurred but not yet reported.

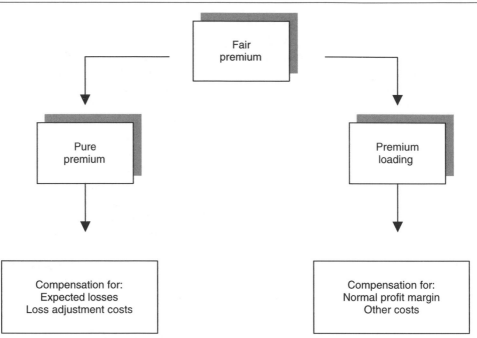

Figure 2.5   Insurance premium pricing components

might suffer financial distress and jeopardize the position of all cedants. Pricing, therefore, cannot be unfair or egregious, and must certainly not be discriminatory. The fair premium of an insurance policy (summarized in Figure 2.5) thus consists of a **pure premium**, which is the amount needed to cover losses and loss adjustment expenses, and a **premium loading**, which is the amount required to cover other expenses and produce an appropriate profit margin.[8] The latter element is essential, as insurers must provide their shareholders with a fair return on capital. In a typical risk/return framework, the riskier the insurer's business, the greater the required profitability, since the variability of claims is higher. A business with more claims variability demands greater capital support, meaning a greater economic return to shareholders. If profit loading is not determined correctly, shareholders will not be compensated fairly and will be unwilling to supply capital.

If risks are independent and homogeneous, it is relatively easy for an insurer to determine how much premium it needs to charge. Exposures that exhibit similar characteristics are grouped together and charged at the same rate, i.e., one reflecting average loss experience. This may be supplemented by certain merit adjustments – a class of rates that may be adjusted up or down based on certain merit criteria, including the **schedule rating** (a rate modified by physical characteristics of cover) or the **experience rating** (a rate modified by past loss experience[9]). However, if risks are heterogeneous and do not lend themselves easily to classification, pricing

---

[8] Insurers create **unearned premium reserves** – a liability representing the unearned portion of gross premiums on outstanding policies. The reserve account is used to pay for possible future losses and refund policies that are cancelled. In fact, unearned premium reserves have an equity component, as the entire gross premium received from clients is set aside, but only the first year contains large costs.

[9] This often includes a retrospective rating where loss experience during a given period is used to determine the premium for that period (e.g., an initial premium is paid at contract inception, and any replenishment or refund is settled at contract expiry); we shall discuss retrospective policies in more detail in Chapter 4.

becomes considerably more complex; rate-setting may occur on the basis of subjective, rather than objective, measures, which may lead to less precise results; as noted earlier, when good information classification is lacking, adverse selection can arise.

Since insurers run diversified books of risks, cannot precisely estimate expected claims, and are faced with information asymmetries, insurance pricing is rarely optimal: in some years insurers do well and in others they do poorly. When an insurer has a bad year it is likely to increase its premium charges, but any change will be based on its reassessment of expected future claims rather than an arbitrary increase to make up for a bad year; indeed, competition helps to enforce this discipline. The use of actuarial pricing techniques, based on average risk statistics, means that some "good" risks are not properly priced (e.g., they may be overpriced from the end-user's perspective). In such cases there may be greater incentives to use ART-related mechanisms.

Naturally, insurers (particularly those that are sensitive to value maximization) strive to charge different premiums for different expected claims. Again, however, there is a cost/benefit tradeoff involved. Reducing information asymmetries to price risks more appropriately may be expensive, and greater than the incremental premiums that can be charged. Insurers are also sensitive to the time value of money; indeed, it is a key source of profit and loss and must be managed properly. In general, the time value of money works to the advantage of insurers, as they receive premiums from cedants upfront (e.g., more value today) but pay claims over a period of time (e.g., less value today). From the cedant's perspective, stable and transparent premium charges are desirable, as they add certainty to the corporate budgeting and loss control/financing process and inject greater predictability into corporate cash flows.

2.3.2 Hard versus soft markets

The insurance market, like most other sectors of the global financial marketplace, goes through cycles that can last for any length of time. During a theoretically "normal" market cycle, insurance supply and demand operate in an equilibrium state, and the fair premium charged by insurers is appropriately borne by cedants. Through a conventional economic supply and demand framework, such as the one depicted in Figure 2.6, we note the equilibrium point N at the intersection of the supply and demand curves, reflecting a supply of insurance at Q_1 at a premium price of P_1.

In practice, this ideal equilibrium state does not appear very frequently or last very long. It is more common for the marketplace to be in a state of disequilibria – where the market is described as being "hard' or "soft". Insurance market cycles are largely driven by industry capacity and investment returns, where capacity is directly linked to insurer/reinsurer capital. When capital levels are strong, insurers have a tendency to reduce premiums and write more cover; and when capital levels have been depleted, the reverse occurs. Investment returns also play a role. Since insurers and reinsurers obtain a portion of their operating revenues from investment portfolios and reinvestment of premiums, healthy returns provide a greater ability to cover losses from weaker underwriting experience; insurers are thus more apt to write cover. When investment returns are poor, the industry has less financial cushion and flexibility, causing a tightening of underwriting standards, contraction in supply and a rise in premiums.

A **soft market** for insurance is characterized by the excess supply of risk capacity, which leads to lower premiums. A soft market might develop when the system is flush with capital that needs to be allocated productively. In such a situation, insurers lower their underwriting standards in order to win incremental business; they may also lower their premiums as

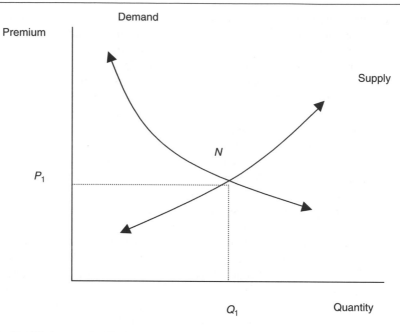

Figure 2.6   Equilibrium market for insurance

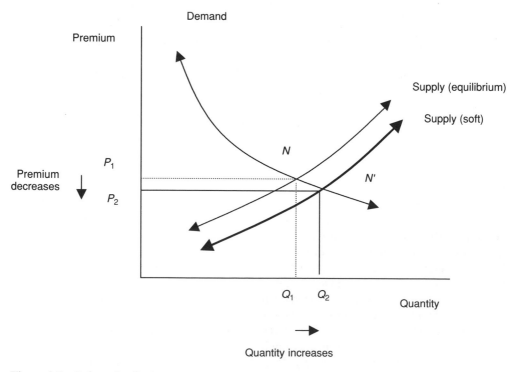

Figure 2.7   Soft market for insurance

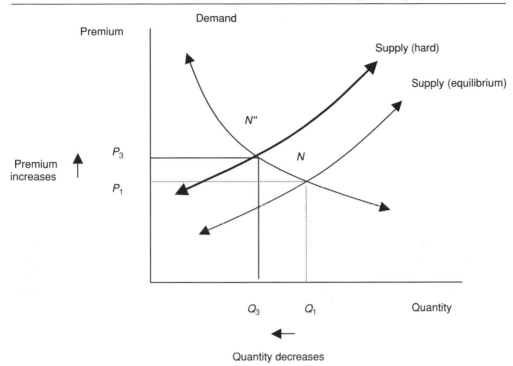

Figure 2.8   Hard market for insurance

additional competitors enter the marketplace. The end result is a shift in the supply curve to the right, reflecting the fact that insurers are willing to provide greater amounts of cover at lower prices. The new equilibrium price of insurance coverage is shown as point N' in Figure 2.7, with premiums declining from P_1 to P_2 and supply increasing from Q_1 to Q_2. In a soft market, traditional insurance coverage is very competitively priced and surfaces as an attractive alternative in the risk management cost/benefit framework.

Excess supply of risk capacity is not a sustainable market state. At some point the lower underwriting standards instituted by insurers as a mechanism for capturing market share, along with lower premium charges, lead to underwriting losses in excess of reserves established to cover actual loss experience. The cycle turns into a **hard market**: insurers reduce the amount of coverage they are willing to write, causing the supply curve to shift to the left (to the new equilibrium point N'', as noted in Figure 2.8). This drives the quantity of cover down and premiums up (i.e., actual premium received (P_3) is greater than the fair equilibrium premium (P_1)). The hard market cycle can be hastened by the onset of some significant disaster that leads to an excess of claims, such as the low-frequency/high-severity scenario that characterizes damaging catastrophes (e.g., hurricanes, earthquakes and terrorism) or the onset of **clash loss** (i.e., a scenario when various insurance lines are impacted by claims simultaneously – e.g., P&C, business interruption, life and health).[10] During a hard insurance market, the alternative risk transfer mechanisms that we consider in the book emerge as compelling options.

---

[10] In fact, the US Insurance Services Office (ISO) estimated that a $50bn catastrophe occurring during the mid- to late-1990s would have caused widespread insurer/reinsurer insolvencies, eliminating up to one-third of US risk capacity.

As the market moves through the hard cycle, the higher level of premiums that can be earned attracts new competitors (i.e., those eager to capture a share of the newly lucrative market). As more insurers join (or rejoin), the supply curve shifts back to the right once again, toward its equilibrium state, and the normal/soft/hard market cycle begins anew. To determine the state of the cycle, insurers/reinsurers often consider the level of the **combined ratio**, which is defined as the ratio of paid losses, loss adjustment expenses and underwriting expenses to premiums. If the ratio is greater than 100, insurance business is unprofitable, suggesting a soft market; this can obviously be beneficial to end-use clients (particularly if they are able to lock in coverage levels for multi-year periods) but quite detrimental to insurers/reinsurers. Unless investment returns are sufficient to offset the loss experience, the market will begin to harden. For instance, if an insurer has paid losses of $80, loss adjustment expenses of $20, and underwriting expenses of $5, against which it has earned premium income of $100, its combined ratio is 105%; for every $1 of premium it collects through underwriting, it loses $0.05. Thus, unless investment income is greater than $0.05, the firm is operating at a loss and will be forced to raise premiums, decrease coverage, or both.

The length of cycles, which might last from one to 10 years, depends on a variety of external factors. For instance, a hard market might be prolonged if the industry is impacted by an unusually high incidence of claims (including several high-severity disasters) and poor investment returns; this might be compounded by regulatory concerns over capital/reserve adequacy that force some insurers/reinsurers to curtail their underwriting activities. Until capital bases can be rebuilt through stronger investment and underwriting results – a process that might take several years to achieve – the market is likely to remain hard; while new entrants might join to take advantage of high pricing, the amount of progress they can make in a short time frame (particularly as primary insurers) may be quite limited.

When supply and demand imbalances exist, risk management markets are not in equilibrium. A lack of equilibrium, particularly from a supply perspective, means that loss-financing coverages may be uncertain. Even if a cedant is willing to pay the premium demanded at the theoretical margin, insurers might not be willing to underwrite the risk. This may occur when the industry is overly concentrated in a particular exposure and experiencing a large amount of claims; further coverage may be uncertain and unavailable at any price. For instance, if the insurance sector has written an excess of mid-Atlantic hurricane coverage over a period of time and is impacted by an unusually high frequency and severity cycle (leading to large P&C claims), future coverage becomes questionable. Those relying on such loss financing may be left in an untenable position.

CASE STUDY

The September 11 terrorist acts and the insurance underwriting cycle

On September 11, 2001, terrorists hijacked four US airliners. Two planes were flown into World Trade Center Towers 1 and 2 in New York City, causing the collapse of the buildings (as well as surrounding properties), a third plane was crashed into the Pentagon complex outside of Washington, DC, and a fourth in the countryside of Pennsylvania. In addition to the tragic loss of thousands of innocent lives, there was a considerable amount of direct and indirect damage to property, infrastructure and services. Not surprisingly, this cash loss had a considerable impact on the insurance/reinsurance sector, which paid out claims across a broad spectrum of exposures, including property damage, business interruption, workers' compensation, health, life, aviation liability, and so forth. Although the four crashes were considered "acts of war" and thus commonly excluded from coverage under most policies, insurance companies did not seek exclusion and generally paid out quite promptly. In fact, the event became the single largest loss ever sustained by the insurance/reinsurance sector, with direct and indirect loss estimates ranging from $30bn to $58bn.[11] The largest impact occurred in the P&C sector, where insurers had provided coverage for property damage, business interruption and aviation; the health/life sector, though important, faced smaller losses. The events of 9/11 were seen as a key test of both the reinsurance and retrocession mechanisms; since many P&C insurers had transferred their exposures to the reinsurance market (which had, itself, transferred a portion via retrocession), there was concern as to whether all reinsurers would have the financial strength to back up all claims.

Table 2.1   Direct loss estimates of 9/11

Category	Estimated loss amounts ($bn)
Life	2.7
Property	8.5
	(including $3.5bn for WTC 1 and 2)
Business interruption	10
Workers' compensation	4
Aviation liability	3.5
Hull	0.5
Other liability	10
Other	1

The underwriting cycle had begun to harden prior to 9/11. After nearly a decade of soft market conditions characterized by fairly loose underwriting standards and sporadic 'large claims losses' (e.g., Hurricane Andrew, 1992; California Northridge Earthquake, 1994; Kobe Earthquake, 1995; UK storms/flooding, 2000), the market cycle began turning in 2000/early 2001. Weaker combined ratios and lower investment returns (a function of both the low interest rate environment and significant equity market corrections) led to a gradual tightening of underwriting standards and a rise in premiums. When the events of 9/11 struck there was an immediate contraction in insurance supply. Certain risks that had once been covered as a matter of course (e.g., terrorist acts) were excised from virtually all policies (leading to the creation of certain government-sponsored terrorist coverage pools). Coverage of certain other exposures was curtailed during the January 2002 renewal season, causing premiums to rise by as much as 25% (premiums continued to rise in the months thereafter, in some cases reaching 50–150% of previous levels for exposures related to general liability, workers' compensation, and property). The hard market cycle that had commenced in 2000 accelerated rapidly, leading to two direct results: the creation of new Bermuda-based reinsurers to supply more risk capacity and take advantage of the higher premium environment, and a review by corporate end-users and others on alternative risk transfer mechanisms that might prove more cost-effective in the new hard market environment. In the event, many reinsurers were formed – including Axis Specialty

[11] Tillinghast has bounded the range between $30bn and $58bn. Hartwig has estimated $40bn of direct costs. Various other estimates have appeared in similar ranges (and depend primarily on items included/excluded from direct and indirect loss estimates).

(Marsh), Allied World (AIG, Goldman Sachs, Chubb), Endurance Re (AON), Arch Re (Arch Capital), DaVinci Re (Renaissance Re), and many others – adding capacity to the market within 6 to 18 months of the event. By late 2002, more than 100 new international insurance incorporations had been processed in Bermuda[12]; many firms had spent the insurance season seeking new accounts in order to take advantage of the rise in premiums. Interestingly, a widely anticipated turn toward ART-related capital markets issues, which are often attractive in hard market cycles, did not immediately follow. However, other forms of ART activity remained buoyant or expanded (e.g., captives, integrated programs, finite policies).

To re-emphasize, market cycles determine pricing, and pricing levels help to guide risk opportunities to the most cost-competitive substitutes or proxies.

2.4   ACCESSING NEW RISK CAPACITY

A firm expecting to make rational risk management decisions in a cost/benefit framework must be able to review as many options as possible. If it cannot, then it becomes a passive price-taker and is unlikely to be able to maximize its enterprise value. Since every risk management market has cycles of supply and demand, new conduits and mechanisms develop to address the shortcomings. If a hard insurance market develops and the marginal premium charged for coverage becomes too expensive for a company, it can turn to other sources to execute its risk plan[13] (e.g., joining a risk retention group, establishing a captive, utilizing derivative contracts, issuing a capital markets instrument, and so forth). The specific mechanism, though obviously important, is secondary to the fact that a company can turn to an alternative technique that is economically rational. When a company is able to access new sources of **risk capacity** – which we consider to be risk coverage that allows exposures to be transferred – it no longer faces coverage uncertainties that can damage enterprise value. As we shall note in subsequent chapters, accessing new types/sources of risk capacity is one of the key drivers and benefits of the alternative market. By using ART products and mechanisms, companies trying to arrange a risk management strategy reduce their reliance on traditional sources of capacity and the likelihood of facing uncertain or expensive coverage. They are no longer passive price-takers and can proactively search for the lowest cost alternatives. Accessing new risk capacity is possible because different intermediaries and capacity suppliers have different specializations, resources and goals and must adhere to different rules, regulations and legal/accounting treatment; these can lead to price differences.

The availability of alternative mechanisms means that properly priced risk capacity should be in continuous supply. For instance, traditional insurance companies are focused on providing single year (renewable) coverage of discrete lines of exposure, while banks specialize in multi-year, bundled risks. These, at any point in time, might have very different supply/demand and pricing dynamics. If a company can access either or a combination of the two when needed, it

---

[12] Not all of the 100+ companies were established, of course. Many sought regulatory approval but eventually decided not to proceed with a full activation of services.

[13] For instance, during 2000 and 2001 a combination of factors related to poor equity markets, economic downturn and an excess of claims from the 9/11 terrorist attacks and floods in North America and Europe, reduced global insurance capacity by an estimated 25% – leading to the price increases expected during a hard market.

reduces or eliminates the uncertainty related to optimal cover at a particular price. As we shall note later, the ART market attempts to bring together the 'best of both worlds'.

While companies and other end-users demand risk capacity, investors supply (directly or indirectly) what is needed. Investors participate in the marketplace when they can achieve returns that are commensurate with the risks they are being asked to assume. If marketplace supply and demand forces suggest that an equilibrium return of $x\%$ is available for a given risk cover, then any return in excess of $x\%$ is likely to be an attractive proposition for investors. Obviously, as more investors attempt to take advantage of the attractive returns, they channel excess capacity into the market, turning a hard market into a soft one, and driving returns back down to the equilibrium point (or below). This ultimately causes a contraction in the supply of capacity. Investors, however, are also cognizant of the returns they can achieve in other risky asset classes, and if it becomes more profitable to invest in global equities than P&C or cat risk, they can reallocate their capital and cause a capacity contraction. The lack of supply will eventually drive returns back up to the point where investors are willing to participate – that is, the level where returns compensate for risks taken. Central to any investor's decision, of course, is the level of diversification that can be achieved by participating in a given market-place. Thus, it is not simply a question of considering whether the absolute returns available in the insurance/reinsurance market are greater or less than those in other asset classes, but whether they are correlated with other elements of the portfolio. A P&C risk that is uncorrelated with the balance of an investor's equity or fixed income portfolio, and yields returns that are slightly lower than those in the balance of the portfolio, might still be a compelling proposition.

Intermediaries play a central role in risk capacity, in several ways: bringing end-use clients and investors together, supplying capacity in their role as investors, and acting as end-users in their role as corporate risk managers. Their role is thus pivotal and fundamental to the concept of market convergence (which we discuss in the next chapter). If intermediaries – including global insurers, reinsurers, commercial banks, investment banks and universal banks – can successfully bring investors and end-users together through their distribution networks, the amount of risk capacity available to underwrite risk is likely to increase. Likewise, if they are willing to act as direct or indirect investors, they can help to build the supply of risk capacity. If they are also on hand to absorb some of the risk capacity by managing their own portfolios of very large and complex risks, they help to ensure that the market moves toward an appropriate level of efficiency and equilibrium pricing.

2.5   DIVERSIFYING THE CREDIT RISK OF INTERMEDIARIES

When corporate end-users arrange risk transfer, risk-financing or hedging solutions with intermediaries they are often exposed to **credit risk**, or the risk of loss if the intermediary, as a counterparty, fails to perform on its contractual obligations. For instance, if a company has entered into a derivative hedging transaction with a bank and the hedge acquires value (offsetting a loss in the company's underlying operations), default by the bank creates a loss for the company. Similarly, if the company purchases an insurance policy from an insurer who defaults when the policy has value (e.g., an insurable loss has occurred, or a claim has been submitted), the company suffers a loss. This dimension of credit risk is an important element of the financial markets in general, and the risk management markets in particular. Any firm active in risk management activities is likely to have credit exposure to intermediaries and must take account of that exposure.[14]

When credit risks are centered with highly rated intermediaries (e.g., A, AA or AAA rated) and the exposures are not large, concentrated or long-term, the credit risk a firm faces may be acceptable. However, when this is not true, exposure has to be managed actively. A company with large or complex financial/operating risks can deal with a number of insurers/reinsurers or financial institutions, which permits diversification of the portfolio of credit exposures. Risks can be channeled to different institutions using a variety of mechanisms, including those provided by the financial market and the ART market, to enable exposures to be spread more evenly. A firm can also use specific structures from the ART market that are actually designed to eliminate the credit risk of the insurer/reinsurer completely (e.g., the issuance of a capital market security or the use of a pure captive eliminates a firm's exposure to the insurer or reinsurer). The ability to diversify, reduce, or eliminate credit risk exposure to intermediaries is thus another driver of activity in the ART market.

Intermediaries are exposed to each other's credit risk. Indeed, many insurers/reinsurers and financial institutions have intricate business relationships that span multiple fronts. For instance, insurers often hold large portfolios of bank liabilities as investments and are thus exposed to bank credit risk; they also rely on banks for contingent credit facilities (e.g., liquidity lines, letters of credit). Banks, in turn, often seek risk cover for aspects of their operations from insurers (e.g., buying credit protection from insurance companies to hedge the credit risks in their loan portfolios, purchasing surety cover, bond insurance or trade credit insurance for specific deals, and so on). Banks may also enter into long-term derivative transactions with financial subsidiaries of insurers/reinsurers. Insurers, of course, routinely purchase reinsurance cover from the reinsurance sector, and are thus exposed to reinsurer credit risk. A symbiotic relationship therefore exists between the sectors; since these types of transaction can generate considerable amounts of credit exposure, they must be managed carefully, sometimes through the specific ART mechanisms we detail in subsequent chapters.

2.6 MANAGING ENTERPRISE RISKS INTELLIGENTLY

The ART market is also driven by demand from corporate and end-use clients who seek new and more intelligent ways of covering traditional and non-traditional exposures. While it is simple for firms to acquire standard insurance/reinsurance (e.g., traditional lines of cover and 1-year maturities) or basic derivative hedges, large companies seeking to manage their risks more wisely require more intricate or comprehensive solutions. This means greater demand for:

- multi-year and multiple peril structures, including programs that extend for 3 to 5 years (and more) and cover risks associated with multiple exposures (e.g., earthquake and hurricane, or business interruption and workers' compensation);
- non-traditional covers, including new risks arising from a changing environment spurred by financial and trade deregulation, terrorism, reputation, intellectual property, technology, geopolitics, fraud, malpractice, non-catastrophic weather, the environment, and so forth;

---

[14] This risk is all too real: for instance, between 1984 and the millennium, an average of 30 to 60 P&C insurers have become insolvent each year.

- flexible coverage mechanisms, including selection at will from derivatives, insurance/reinsurance, capital markets instruments, captives, and so on;
- integrated risk programs, including platforms that group together seemingly diverse exposures in a customized fashion to produce the most price- and resource-efficient coverage possible.

Since a comparative advantage in arranging a risk exposure might differ from that of assuming or managing the risk, the ART market can help to direct the risk to the institution, product or solution where the capability and advantage exists.

2.7 REDUCING TAXES

Tax matters can feature prominently in any economic decision. An instrument, vehicle or transaction that lowers taxes (all other variables being equal) will ultimately boost operating/net income and, thus, enterprise value. It is therefore important to understand the tax impact of various risk management techniques.

Consider, for instance, the tax treatment of insurance contracts. In many national tax jurisdictions insurance premiums paid by a company are treated as an ordinary and necessary business expense and deducted against income as incurred; this deductibility boosts net income. Similarly, insurance proceeds received in the aftermath of a loss and claim are generally not taxed (unless, for example, the proceeds are greater than the damaged property's tax basis or represent lost business profits); this, again, can increase a firm's net income. A firm that is uninsured and suffers a loss can deduct the uninsured portion of the loss from income (e.g., for P&C losses a firm can deduct the lower of the difference between fair market value before and after the loss, or the adjusted book value of the property). The source of the insurance can also factor into the tax equation. For instance, a US firm buying insurance from an offshore insurer will face a higher cost as it is essentially paying, through the premium, an excise tax to the US Treasury. Insurers themselves can receive special exemptions from current taxes by pooling risks. The tax treatment of captives depends on the type of captive a company uses. Although we shall explore the issue at greater length in Chapter 5, a firm that uses a group, senior or even sister captive can generally deduct the insurance premium paid to the captive as an ordinary business expense. In contrast, deductibility may not be possible if a company uses a pure captive that underwrites little, or no, third-party business.

The tax treatment of derivatives is much less transparent and must be considered carefully. In many jurisdictions rules remain subjective and depend on the nature of the underlying transaction and reference index. However, the central tax benefit often hinges on whether a derivative is considered to be a hedge for risk management purposes or is actually a speculative position. If it can legitimately be considered to be a hedge, then the firm can account for derivative gains/losses under ordinary income/loss deductibility. A swap or option that limits balance sheet exposure to interest rates, commodity or currency risks might qualify as a tax hedge; and 'anticipatory' hedging might also be permissible. In contrast, a derivative that protects revenue streams or net income against price/volatility risks may not always be considered to be a tax hedge. If a derivative is not a hedge, then derivative losses become capital losses and can generally only be deducted against capital gains (they are otherwise forfeited).

Tax deductibility issues are not limited to insurance, reinsurance and derivative contracts. Loss control mechanisms that lower the actual risk exposures of a firm through protective measures may also be deductible. For instance, under some accounting regimes loss control expenses such as training and education related to safety, hazards, inspection, and so on, can be deducted from income immediately. Loss control measures that take the form of capital assets (e.g., sprinkler systems, safety fencing, security, and so on) are depreciated over the useful life of the asset and deducted in each relevant period.

Although tax issues related to risk management and corporate matters are obviously complex – and depend largely on location, product, timing, and so on – it is important to emphasize that different risk management techniques attract different tax treatments that must be considered in light of cost/benefit tradeoffs.

2.8   OVERCOMING REGULATORY BARRIERS

Insurance/reinsurance companies and financial institutions are regulated by different authorities and are often required to adhere to unique rules. As a result, activity in the ART market is influenced by attempts to overcome regulatory barriers that might otherwise limit or prohibit business (this is distinct from capitalizing on deregulation, which we consider below). Overcoming regulatory barriers requires the nature of the risk management product being created or used to be carefully considered. For example, it is important to determine whether a product is considered to be insurance or a derivative by the national regulator (and, if a contract is a derivative, whether it is a hedge and whether the intermediary is authorized to write the contract). This has a bearing on regulatory and tax treatment and impacts costs/benefits for end-users and intermediaries. If a cedant and insurer operating under English Law agree through a risk transfer product to the payment of a specific value – whether or not a loss has occurred – the product will be considered an 'unenforceable wager' and will not carry the same loss, tax and accounting treatment as an insurance contract. Such distinctions must be understood in advance of dealing.

Insurers generally face more stringent regulations than reinsurers because regulators feel greater pressure to protect individual policyholders against the prospect of insurer insolvency. In many countries insurance companies are regulated by state or national regulatory agencies, which apply strict rules on underwriting, investment and capital prudency standards. Reinsurers, in contrast, operate on an international, cross-border scale. Their business is directed primarily toward the professional market and, as they are subjected to relatively less stringent regulatory rules and scrutiny, they can underwrite a greater variety and concentration of risks than primary insurers. The regulatory framework thus makes it easier to direct certain ART-related business to the reinsurance, rather than the insurance, market. To 'circumvent' restrictions that might otherwise impede business, some major insurers have established reinsurance subsidiaries to deal in select products and risks on an offshore basis. Some have also developed capital market subsidiaries to offer derivative and other financial instruments to their professional client base.

In a similar light, regulations typically prevent banks from writing primary insurance or reinsurance. In order to access the market as a supplier of insurance/reinsurance capacity, some choose to link into the market through separate insurance/reinsurance subsidiaries and Bermuda transformers (as discussed in Chapter 9). In some cases regulatory barriers direct business/risk management flows; for example, banks have demonstrated significant demand for credit enhancement from the insurance sector as they can arbitrage the cost of capital spread that arises from regulatory differences. Banks that face a regulatory capital charge on the risk of loans they have extended can transfer the risk to the insurance sector (via collateralized debt obligations (CDOs) and credit derivatives/insurance), which are subject to a different set of charges. Since banks and insurers assess technical reserves against expected losses and capital for unexpected losses in different ways, the opportunity for a 'regulatory arbitrage' exists: e.g., insurers assume credit risks that banks want to shed in order to lower their capital charges. In some countries insurance regulators prohibit companies with individual credit risks to use credit derivatives, but they may permit the use of insurance/reinsurance contracts. The same often occurs in the weather derivatives/insurance market. These are all examples of regulatory arbitrages that help to promote the growth of the ART market.

2.9   CAPITALIZING ON DEREGULATION

While regulatory barriers exist between different market segments and inhibit the type and amount of risk management business that can be conducted by specific institutions, deregulation forces are helping to promote greater cross-sector activity. This deregulation leads to **convergence** – which we define as a cross-sector fusion of business activities – with insurers and financial institutions participating in each other's markets through the creation of mechanisms that allow assumption and transfer of insurance and financial risks. Through deregulation, insurers/reinsurers and financial institutions actively offer products, services and solutions in each other's areas of traditional expertise; by doing so they gradually assume the appearance of broader-based financial conglomerates. Thus, we may observe banks and securities firms offering insurance-related products and services and attempting to solve risk management problems that have traditionally been associated with insurance risks. It is increasingly common, for instance, for commercial banks to sell life insurance, long-term health care/disability cover, and annuities, and for investment banks to absorb catastrophe risk, political risk, and so forth. Insurers and reinsurers, for their part, offer banking and investment services and deal actively in a range of financial risks, including credit and market risks. We shall consider some of the specific cross-sector ART activities that each of these groups performs in the next chapter, but for now note that, as a result of deregulation, the boundaries that once defined these distinct industry sectors are no longer applicable. This makes it simpler for a single intermediary to offer a range of financial, insurance-based or hybrid/ART-based solutions; firms that can consolidate risk management programs (i.e., programs that simultaneously manage credit and market risks, and certain insurance risks, in a multi-year form and with appropriate coverage layers) produce a valuable and convenient product/service for clients.

In the US, product and market convergence has been aided by the passage of the 1999 Financial Modernization Act (i.e., the Gramm–Leach–Bliley Act), which eliminated the 1933 Glass–Steagall Act and Depression-era legislation that prohibited banks, investment banks and insurance companies from encroaching on each other's territory. For example, through this legislative change, an insurer can own a bank, a bank can grant loans and underwrite insurance, and holding companies can be created to control subsidiaries that offer banking, insurance and investments. This leads to greater cross-industry mergers and acquisitions, (e.g., Citibank/Salomon/Travelers, Merrill Lynch/ML Insurance, ML Bank) the creation of multi-service platforms, and offers more integrated products and services, including those characteristics of the ART market. In the UK and Continental Europe, regulations have permitted cross-industry consolidation for years, and a number of hybrid 'bancassurance' organizations have developed to provide combined banking/insurance services (e.g., Allianz/Dresdner, ING, Lloyds/Scottish Widows), and so forth. Through these combined platforms, firms can structurally and organizationally create different risk management products/services in a much more transparent and efficient manner, which ultimately benefits the end-use clients.

Regardless of the specific form of development and delivery, the key market drivers we have mentioned in this chapter have been critical to the expansion of the ART market. Indeed, many of these forces will continue to fuel further innovation and activity in coming years as end-users and intermediaries gradually realize the particular advantages that can be obtained from the use of alternative solutions.

3

The ART Market and its Participants

In the first two chapters we have considered basic concepts related to risk and the theoretical motivations that drive risk management decisions. We now turn our attention to a general discussion of ART, reviewing the characteristics of the marketplace, including scope, origin, market participants, and convergence. As we develop the ART theme by considering products, vehicles, and solutions in the chapters that follow we shall revert to several fundamental issues covered in this section.

3.1 A DEFINITION OF ART

The ART market is a broad-based sector that defies precise classification. Indeed, its scope and coverage varies considerably among practitioners, end-users, and regulators, so that any definition is based, to some degree, on opinion. To review the definition we presented in Chapter 1, we note once again that the ART market is the *combined risk management marketplace for innovative insurance and capital market solutions*, while ART is *a product, channel or solution that transfers risk exposures between the insurance and capital markets to achieve stated risk management goals*. In its broadest sense ART can be viewed as an all-encompassing sector that involves multiple asset classes and risks, conduits, products, terms, industries, and legal vehicles. To create an optimal ART-based risk management plan, multiple products, vehicles, and solutions are often used in combination.

To help to focus our discussion, we segment ART into three categories: products, vehicles, and solutions.

- *Products* Any instrument or structure that is used to achieve a defined risk management goal. Within this category we include:
  - Select insurance/reinsurance products
  - Multi-risk products
  - Insurance-linked capital markets issues
  - Contingent capital structures
  - Insurance derivatives.
- *Vehicles* Any channel that is used to achieve risk management goals. Within this category we include:
  - Captives and risk retention groups
  - Special-purpose vehicles/reinsurers
  - Bermuda transformers
  - Capital markets subsidiaries.
- *Solutions* Any broad program that uses multiple instruments or vehicles to manage risk exposures on a consolidated basis. Within this category we include:
  - Enterprise risk management programs.

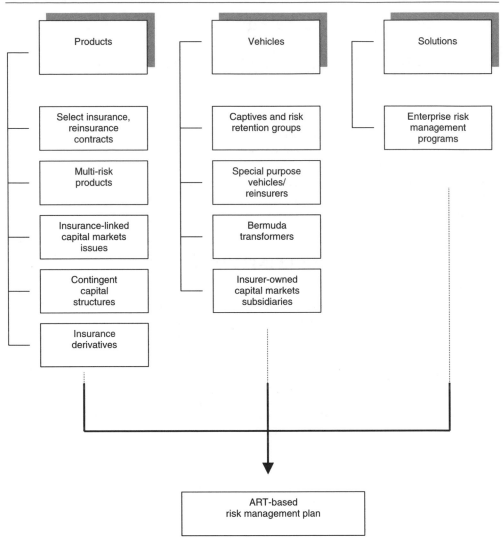

Figure 3.1 Categories of ART

We consider each of these issues, summarized in Figure 3.1, at length in the balance of the book. In fact the three segments form a central core in risk management as they allow greater, and more efficient, dispersion of risk exposures throughout the financial system. Investors, end-users and intermediaries can benefit by using the products, vehicles, and solutions mentioned above to manage risks. However, to enable implementation to be successful, appropriate skills, resources, and infrastructure must exist. If an individual firm cannot properly consider, measure, manage, and monitor a wide array of insurance and financial risks, or if an investor or capacity supplier cannot properly evaluate risk and return tradeoffs, then incorrect risk and investment management decisions can result. ART can only be successful when it forms part of a robust risk management process.

3.2 ORIGINS AND BACKGROUND OF ART

Since the definition of ART is broad, and at least somewhat subjective, it is difficult to point to a precise time or location when the market actually "started". Indeed, its evolution has been gradual – a characteristic that remains true to the present time. However, since an important element of the sector involves self-insurance, risk retention, and captives (which we consider in Chapter 5), it is generally agreed that growing use of these techniques/vehicles during the late 1960s and early 1970s marks the informal start of the ART market. By the time many of the world's largest corporate risk managers had established retention and captive programs, new techniques of risk transfer and risk financing began to appear. During the 1980s and 1990s risk-financing products – which focused primarily on the timing, rather than the transfer, of risks and cash flows – began to take greater hold. Various types of finite risk programs, which we discuss in Chapter 4, spurred growth in the ART market during this period. By the mid- to late-1990s, and into the new millennium, a combination of market cycles, product innovation, and deregulation ushered in a new wave of risk management mechanisms, including multi-risk products, contingent capital instruments, securitizations, and insurance-related derivatives (which we review in Chapters 6 through 9). These helped to foster advances in enterprise risk management in the late 1990s and early millennium (as discussed in Chapter 10); in fact, the future of the ART market rests heavily on further expansion in integrated approaches to risk management. The core of the ART market thus developed in incremental stages over a 30-year period.

As the ART market has evolved through various phases, the fundamental drivers discussed in the previous chapter, including value maximization, market cycles/capacity, taxes, and regulation/deregulation forces, have guided growth and innovation. Managing corporate risks in order to maximize enterprise value has become more critical than ever, and any marketplace or mechanism that can offer cost-effective risk solutions becomes an important element of the system. In fact, certain market environment variables seem to be accelerating the growth process, including those related to financial failures, credit market expansion, and new sources of risk. For instance, the financial and corporate failures/scandals of the late twentieth and early twenty-first centuries have led to a significant amount of liability and litigation; in some cases investors have pursued companies, boards, and executives for restitution, and insurers/reinsurers providing cover have been forced to make payments; more of this activity might appear in the future, meaning that companies and risk managers need to be attuned to mechanisms providing coverage against breaches by directors and officers, fraud, environmental liabilities,[1] and so on. Intermediaries will also have to consider new ways of dealing with these potential liabilities. The growing market for credit instruments – loans, bonds, securitized structures, and derivatives – has indicated a turn toward more active and dynamic management of credit exposures, placing additional demands on the ART market and its participants. Indeed, the credit dimension of risk management promises to grow even more rapidly as new issuers/borrowers access capital and investors reallocate their portfolios. Tools that can help to manage, transfer, or replicate credit risks have been, and will continue to be, prevalent. New sources of risk have also appeared and are changing the risk management landscape; companies are demanding a range of new covers, including those once widely regarded as 'uninsurable'. For instance, risks related to intellectual property, terrorism, complex financial

---

[1] For instance, asbestos claims remain an ongoing problem for the insurance industry at large; the large amount of claims suggest that insurance reserves may be $50bn short of what may ultimately be required, and the system may have to follow a 'pay as you go' process for some time.

indicators, complicated liability/litigation, illiquidity, 'cybercrime,' and so on, lend themselves to some of the solutions of the ART market. While these may contribute to further ART growth in future years, they present considerable challenges. Any new source of risk or disruption in the financial process makes the evaluation and management of exposures more challenging. The lack of data and loss experience, and the changing nature of financial relationships and market variables, places a growing burden on risk management providers and end-users. Traditional insurance/reinsurance providers that are not able to cope with new dimensions of risk may lose business to other intermediaries with more sophisticated analytics and/or greater risk appetite. The face of the ART market will thus continue to change further in coming years.

Some aspects of the ART market are very global in nature, while others are associated with national or regional markets. For instance, risk retention groups and multi-trigger products are particularly popular in the US and are used by an ever-growing segment of the marketplace; they are, however, less common in Europe and Asia. Captives, in contrast, are extremely popular with companies and insurers around the world – so popular, in fact, that a number of 'captive friendly' tax jurisdictions have developed in various locations to service local demand for captive business. The same is true of insurance-linked securitizations: global issuers have participated actively since the late 1990s.

ART products and solutions are characterized by a high degree of customization. ART is a bespoke, sometimes time-consuming, process that is intended to resolve very specific risk management goals. Unlike many other financial or insurance products, ART instruments and solutions are generally not 'commoditized' for long periods of time (if ever). Many structures must be tailored to suit the specific requirements of each client and supplier of risk capacity/financing, as well as local rules and regulations. Only when significant experience has been gained might a particular product/service become more standardized and available through a larger number of intermediaries to a greater number of end-users (even then, however, bespoke features remain apparent to some degree).

3.3 MARKET PARTICIPANTS

The ART market has managed to grow and innovate through supply and demand forces. It is common, in a traditional framework, to consider risk management in two distinct ways: those who demand particular services (e.g., corporate end-users and investors) and those who can supply them (e.g., intermediaries). End-users need risk solutions that can protect economic capital, minimize financial distress, and help to maximize enterprise value. Investors demand capital deployment opportunities with returns that reflect the risks taken; if they can successfully identify such opportunities, they supply the marketplace with much-needed risk capital. Intermediaries bridge the gap, uniting the two by creating solutions and delivering investment capital/risk capacity. Those responsible for designing and marketing particular risk products/services and supplying risk capacity are often the end-users or investors. Accordingly, at any point in a market or product development cycle an institution may supply or demand services or capital (within the bounds of applicable regulation, of course). To help to illustrate this point we consider some of the key participants in the ART market – including insurers and reinsurers, financial institutions, corporate end-users, investors, and brokers – and the various roles they can play.

3.3.1 Insurers and reinsurers

Insurers and reinsurers supply risk capacity in a number of traditional insurance lines (e.g., P&C, liability, health, auto, and so on). In the normal course of business they are involved in:

- underwriting (i.e., selecting and classifying applicants through particular standards and in relation to the existing portfolio of risky business);
- rate-making (i.e., valuing, in an actuarial framework, risk exposures being covered to ensure appropriate premium loading);
- settling claims (i.e., verifying and paying losses);
- managing investments (i.e., investing internal investment assets in a range of debt and equity securities);
- managing risks (e.g., using reinsurance/retrocession, derivatives and other techniques to balance internal risks, particularly those associated with liabilities).

Apart from these core activities, insurers and reinsurers are significant participants in the ART market: they design and market ART products, manage their own risk exposures through ART-related mechanisms, invest policyholder funds in a range of ART-related assets (e.g., catastrophe bonds, credit transfer instruments), and supply specific layers of risk capacity through ART instruments. While some of the expansion of insurers/reinsurers into ART arises from their desire to service client requirements and manage their own risks, it is also driven by the need to find new sources of revenue with appropriate margins. Offering ART services diversifies revenues among a broader base of companies, sectors, and exposures, and helps insurers to manage business through favorable/unfavorable market and pricing cycles.

Insurers, including many of the world's largest, may be organized as joint stock companies (i.e., standard, limited liability incorporated entities, with investors supplying equity capital and *de-facto* owning, if not controlling, the firms) or mutual organizations[2] (i.e., combined ownership with policyholders supplying necessary capital).[3] As business growth has led to the need for more capital, various large mutual insurers have demutualized, gaining access to external equity capital. The incidence of insurance industry consolidations has also accelerated since the mid 1990s as various firms have sought to expand their balance sheets and distribution networks. Lloyds of London – a central focus of the insurance and reinsurance market – is not an insurance company *per se*, but an association that provides services to members and syndicates (who may, themselves, be joint stock or mutual organizations). Reinsurers, acting as insurers to the insurance industry, are typically organized as joint stock companies, and conduct most of their business in the professional market. Many are incorporated in Bermuda, where they can take advantage of favorable tax treatment and a relatively flexible, though still secure, regulatory environment.

While insurers have historically focused strictly on traditional insurance business (and many, it should be noted, continue to do so), some of the largest have expanded their operating scope in recent years to the point where they are well represented in diverse businesses and have assumed the form of broad financial conglomerates. Though most insurers continue to preserve an insurance focus (e.g., a core business of P&C, liability, health, life cover based on standard

---

[2] Mutual organizations can grant policyholders dividends or rate reductions if operations are profitable; alternatively, if losses are excessive, they may issue assessable policies on which policyholders must make good.

[3] A third type of insurance firm, the reciprocal exchange, is effectively an unincorporated mutual and not encountered very frequently.

one-year terms and strict actuarially driven pricing) those on the leading edge create new products, extend underwriting terms, and incorporate financing elements into their policies (e.g., financing via finite contracts). Some of the expansion is evident in the credit risk transfer market, where various firms actively underwrite credit risks through enhancements, financial guarantees, and credit wraps. For instance, monoline insurance companies and P&C insurers routinely enhance asset-backed securities[4] and senior tranches of **collateralized debt obligations** (CDOs, securitized pools of credit) that are originated by banks. Even when a bank does not require credit insurance/credit wrap (e.g., no funding requirement) it might turn to a monoline to buy credit protection via a portfolio credit default swap. Monoline insurance companies[5] routinely underwrite financial guarantee insurance to cover bondholders and must therefore be extremely informed about credit risks (they tend to underwrite low-frequency/high-severity events because of their risk-averse underwriting standards, which help them to preserve AAA ratings). Some insurers have even established capital market subsidiaries in order to offer a range of financial and insurance-related derivatives – the traditional domain of banks and securities firms. Insurers, as investors and asset managers, have also acquired considerable expertise in the analysis and trading of financial instruments and credit portfolios, which, again, has historically been the domain of banking firms. P&C insurers, monolines, and life insurers are significant investors in credit instruments, either directly (through the purchase of asset-backed securities, CDOs) or synthetically (through the sale of credit protection on various CDO tranches and portfolio credit default insurance/swaps); while life insurers often invest in mezzanine and equity tranches of CDOs. The insurance sector also transfers market risk, by guaranteeing returns on particular products sold to cedants or expressing direct views on classes of market risk. For instance, some P&C insurers sell long-dated options on a variety of equity indexes, either directly (e.g., straight sales of options) or indirectly (e.g., providing downside protection in principal-guaranteed equity funds). Life insurers sell options on various other market references, including interest rates and currencies (separately, they are also significant buyers of swap options and interest rate floors to protect their guaranteed liability exposures). Though the margins on this business are generally acceptable (though not as wide as in the credit sector), the risks can be challenging to manage. Valuing and hedging complex, illiquid, and long-dated options are demanding tasks.[6] However, the fact that they must routinely deal in a variety of financial instruments and risks means that they are acquiring many of the skills that have historically been associated with the banking sector.

Reinsurers are also expanding their scope and some are assuming the appearance of integrated financial institutions. In fact, reinsurers have acquired significant financial capabilities in recent years (to complement their core insurance and reinsurance expertise) and can be

---

[4] Some asset-backed programs, particularly in the commercial paper market, require bank facilities as a backup in order to achieve suitable credit ratings; accordingly, banks actually bear a large amount of credit risk unless third-party enhancement is available through overcollateralization, a monoline guarantee, or unconditional surety programs.

[5] Monolines were originally established in the 1970s in the US to provide municipal bond investors with guarantees of principal and interest. During the 1980s they expanded their coverage to the asset-backed securities market, and in the 1990s they made the logical progression to covering CDOs and other credit structures.

[6] For instance, in the late 1990s UK life insurers purchased large amounts of long-dated sterling swaptions to hedge deferred annuities and cover reinvestment risks (e.g., 30-year investment products with guaranteed minimum returns). Such hedges were very difficult to create as they were illiquid, long-dated, and very credit intensive. In fact, many of the investment banks that helped to arrange the hedges by selling the cover had difficulties with their own hedges, and some suffered losses. Since banks generally did not want to deal with the credit risks of insurers on such a long-dated basis, they were required to consider alternative mechanisms, e.g., contracting with supranational organizations such as the World Bank and European Investment Bank to have them issue 40-year sterling notes with interest rates and amortization schedules linked to swap rates and mortality rates; the life insurance companies could then purchase the notes as hedges for their own guaranteed annuity operations.

regarded as very sophisticated players in different aspects of risk and investment management. These firms are active across a wide range of traditional insurance and ART businesses. For instance, reinsurers routinely underwrite credit protection for insurers on an individual obligor basis (e.g., an insurer might buy a mezzanine tranche of a CDO, taking the first 5% of losses; it may then approach a reinsurer to obtain protection on individual credits within that 'first loss' piece). They also provide insurers with hedges on their guaranteed annuity business and some buy and sell derivatives via dedicated capital market subsidiaries authorized to engage in such business.

As noted, insurers and reinsurers participate in the ART market, in part, to diversify their revenue streams. Rather than being exposed solely to the market cycles that define the magnitude and quality of industry earnings, many institutions are eager to continue diversification into other, hopefully uncorrelated, businesses. This can help to smooth out some of the earnings volatility that might otherwise arise.

3.3.2   Investment, commercial, and universal banks

Investment banks, commercial banks, and universal (or integrated) banks are focused primarily on originating and managing financial risks. Similar to insurers, they have very specific duties and functions, which they perform to varying degrees (depending on regulatory rules, specific expertise, and corporate strategy). These can include:

- originating credit facilities and loans;
- underwriting capital markets securities (e.g., equities, bonds) on a primary basis;
- trading assets (e.g., equities, bonds, loans, derivatives, foreign exchange) on a secondary basis;
- developing structured products and other synthetic assets (via cash products and derivatives);
- providing wealth management, risk management, and corporate finance advice.

Most banks have considerable expertise in designing products and pricing and trading multi-year, bundled risks (e.g., credit, market, liquidity). While that remains their core business, the most innovative have expanded into the insurance world and regularly assume insurance-related risks. As with insurers, financial institutions are searching for opportunities to expand and diversify revenues in uncorrelated areas, including insurance and ART. For instance, several large investment and universal banks have been at the forefront of insurance-related capital market issues (e.g., catastrophe bonds, contingent capital structures), and various others have actively sought to transfer capital markets risks to the reinsurance market through their own dedicated reinsurance subsidiaries, captives, and Bermuda transformers. Some have also become involved in trading insurance related-derivatives (e.g., weather derivatives). More generally, some of the world's largest banks own insurance subsidiaries that permit them to underwrite certain types of life and annuity covers for their clients (as part of a total wealth management platform).

In addition to revenue diversification, financial institutions may be active in ART for internal risk management purposes. Many banks are eager to transfer their risks in order to lower capital charges and write new business. In many cases risks that they originate, particularly in the credit markets, are passed to the insurance/reinsurance sector, who may have some comparative advantage in assuming exposures as a result of unique regulations and diversification, pricing, and risk management policies. In fact, banks have actively worked with insurers in recent years in transferring credit risks. As noted above, insurers provide a variety of covers on pools of corporate credit risk and also act as investors in a range of tranches (primarily those that rated investment grade).[7] Banks routinely create customized trading desk CDOs and portfolio default swaps for insurers, who essentially sell them the required protection.

Various mergers and acquisitions have occurred within the banking universe in recent years as firms attempt to create greater operating efficiencies, financial strength and broader business and distribution networks. National and cross-border consolidations within the investment banking and commercial banking sectors have occurred regularly since the mid-1990s.[8] It is also worth noting that in some instances financial institutions and insurance companies have merged their operations, creating very broad-based financial conglomerates that can offer insurance, reinsurance, and banking products.[9] These firms are arguably well positioned to offer integrated insurance/banking products and solutions.

3.3.3   Corporate end-users

Corporate end-users that actively manage their risks demand solutions that are appropriate and flexible. While companies in many industries and locations use risk management mechanisms from the traditional markets (e.g., insurance, financial derivatives), some have also migrated to the ART market to make use of finite programs, risk retention techniques, captives, and contingent securities. Indeed, large companies, primarily from the US and Europe, have been particularly active in captives and other self-insurance programs; some have also begun to participate in insurance-related derivatives and integrated risk management programs. Most industry sectors can take advantage of ART market mechanisms: automobiles, heavy industry, technology, raw materials, media/entertainment, integrated petrochemicals, energy, transportation, aviation, food/beverage, hospitality, and retail, among others, are represented in some part of the ART market. In addition, insurers and banks become end-users themselves when they implement ART solutions for their own risk management purposes.

The most sophisticated corporate end-users are willing and able to implement a variety of risk management solutions. There is some indication that large global corporations remain focused on retentions/self-insurance and demand coverage of unique (and what might have once been considered uninsurable) risks; they also appear to be more intently focused on enterprise/integrated risk solutions. Rather than allocating capital on an incremental basis to manage discrete risk exposures, the most advanced corporate end-users review and manage their exposures on a holistic, portfolio basis. Interest is strong enough that the practice of hedging, transferring, or retaining individual risks in isolation may decline over the medium term. Smaller firms, however, still are poorly represented in the ART market. Many continue to focus on traditional vehicles and services, perhaps not realizing they can reduce risk management expenses and boost enterprise value through the use of alternative processes. In fact, they may not be receiving sufficient attention from brokers and intermediaries, who often target the very largest companies as priority clients.

---

[7] A number of insurers experienced credit losses on sub-investment grade and subordinated tranches in the late 1990s and 2001/2002 and have attempted to redirect their investment focus to the higher quality tranches.

[8] For instance, JP Morgan/Chase, Deutsche/Bankers Trust/Alex Brown, UBS/Warburg Dillon Read/Paine Webber, Citibank/Salmon Brothers, Credit Suisse/CSFB/DLJ, and so on.

[9] For instance, Citibank/Travelers, ING, Allianz/Dresdner, Lloyds/Scottish Widows, and so forth. In the US, deregulation measures passed in 1999 (e.g., the Financial Services Modernization Act (Gramm–Leach–Bliley)) made it possible for banks to be more directly and comprehensively involved in the insurance business. In countries such as the UK, the Netherlands, France, and Germany, cross-industry combinations have been permitted for years. In others, such as Japan, they are not permitted.

3.3.4   Investors/capital providers

Investors provide the capital, or risk capacity, that permits specific products and programs to be arranged. They are vital to the ART market, as they allow risks to be assumed, transferred, hedged or otherwise transformed. In fact, without this capital, the ART market would simply cease to function. Investors are generally large institutions that seek adequate returns on their investment portfolios through the provision of different forms of capital. We include in this category insurers and reinsurers, banks, investment funds (mutual funds, unit trusts), pension funds, and hedge funds. For instance, we have noted immediately above that insurers are very significant credit investors; they may decide to invest because credit risks are generally uncorrelated with other assets in their P&C portfolios (or they may believe that particular risks have been 'mispriced.') In many instances insurers, as investors, approach investment banks directly to have them craft specific CDOs and credit portfolios. In fact insurers and reinsurers have been active as credit investors for many years, buying loans and bonds; their credit capacity activities have increased in recent years through the mechanisms mentioned above (e.g., as intermediaries on alternative credit products). Hedge funds and other dedicated investment funds have become important suppliers of investment capital in sectors such as credit risk, catastrophe risk and, more recently, weather risk. As we shall note in Chapter 7, a core base of institutional investors has developed, since the turn of the millennium, to invest regularly in new securitized catastrophic risk issues. Most now realize that insurance-linked securities can provide a compelling investment combination of high returns for risks that are generally uncorrelated with other "traditional" financial asset classes. Various large banks with proprietary investment portfolios also emerge as regular buyers of catastrophe-based issues. Investors can also act as purchasers of securities floated under a contingent of capital facilities. Though the initial risk funding commitment rests with the arranger, in practice investors are on hand to take up contingently issued notes, and are thus the true suppliers of risk capacity.

3.3.5   Insurance agents and brokers

The insurance/reinsurance sector operates through a unique network of agents and brokers; most of these 'intermediaries' are involved in helping to arrange particular elements of risk management business, including ART-related deals. In many countries agents and brokers must be used to negotiate and conclude insurance-related business; failure to do so can be a breach of local regulation or law. Insurance agents legally represent insurers and have the authority to act on their behalf; they are paid directly by the insurers they represent. P&C agents can typically bind insurance companies on specific covers. Insurance brokers, in contrast, legally represent cedants and therefore have no authority to bind insurers. They can solicit and accept applications for cover,[10] but none of these is effective until an insurer actually accepts the proposal. The insurers that ultimately write a given cover pay brokers commissions. Some insurance brokers have emerged as important players in the ART market, helping cedants to analyze complex risks and develop appropriate solutions. They can provide considerable assistance with integrated policies and enterprise risk management programs, where extensive analysis and negotiations may be involved, and can help a client company to source the best possible coverage of risks – including those that cross from the insurance sector to the financial arena. In fact, some portion of the integrated risk business would be slowed without their participation.

---

[10] In the US specialized brokers often help 'non-admitted' insurers to place their surplus lines policies.

Table 3.1   The roles of ART market participants

	Insurers/ reinsurers	Financial institutions	Corporate end-users	Institutional investors	Agents/ brokers
Product development	✓	✓			✓
Risk advisory	✓	✓			✓
Risk capacity (provider)	✓	✓		✓	
Risk capacity (user)	✓	✓	✓		

The various functions that each of the above sectors play in the ART market is highlighted in Table 3.1. There are, of course, other participants in the sector, including those that provide credit ratings of counterparties and specific ART-related deals (e.g., catastrophe bonds, collateralized debt obligations, and so on) and those that develop sophisticated actuarial and financial mathematics models to quantify different elements of risk. Although they are important, we shall not consider them in greater detail.

3.4   PRODUCT AND MARKET CONVERGENCE

The ART marketplace and its products and solutions are considered 'alternative' because they pierce the boundaries of conventional risk management concepts and techniques (e.g., pure insurance, reinsurance, derivatives), calling on diverse financial engineering mechanisms from a number of different sectors and drawing in capital from a broad range of sources. This leads to greater customization, flexibility, and cross-sector integration. Indeed, one of the most noticeable aspects of the ART market is the degree to which once-distinct markets have been drawn together, as noted in Figure 3.2. Convergence, which we have already noted is a cross-sector fusion where insurers and financial institutions participate in each other's markets, is well underway. While the insurance, reinsurance, and financial markets were once very separate – with individual institutions performing well-defined functions within very strict, and clearly defined, boundaries – this is no longer true, primarily as a result of the regulatory and competitive forces we have mentioned in the previous chapter. Traditional barriers that once existed are now gone; where they remain, regulatory arbitrage structures are routinely

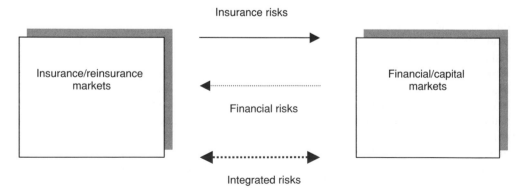

Figure 3.2   General insurance/financial convergence

developed. This allows each sector to develop new profit opportunities, earnings diversification, and risk portfolio diversification.

The convergence movement is expanding. Insurers and reinsurers routinely accept and repackage financial risks and offer a range of banking and financial services; banks, in turn, accept and manage certain insurance risks and write various classes of insurance. The two sectors also develop consolidated programs that include aspects of insurance and financial risk, and use many of the same instruments and solutions for their own internal risk management purposes. Both groups, along with hedge funds, pension funds, mutual funds, and other institutional investors, supply the markets with risk capacity in exchange for attractive investment opportunities. The interdependencies are therefore very intricate. They exist, in large measure, because improved risk management solutions can be achieved as each sector adds relevant expertise/skills and takes advantage of competitive advantages/regulatory relief.

Consider various simple examples of convergence. We have already noted that it is common for insurers and reinsurers to take a significant amount of credit risk. Though they have been traditional credit investors for a number of years (e.g., buying loans and bonds), they are now also extremely active in selling portfolio credit default swaps (as insurance or derivatives), underwriting the credit risks of particular CDO[11] tranches, and so forth. Insurers and reinsurers are also significant participants in a variety of market risks, buying and selling equity, interest rate, and currency market risks through various parts of their businesses. The presence of insurers and reinsurers in credit and market risks marks a clear 'encroachment' on the domain of banking institutions. Banks, in turn, have been very active in assuming various insurance-related risks, often by applying capital markets and structuring techniques to risk transactions related to catastrophe, non-catastrophic weather, and so forth. Banks use their distribution networks to place a variety of insurance risks with institutional investors and some have established reinsurance transformers to deal directly with insurers on an insurance contract basis. It is also true that banks own insurance companies, and vice versa, so they are able to deal in a very broad range of businesses, including the hybrid structures that are so characteristic of ART. These are just several simple examples of the insurance/financial market convergence that is underway, and is indicative of growing interdependence. Insurers, reinsurers, and financial institutions rely on each other to create, assume, and transfer a variety of exposures, meaning that the linkages between the markets are becoming stronger. Though regulatory restrictions still determine the activities that institutions may undertake, there is already a considerable overlap, and further deregulation will bring the markets even closer together over time.

Convergence is not limited to taking and accepting different classes of risk. Aspects of intellectual property, marketing, pricing, and distribution have also started to fuse. For instance, insurance companies have traditionally based their rate-making on actuarial techniques; investment banks, in contrast, have tended to price derivatives through financial mathematics (based on closed-form analytic or simulation-based processes). As the two industries converge – not only in ART, but also in other financial services – the opportunities for considering alternative pricing approaches are growing (e.g., use of simulation processes in insurance pricing, the application of extreme value theory in examining low-frequency financial and non-financial

---

[11] The CDO market has grown rapidly and become an important risk transfer marketplace; by the end of 2002, the market for US and European CDOs had grown to more than $300bn in size – from a standing start in the mid-1990s.

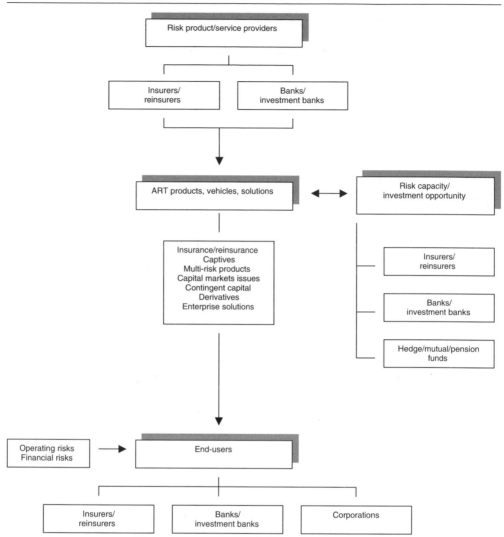

Figure 3.3   General insurance/financial convergence

catastrophes, and so forth). Likewise, as more universal banks and 'bancassurance' groups form, the joint marketing of financial and insurance-based products grows – e.g., through the concept of 'one-stop shopping' for individual consumers (banking, investment management, and personal insurance) and companies (banking, investment management, corporate finance, and insurance services). Figure 3.3 summarizes key aspects of the convergence movement.

Part II
Insurance and Reinsurance

4

Primary Insurance/Reinsurance Contracts

We know from Chapter 1 that insurance and reinsurance contracts are important elements of the corporate risk management market and are widely used in loss-financing programs. Indeed, insurance is so important that few companies operate without some amount of coverage. When accompanied by appropriate reinvestment, insurance can lead to direct and indirect enterprise value gains. Examining the costs/benefits available under different products and structures, and selecting the one that maximizes net cash flows, can create direct enterprise value. Making external stakeholders (e.g., creditors, investors, regulators, suppliers) aware that the firm is operating with a prudent level of post-loss coverage can create indirect value. Though a detailed review of insurance is well beyond the scope of this book, we consider several elemental insurance/reinsurance products in this chapter and their specific role in the ART market.

4.1 INSURANCE CONCEPTS

To begin our discussion on insurance/reinsurance products, we first review the essential features of any contract that is designed to cover an insurable risk. In order for a contract to be considered insurance, it must generally feature the following minimum characteristics[1]:

- The contract must cover an insurable risk with respect to some **fortuitous events** – one that is unforeseen, unexpected, or accidental.
- A sufficiently large number of homogeneous exposure units must exist, in order to make the losses somewhat predictable and measurable; the losses should be non-catastrophic.
- The cedant must have an insurable interest and be able to demonstrate an actual economic loss.
- The risk of loss must be specifically transferred under a contract providing indemnity and involve appropriate consideration (i.e., exchange of risk for upfront premium payment[2]).
- All dealing must be in 'utmost good faith' through the conveyance of material representations.
- The right of **subrogation**, or the transfer of loss recovery rights from cedant to insurer, must exist.[3]

If an insurance contract is to be binding, it must include offer/acceptance and consideration (e.g., fair value given by each party); it must also be executed with knowledge and legal purpose. The contract itself is an aleatory, rather than commutative, one, meaning that values

---

[1] More comprehensive definitions have been put forth regarding insurance and insurable risks, including the existence of highly random losses, small average loss on occurrence, short time between average losses, limits on maximum possible loss, minimal opportunity for moral hazard, high insurance premiums, and coverage consistent with public policy and applicable law.

[2] As noted earlier, premiums are paid by the cedant to the insurer upfront but are only 'earned' by the insurer as time passes and the contract draws closer to expiry. During the contract period the premium balance is held in an unearned premium account.

[3] This concept enforces the principle of indemnity, which indicates that the maximum gain should be limited to the maximum loss, and not some multiple.

exchanged may be unequal and uncertain. Indeed, we recall from Chapter 2 that this is true, as the fair premium charged for insurance cover is based primarily on pure premium, which is a statistically expected loss (plus premium loading); in some cases this will be more, and in some cases less, than actual loss experience.

Insurance therefore represents the transfer of fortuitous losses from the cedant (who pays an economically fair premium) to the insurer (who agrees to provide relevant indemnification). Insurers generally only insure pure risks,[4] based on a large number of non-catastrophic exposure units.[5] They seek to avoid catastrophic losses, which we consider to be a large number of exposure unit losses occurring at the same time (e.g., a concentration of risks that are impacted simultaneously), by diversifying correctly and using reinsurance mechanisms (they may also, of course, turn to certain ART products). If catastrophic loss occurs, then the pooling process has failed and premiums will have to be increased. There are, of course, exceptions to these guidelines (e.g., some insurers underwrite risks where the expected loss is difficult to estimate or the potential for a catastrophic outcome exists). However, where the rules are inviolable, an ART mechanism can be considered as a supplement or substitute.

Unlike derivative contracts, which transfer risk without regard to whether the purchaser suffers a loss, an insurance contract is based on insurable interest and requires proof of loss. This is a central difference between the two mechanisms, and one that limits the ability of companies to use insurance as a 'gaming', or speculative, instrument. Though insurance documentation requirements are jurisdiction-specific, a contract is often documented through a policy with **declarations** (specific insurance contract terms and attestations), an application, and schedules/endorsements. Declarations contain details on the cedant, coverage period, property description, coverage type, premium, deductibles, coinsurance, and caps. The document also references conditions related to cancellation, changes, examination and inspections, and transfer of rights.

4.2   INSURANCE AND LOSS FINANCING

Loss financing, as noted in Chapter 1, comprises hedging, retention, and transfer. *Hedging*, which is based on shifting risk from one party to another, is most often (though not exclusively) associated with derivative contracts,[6] which we shall consider at greater length in Chapter 9. *Retention*, as we have indicated, relates to risks that a firm opts to preserve and manage in what it perceives to be a more efficient and cost-effective manner. Retention can be accomplished through partial insurance (i.e., standard insurance contracts with higher deductibles, broader exposure exclusions, lower policy caps and/or greater copay/coinsurance features). It can also be achieved through certain dedicated insurance products that act primarily as risk-financing, rather than risk transfer, mechanisms. As we shall note below, some insurance products, including loss experience contracts and finite programs, do not transfer much of a cedant's risk, but shift the timing of cash flows associated with premiums, investment income, and loss experience; they can therefore be considered forms of retention. We shall consider

---

[4] Speculative risks may be uninsurable as they have a greater probability of generating large losses; in addition, losses (including those in the extreme tail of the relevant statistical distribution) are difficult to estimate.

[5] As we have noted, measurable loss is important because insurers must know where to price the risk capacity they are granting. As part of the process, insurance must also be able to establish appropriate loss reserves to cover future claims; such loss reserves are often divided into several categories, including losses reported and adjusted, losses reported but not yet adjusted, and losses incurred but not yet reported.

[6] Certain types of insurance contracts can also be considered forms of hedging, e.g., credit insurance covering a specific credit default risk.

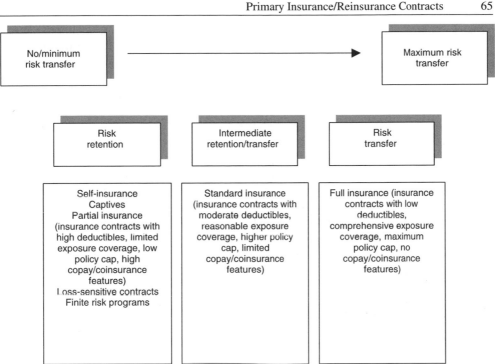

Figure 4.1   Risk retention versus risk transfer

several of these risk financing/retention products below. Risk retention can also be achieved through various captive structures, as described in the next chapter. *Risk transfer*, in contrast, is centered on shifting risks from cedant to insurer through conventional insurance products. In such instances little, or no, risk is retained or financed, meaning that most of the potential loss burden is passed to the insurer. Many standard insurance contracts, particularly those with low deductibles, low/no copay features, and high policy caps, are considered to be risk transfer mechanisms.

Within the general category of risk retention/transfer we note a spectrum of risk transferability that moves from the minimum (e.g., retention via structural features in standard contracts, dedicated risk-financing products, captives) to the maximum (e.g., full transfer via structural features in standard products). Use of one versus the other reverts to our discussion in Chapter 2 regarding risk governance and risk tolerance levels, and cost/benefit tradeoffs arising from the search for maximum enterprise value. Figure 4.1 summarizes the spectrum of risk retention/transfer possibilities.

4.3   PRIMARY INSURANCE CONTRACTS

4.3.1   Maximum risk transfer contracts

Full insurance

We know that the standard insurance policy transfers risk from the cedant to the insurer in exchange for payment of premium. Full insurance can be considered to be a maximum risk transfer contract: the goal is to shift as much exposure as possible at an appropriate price (i.e., the fair premium discussed earlier). Full insurance is generally characterized by *small deductibles, large policy caps, limited (or no) copay/coinsurance,* and *limited exclusions.* In creating a contract of this type the cedant is maximizing its premium payment (cost) in exchange for what it perceives to be greater risk transfer advantages (benefit). A traditional contract is based on an upfront premium payment for one year of cover.

As indicated in Chapter 1, various classes and subclasses of full insurance coverage are available, including marine insurance (e.g., hull, cargo, freight, liability) and non-marine insurance (e.g., life, health, and commercial P&C). Each subclass can be further divided into specific coverages. For instance, within the P&C sector policies can be written against property damage, business interruption, liability, directors and officers' liability, employ benefits/workers' compensation, home, automobile, and so forth. In addition, some insurers also offer insurance coverage of other types of corporate risks,[7] including those related to corporate finance transactions (e.g., coverage of representations and warranties,[8] tax opinions,[9] contingent tax liabilities, aborted acquisition bids, and so forth). These covers are designed to indemnify a company against any potential problems/losses arising in the aftermath of a corporate control transaction and might, in certain instances, be viewed as a substitute for undertaking a thorough due diligence exercise.

4.3.2   Minimal risk transfer contracts

Risks can be retained through a number of different vehicles, including self-insurance, risk retention programs, and captives (which we consider in detail in the next chapter), and partial insurance, loss sensitive contracts, and finite risk programs, which we discuss below.

Partial insurance

Partial insurance, a common form of risk retention, is a standard insurance contract that is tailored so that the cedant retains more, and thus transfers less, exposure (any customization of standard coverage is known as a **manuscript policy**). This results in a lower premium payment from the cedant to the insurer, consistent with the cedant's desired cost/benefit tradeoff. Partial insurance is created by altering deductibles, policy caps, copay/coinsurance features, and policy coverage/exclusions.

The characteristics of insurance are commonly altered through the *deductible,* which can be set on an individual loss basis or in aggregate (i.e., the sum of all loss events occurring during the coverage period). The greater the deductible, the greater the retention and the lower the transfer. For instance, a standard insurance policy for a risk averse company seeking to shift a significant amount of risk might feature a $1 million policy cap and a $100 000 aggregate deductible. After the first $100 000 of losses (which may come from a single event or many smaller ones), the

---

[7] In fact, Lloyds has offered a variety of corporate financing covers since the 1980s, but others have joined the marketplace in recent years.

[8] Representations (or 'reps') and warranties cover is designed to eliminate or reduce the risk related to future breach of reps and warranties by sellers or buyers of a company (or its assets), including those related to intellectual property, cash flows, tax, product and environmental liabilities, and so forth. Either, or both, parties may purchase the cover. If the seller purchases the insurance, the insurer underwrites an indemnity obligation payable to the buyer, and if the buyer purchases the insurance, the insurer underwrites the risk and cost of pursuing a seller in a breach. The cover can be useful in situations where valuation is difficult, e.g., intellectual property and intangibles.

[9] Tax opinion cover is designed to manage the risk of a tax challenge by a tax authority, i.e., a tax benefit is not considered favorably and results in a tax liability. This is particularly important in an era where tax shelters are still widely used, but periodically challenged by the tax authorities.

next $900 000 of losses is fully covered. A risk-taking company seeking to retain more risk might increase the deductible to $400 000 and thus be liable for the first $400 000, rather than $100 000, of losses; the insurer *de facto* provides $600 000 of loss coverage as a second layer. In the first example the company retains $100 000 of risk and transfers $900 000, in the second the firm retains $400 000 and transfers $600 000. In fact, while this may be precisely what the risk-taking company wants, insurers tend not to favor high deductible policies since pricing of the fair premium is difficult (i.e., it is very complicated to estimate the magnitude of the tail of the distribution). In addition, the insurer loses incremental investment income from the lower amount of reinvested premium.

A *policy cap* can also be used to define a level of risk retention by placing a limit on the insurer's loss payment liability to the cedant. The smaller the cap, the greater the ultimate retention and the lower the transfer. For instance, a company might contract with an insurer on business interruption coverage and cap the policy at $1 million; if an insurable event occurs and generates $2 million of business interruption losses, the insurer bears the first $1 million (assuming no deductible) and the company the second $1 million. Through this mechanism the company has effectively increased its risk retention by accepting any potential losses greater than $1 million. As with deductibles, policy caps can be set on a per occurrence or aggregate basis. Unlike deductibles, caps force the cedant to accept risk of loss in excess of the cap, meaning the amounts may be unpredictable and potentially large. In fact, through a cap the company remains uninsured in the tail of the distribution, which is precisely where coverage is most often needed (e.g., coverage of a catastrophic event that might otherwise precipitate financial distress); recall from our generalization in Chapter 1 that high severity/low frequency events are precisely the ones that a company should consider protecting against. Insurers, in turn, favor the inclusion of policy caps for the same reason: they need not be as precise in estimating the tail of the curve.

Risk transfer can also be limited through *copay/coinsurance* features, where cedant and insurer share in a certain amount of losses. The greater the cedant's share of a copay, the greater the retention, and the lower the transfer. Coinsurance payments can be determined in various ways. For instance, the insurer might agree to pay a set proportion of the actual cash value of the loss, with the cedant bearing the balance. Alternatively, the amount a cedant can recover from the insurer might be set as function of the amount of insurance carried relative to the amount required, multiplied by the actual loss experience. The insurer and cedant thus share in each loss on a predetermined percentage basis (depending on the cedant's own risk appetite); the premium payable to the insurer is a function of both the full premium and the proportion of risk retained.

Policy coverage/exclusions are another form of risk retention. By specifically defining the scope of desired coverage, the cedant indicates the risks it is willing to retain and those it wants to transfer. The more exclusions a policy contains (either as broad categories of risk – e.g., catastrophic P&C – or a specific event – e.g., North Atlantic hurricanes) the greater the implicit risk retention and the lower the transfer. Policies with less exclusions provide greater transfer and, by definition, less retention. In some policies all risks within a category (e.g., property damage) might be covered unless they are specifically excluded; the cedant is responsible for identifying and specifically excluding exposures that it wants to retain. In some cases, of course, the insurer will exclude coverage of certain risks, including those reflecting lack of insurability, extraordinary risks/hazards or excessive risk of moral hazard; the cedant is therefore forced to retain the risks or seek alternative solution. Figure 4.2 summarizes the mechanics for converting a full insurance policy into a partial one.

Ultimately, partial insurance is an effective way for a company to retain a particular amount and class of risk. In considering the cost/benefit tradeoffs, it is relatively straightforward for a

Table 4.1 Example of costs versus coverage benefits of various partial insurance options

Scenario	Cost	Coverage Benefit			
	Premium	Deductible	Cap	Coinsurance	Exclusions
1	$5m	$0	$10m	0%	None
2	$4m	$1m	$8m	5%	No D&O
3	$3m	$2m	$7m	10%	No interruption
4	$2m	$3m	$6m	15%	No earthquake
5	$2m	$3m	$5m	10%	No D&O
6	$1m	$5m	$7m	5%	None

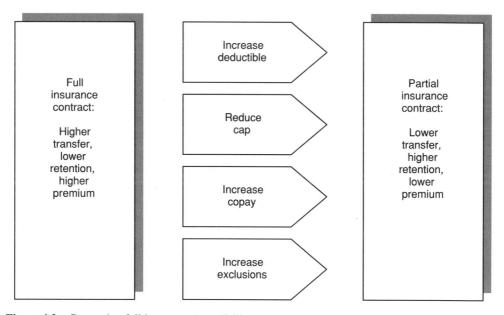

Figure 4.2   Converting full insurance to partial insurance

firm seeking a mix of risk retention/transfer to run scenarios of expected loss versus premium using a range of deductibles, caps, coinsurance, and coverage exclusion scenarios; this yields the aggregate enterprise value under each potential scenario and can help to guide the overall risk management strategy. Table 4.1 contains a very simplified example of this approach (actual scenario analysis is obviously much more detailed and would involve dozens of iterations and options).

Loss-sensitive contracts

Loss-sensitive contracts, partial insurance contracts with premiums that generally depend on loss experience, comprise a second category of minimal risk transfer instruments They are available in various forms, including experience-rated policies, large deductible policies, retrospectively rated policies and investment credit programs. Loss-sensitive contracts differ from conventional fixed premium insurance contracts in several ways: premiums depend on losses that occur during a specified period, payouts are typically not determined until some

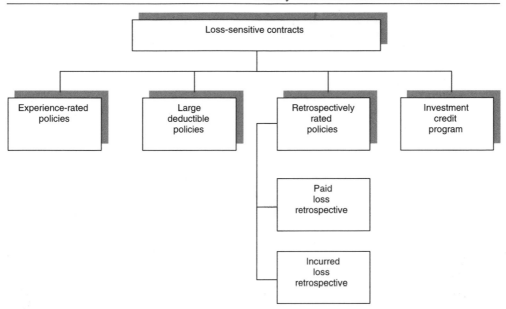

Figure 4.3 Loss-sensitive contracts

period of time has passed, and the cedant is allowed to retain a greater amount of risk. It is not unusual under a loss-sensitive contract for the insurer to cover a cedant's entire loss before determining, and then receiving, premium; under this structure it is easy to see how loss-sensitive contracts have a greater element of risk financing than conventional fixed premium instruments. Indeed, since the insurer is *de facto* granting the cedant a loan, it often requires the posting of security or collateral in order to minimize or eliminate any resulting credit risk. Common loss-sensitive contracts are summarized in Figure 4.3.

The **experience-rated policy** (ERP) is a contract where the insurer charges the cedant a premium that is directly related to the cedant's past loss experience: the greater the past losses, the higher the premium. This provides at least two benefits, including a reduction in moral hazard and a more robust mechanism for estimating expected future losses. If moral hazard is excluded from the pricing algorithm, the cedant benefits through a cheaper policy. While the ERP has less risk retention/financing than other contracts we consider below, it must rightly be considered a loss-sensitive instrument since an element of future premium is dependent on the experience of past loss.

The **large deductible policy** (LDP), as the name suggests, features a deductible that is much larger than one found on a typical fixed premium contract. The cedant retains, and in a loss situation finances, a much larger amount of risk, and thus pays the insurer a smaller premium (consistent with our discussion of partial insurance above). Since it is common for the insurer to pay all losses and then seek reimbursement from the cedant, the large deductible means that the insurer temporarily finances any loss on behalf of the cedant. Consider, for example, an insurer writing a conventional policy with a $10m cap and $1m deductible with Cedant A, and an LDP policy with a $10m cap and a $9m deductible with Cedant B. If a $10m loss occurs, the insurer immediately pays the $10m under each policy and then seeks reimbursement from A and B, in the amount of $1m and $9m respectively. Until it has been reimbursed – a period that may cover several months – the insurer is essentially financing the $1m for A and the $9m for

B. Cedant B, holding the LDP, has also paid a lower premium than A since it has retained more risk; its primary goal, however, has been to retain and finance, rather than transfer, exposure.

The **retrospectively rated policy** (RRP) is a contract requiring the cedant to pay an initial premium and, at some future time, make an additional premium payment (i.e., a retrospective premium) or receive a refund (i.e., a retrospective refund), depending on the size of any losses that occur. The RRP therefore 'looks back' to determine the type of cash flow adjustment that needs to be made. Maximum and minimum levels bound most RRPs in order to inject a greater amount of certainty into the loss estimate process. For instance, the retrospective premium might be set at 80% of losses, with a minimum of $1m and a maximum of $5m; the cedant and insurer are then governed by these contractual constraints. Since the retrospective premium/refund cannot be determined until losses, adjustments and/or loss estimates have occurred, the RRP preserves retention and financing, rather than transfer, characteristics. The RRP is available in two forms: the **paid loss retrospective policy**, a contract where the cedant's incremental premium is due when the insurer makes actual payments (a period that might span several years, suggesting a multi-year risk financing) and the **incurred loss retrospective policy**, a contract where the cedant's incremental premium is payable during the year based on the insurer's best estimate of losses (e.g., actual losses plus an estimate of future losses). The paid loss retro structure has a greater dimension of risk financing, since no 'intervening' premium replenishment is required. Again, the financing element of RRPs often requires cedants to post collateral with the insurer.

Though LDPs and RRPs are relatively popular, two potential disadvantages can surface: cedants must often post collateral to secure financing exposure and they have to pay taxes on investment earnings. To circumvent these two hurdles the insurance sector has developed the **investment credit program** (ICP), a tax-advantaged loss-sensitive structure that contains elements of financing and transfer. Under the ICP the cedant pays the insurer an amount designed to cover expected losses up to some desired deducible. The insurer places the funds in a trust account and uses them to cover losses as they occur. If the trust account moves into deficit, the cedant pays in an additional premium, and if it builds to a surplus, the excess is fully refunded (in contrast to the finite programs we discuss below, which generally split any surplus balance between the cedant and insurer). As long as the ICP is structured with an appropriate premium/expected loss threshold that transfers some risk to the insurer, it qualifies as insurance and is accorded relevant insurance-related tax benefits. In addition, since funds are held in trust (and cannot be withdrawn by the cedant) collateral is not required and investment earnings are not taxed. Figure 4.4 summarizes the cash flows of the ICP.

It is worth noting that institutions often use loss-sensitive contracts to capitalize on favorable tax treatment. Insurance premiums associated with the policies are deductible, providing a direct tax advantage. In addition, while retained losses can only be deducted when they are paid, insured losses can be deducted when they are incurred (which might occur during an earlier period).

Finite risk programs

Finite risk programs, which have been in existence in basic form for several decades (e.g., the first standardized 'time and distance' contracts date back to the 1980s),[10] are minimal

---

[10] Through the time and distance program an insurer/reinsurer agrees to pay an agreed schedule of loss payments in the future without assuming any losses that are greater than those in the schedule. The cedant pays a specified premium, which is effectively the

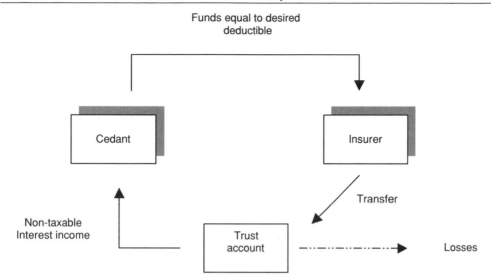

Figure 4.4   Investment credit program

risk transfer contracts that are widely used to fill gaps appearing in the traditional insurance market. In fact, finite programs are a popular form of risk financing, used by companies who are primarily interested in retaining, managing, and financing, rather than transferring, exposures.[11] Finite programs can be structured in many different forms and we consider several of the most common in this section, including retrospective finite programs (encompassing loss portfolio transfers, adverse development cover, and retrospective aggregate loss cover) and prospective finite programs. These are summarized in Figure 4.5. Though other variations exist, most are based on similar principles. Finite risk programs can be structured as primary insurance (between cedant and insurer) as well as reinsurance (between insurer as cedant and reinsurer, further to our discussion on reinsurance later in the chapter).

Finite contracts are used to manage the risks associated with loss exposures or the rate of loss accrual, and serve primarily as cash flow timing, rather than loss transfer, mechanisms; accordingly, they offer balance sheet and cash flow protection rather than capital protection. Finite structures are primarily concerned with the timing risks between losses, investment income and reserve accrual over a multi-period horizon, and how these elements can be structured in order to smooth cash flows. A finite contract cannot be viewed as a simple one-year risk cover for an isolated exposure – it must be considered a multi-year program that impacts broader corporate cash flows. Though the ultimate goal is not to transfer a significant amount of risk, the benefits achieved from risk financing must still be regarded as important and beneficial, e.g., reducing cash flow variability, lowering the cost of capital, decreasing the probability of financial distress, and increasing debt capacity; each of these features can be useful in the

---

NPV of true loss payments; in fact, there is so little risk transfer embodied in the program that it is not even viewed as an insurance contract in the US.

[11] To further demonstrate the idea of insurance/capital markets convergence, it is worth noting that many finite contracts can actually be regarded as **total return swaps** (TRSs) – over-the-counter derivatives that synthetically replicate the timing and magnitude of a cash flow position. Though we shall discuss derivatives at greater length in Chapter 9, we note at this juncture that finite contracts that shift losses to subsequent periods are simply mechanisms for reshaping cash flows, which is precisely what TRSs do. Though certain tax and accounting differences exist, the concepts behind the basic structures are quite similar.

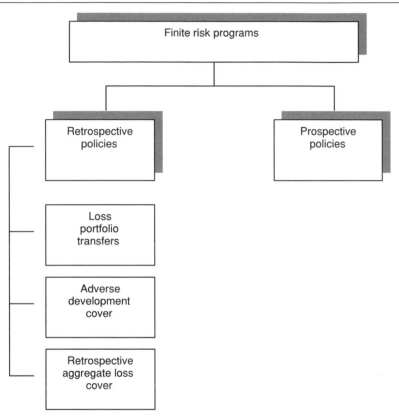

Figure 4.5   Finite risk programs

enterprise value maximization process. In addition, finite products that meet certain criteria related to structure and risk transfer are considered insurance contracts and generate tax benefits; the more risk transferred, the greater the tax benefits.

Finite risk policies are economically attractive when the market for traditional insurance hardens; in such cases products that transfer less exposure are often more competitively priced than full insurance. (This, however, still depends on the market environment. For instance, in the post-September 11, 2001, market cycle – which accelerated the hardening that was already underway – demand for finite products should have expanded noticeably. Unfortunately, this period coincided with a number of corporate bankruptcies and financial reporting scandals in the US and Europe,[12] calling into question mechanisms that legitimately (or otherwise) shift/smooth earnings and cash flows. Some equity analysts covering the stocks of companies using finite techniques to manage cash flow timing published negative reports that kept various companies from accessing or expanding their finite programs; this lasted for a period of up to two years, after which the legitimate nature of finite risk products began to emerge once again.) It is important to remember that finite policies are not strictly about accounting treatment,

---

[12] Enron, WorldCom, Tyco, HealthSouth, Swissair, Lernout and Hauspie, and a host of others, either filed for bankruptcy or were forced to restate earnings (sometimes by rather significant amounts).

though the products can certainly help narrow differences between current accounting and financial enterprise value.[13]

CASE STUDY

A finite risk program

Company XYZ wishes to create greater stability in its corporate cash flows and budgeting process, but still wants to transfer a certain amount of risk arising from its P&C exposures. Company management believes that more stable cash flows will appeal to investors and lead, ultimately, to higher valuations.

After discussing the matter with its broker, the company decides to create a 3-year finite policy where it pays $2m premium per year into an experience account that earns 5% interest on the balance (taxable at XYZ's marginal corporate rate of 34%). XYZ favors this arrangement because the $2m reflects the certain, predictable cash outflow of the company. In order to establish and maintain the program, XYZ must pay Insurer ABC an annual fee equal to 10% of premium. Losses will be funded through the account; any shortfall during the three years will be 90% paid by XYZ and 10% by ABC. ABC caps its total payment at $3m over the life of the program.

Over each of the next three years, actual loss experience amounts to $1m, $2m, and $5m. Table 4.2 reflects the cash flow effects of the finite program.

Table 4.2   XYZ's finite program

Item	Year 1	Year 2	Year 3
Previous balance	$0	$860	$747
Premium deposit	$2000	$2000	$2000
Fee	−$200	−$200	−$200
Beginning balance	$1800	$2660	$2547
Claims	−$1000	−$2000	$5000
After-tax interest	$60	$87	$85
Ending balance	$860	$747	−$2368

Since the account has a deficit of nearly $2.4m at the end of year 3, XYZ will fund nearly $2.2m and ABC will cover the balance; in fact, the company may fund the shortfall in installments (e.g., over a further 2- or 3-year period) in order to continue smoothing cash flows, which is its primary goal in creating the program. The main point to note is that XYZ's cash flows have been made less volatile by the use of the finite mechanism. Rather than facing losses of $1m, $2m, and $5m over each of the three years, it has been able to budget a steady cash outflow of $2m per year (disregarding fees and after-tax interest income), and can arrange to smooth the $2.2m shortfall once again through an extension of the program.

---

[13] For instance, Generally Accepted Accounting Principles (GAAP) and International Accounting Standards (IAS) are not well suited for industry sectors with long cycles, such as insurance; in addition, they tend not to favor industries where *ex-ante* knowledge of corporate costs is not known precisely (e.g., in insurance, claims as a "cost" of the business can only be estimated – but never precisely). Accordingly, finite products can help even out some of the accounting discrepancies that might arise from application of GAAP or IAS rules to industries that may not be in complete synchronicity.

Though full insurance and finite programs are both subject to some level of underwriting, credit, investment, and cash flow risks they represent different risk management alternatives:

- Full insurance typically involves a single-year cover, while finite programs are generally multi-year programs.
- Full insurance results in risk transfer (e.g., the insurer grants a large cap), while finite programs result primarily in risk financing (e.g., the insurer grants a very small cap).
- Through full insurance the insurer retains the entire premium in exchange for bearing risks, under finite programs the cedant and insurer share in profits derived from a split of risks, financing, and investment.
- With full insurance the premium is dependent largely on expected loss experience and underwriting costs, while under finite programs it depends primarily on investment income.

In order to qualify as insurance from an accounting and regulatory perspective, finite programs must involve some risk transfer. While they never feature as much risk transfer as standard insurance policies, a certain amount of exposure must be passed to the insurer; in general, the greater the tenor of the finite program the larger the amount of risk transfer. Gross premiums on a finite contract can be quite high, but include profit sharing between the cedant and insurer, meaning that the net cost can compare favorably with other mechanisms. In fact, over the long-term, finite risk programs can be cheaper than other risk transfer mechanisms because of a strong link with the cedant's loss experience.

The total realized cost (e.g., the net effective premium) on a finite program is ultimately a function of actual loss experienced. If losses are low, the cedant receives a premium refund, and if they are high, it will have to increase its payment contributions. Mechanically, premiums and investment income are credited to an 'experience account' while losses and fees are debited. The net remaining balance is then shared between the cedant and insurer on a pre-agreed basis at the end of the contract term. If loss experience is greater than originally estimated, the cedant places additional funds in the account in the form of 'premium' (the amount depends on the specific *ex-ante* loss-sharing agreement with the insurer). Finite contracts generally expose the insurer to limited downside as a result of policy caps (which may be instituted in aggregate, per occurrence or per year); in addition, most contracts feature deductibles, requiring the cedant to take the first loss exposure.

Retrospective finite policies

A **retrospective finite policy** (also known as a post-funded policy) is a finite contract that manages the timing risks of liabilities that already exist and losses that have already occurred. For instance, a company involved in a merger or acquisition might use a retrospective policy to finance (e.g., smooth) past liabilities that have been incurred but not yet reported; this adds greater transparency to the acquisition process and permits easier valuation. Though various retrospective structures exist, we focus our attention on loss portfolio transfers, adverse development cover, and retrospective aggregate loss cover. Although they operate on similar principles, each one has slightly different characteristics that influence the degree to which risks are financed and transferred (i.e., the nature of timing risk and underwriting risk).

The **loss portfolio transfer** (LPT) allows a firm to cede unclaimed losses from previous liabilities in the form of an entire portfolio. The cedant pays the insurer a fee, premium and the present value of net reserves to cover existing portfolio liabilities. The amount of timing risk that can be shifted is usually limited through aggregate loss limits and pre-set exclusions. The LPT thus transforms uncertain 'lump sum' liabilities into certain liabilities, with a present value that is equal to the NPV of unrealized losses. The cedant is effectively transferring the risk of losses occurring more rapidly than expected. If actual losses occur more slowly, the cedant and insurer can take advantage of the advantageous cash flows and share profits obtained from investment income. The cedant's payments are generally tax deductible, as are the insurer's incurred losses. Fundamentally, the LPT structure eliminates the uncertainty of past liabilities on cash flows (e.g., such as might arise from environmental or product liability claims), since the insurer assumes the risk of unexpectedly rapid claims settlements (which, for the cedant, would imply lower earnings potential via investment income on cash flow). LPTs allow a cedant to exit a business line more rapidly than might otherwise be possible, facilitate corporate control transactions, and free up capital to take on other risks; they are particularly suitable for long-tailed exposures, since the main element of the contract relates to time. In fact, LPTs have become popular with insurers in recent years; reinsurers actively manage the reserves of an insurer for outstanding losses on retrospective cover, taking over the insurer's liabilities so that it can continue to write primary business. Within the broad category of retrospective policies, LPTs are characterized by a greater shifting of timing risk, rather than underwriting risk.

An **adverse development cover** (ADC) is a finite contract that is conceptually similar to an LPT (i.e., the same motivations regarding the conversion of uncertain lump sum losses for certain losses) but broader in scope. Through an ADC a cedant again seeks to shift the timing of losses that have already occurred (as in an LPT) but can also include losses that have been incurred but not yet reported. Unlike LPTs, ADCs do not involve the transfer of liability/claim reserves; the cedant pays a premium for the transfer of losses exceeding a level that has already been reserved. This essentially means that financing is on existing liabilities in excess of reserves, with the insurer providing compensation for losses above an attachment point. Like LPTs, ADCs are typically capped, though a cedant can seek multiple layers of coverage. If LPTs represent a straight-line function of losses over time, ADCs can be viewed as an increasing function beyond the attachment point. Indeed, since ADCs feature more underwriting risk than LPTs, premiums are usually higher. Policies tend to be long-dated and are often used in the catastrophic reinsurance markets as a form of retrospective excess of loss cover (as discussed below). Within the group of retrospective policies, ADCs are distinguished by a greater shifting of underwriting risk rather than timing risk.

The **retrospective aggregate loss cover** (RALC) is similar to the LPT, but replaces reserves established for an unknown liability with a fixed payment. Under a typical structure the cedant finances existing losses and losses incurred but not yet reported through a premium payment equal to the value of reserves, and cedes liabilities to the insurer, just as it would through an LPT. However, the cedant must also pay for losses above a specified amount when they are incurred and thus retains some timing risk. The RALC provides some excess protection on underwriting risk (like an ADC) and thus features a greater amount of risk transfer than the LPT, though not as much as the ADC. Within the group of retrospective policies, RALCs shift timing and underwriting risk.

Figure 4.6 summarizes the underwriting risk/timing risk tradeoff between the major retrospective policies we have described above.

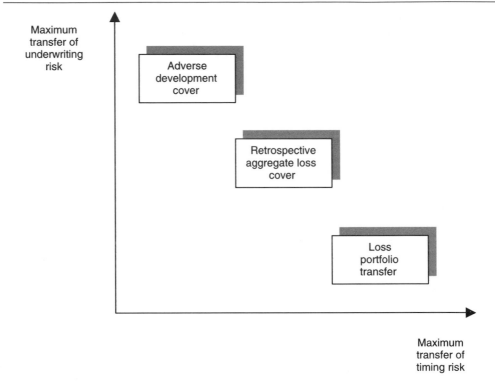

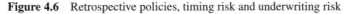

Figure 4.6   Retrospective policies, timing risk and underwriting risk

Prospective policies

A **prospective finite policy** is similar in concept to a retrospective policy, except that it covers the timing risks associated with future or expected liabilities rather than those that have already occurred. Prospective policies can be structured as insurance (i.e., between the ceding company and the primary insurer) or reinsurance (i.e., between the ceding insurer and reinsurer); we consider two forms of the prospective finite reinsurance structure later in the chapter.

4.3.3 Layered insurance coverage

It is common in the risk management market for cedants to layer their insurance coverage in order to obtain an optimal mix of cover at the best possible price. Layering insurance coverage also permits a cedant to use different policies to address different levels and types of risk (this emerges as an important mechanism when building an integrated risk program, as we shall discuss in Chapter 10). In its simplest form, layered coverage on a primary basis calls for insurers to provide cedants with relevant loss cover by attaching at specific levels that relate to their own risk tolerance, portfolio composition and expertise. Some insurers prefer to accept risks that are smaller in size but more likely to result in loss. These insurers attach "closer to the mean" of the loss distribution and can be viewed as the "first loss" piece of coverage; they provide the first dollar of payout to the cedant after any deductible has been exhausted. Though they may have to pay out on a loss first, the losses are more predictable and, arguably, more

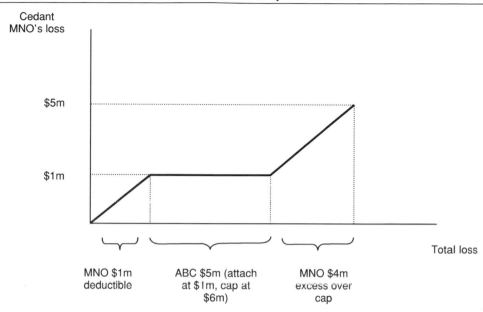

Cedant
MNO's loss

$5m

$1m

Total loss

MNO $1m
deductible

ABC $5m (attach
at $1m, cap at
$6m)

MNO $4m
excess over
cap

Figure 4.7 Layered coverage: Example 1

manageable. In addition, the premiums insurers earn in providing first loss cover are generally larger. Some insurers prefer to cover risks that are larger but less likely to result in loss; they attach "farther away from the mean" and thus provide excess layer coverage. The insurer in this position is effectively taking the second (or third, or higher) layer, and will not be called on to perform until the deductible and first loss layer is exhausted. The cedant benefits when specific attachment points coincide with each insurer's expertise and portfolio construct. For instance, an insurer that writes first loss cover as a result of its expertise in managing such risks is likely to give the cedant better pricing than an insurer that is used to writing excess loss covers (and vice versa). Relative pricing advantages can thus flow to the client.

Consider a simple example of layered coverage where the Company MNO, as cedant, retains $1m of risk and Insurer ABC provides coverage of $5m beyond the deductible (i.e., ABC attaches at $1m and is capped at $6m). If a $10m loss occurs, MNO pays $5m (i.e., the first $1m via the deductible, plus the difference between the cap and the loss ($10m − $6m); Insurer ABC pays $5m of the loss as well. Figure 4.7 illustrates the coverage.

Assuming that MNO does not want to bear the excess losses, it may be willing to pay for coverage beyond the $6m cap (to $10m, for example). However, if ABC does not wish to take exposure beyond the original cap, two alternatives are possible: ABC can write the entire exposure ($10m cap, or $9m exposure) and reinsure the portion it does not want in the reinsurance market, or MNO's broker can identify another insurer, CDE, who is interested in writing excess layer coverage. Though the economic effect is the same to the cedant, the two alternatives feature differences related to ceding commissions and taxes. Let us first continue the example using Insurer CDE as an excess layer provider. Under the new scenario, MNO continues to retain $1m of risk through the deductible, ABC attaches at $1m and is capped at $6m, and CDE attaches at $6m and is capped at $10m. If the same $10m loss occurs, MNO pays $1m, ABC $5m, and CDE $4m. This profile is illustrated in Figure 4.8. If an $11m loss

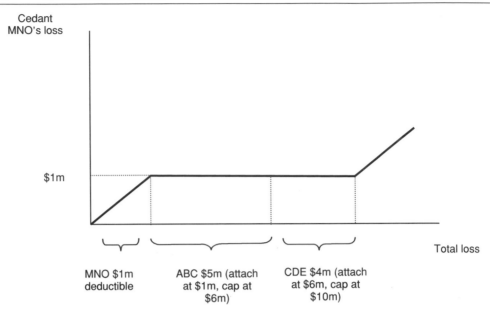

Figure 4.8   Layered coverage: Example 2

occurs, MNO pays $2m (e.g., the deductible and the $1m slice above CDE's cap), while the two insurers continue to face the same maximum losses of $5m and $4m.

In practice, it may be easier for ABC to take the entire risk on its own books and then reinsure the portion it does not want in the reinsurance market.[14] If it chooses to do so, the entire process is generally invisible to the cedant, which is typically only aware of the primary insurer's participation. If a claim is made under the policy, the primary insurer provides the cedant with a full payment as defined under the policy, and recovers its own loss payment from the reinsurer. Continuing with our example, we can imagine the following: instead of having CDE join as a second primary insurer writing excess layer coverage (e.g., $6m attachment and $10m cap), ABC might provide a full policy attaching at $1m and capping out at $10m; it then accesses the reinsurance market and finds Reinsurer XYZ, who is willing to write cover on the excess layer from $6m to $10m. In exchange for a pass-through of the relevant share of the premium from the cedant, XYZ pays ABC a ceding commission. If a $10m loss occurs, MNO continues to bear $1m of losses via the deductible, ABC loses $9m on a gross basis (e.g., $1m attachment and $10m cap) but only $5m on a net basis (e.g., recovery of $4m from XYZ), while XYZ loses $4m (e.g., $6m attachment and $10m cap). Figure 4.9 illustrates this version of the example. We consider more detailed forms of vertical and horizontal reinsurance layering in the next section.

4.4   REINSURANCE AND RETROCESSION CONTRACTS

Reinsurance and retrocession contracts are central to the effective management of insurance risks and the creation of risk capacity and alternative risk products. In its most fundamental form

---

[14] A parallel exists in the loan/credit default swap market, where an originating bank might grant a loan to a client and preserve the entire credit on its book (if it is economical to do so from a funding and capital charge perspective). However, in order to protect its risk exposure it may purchase a credit default swap or option from a third party, thus covering a portion of the loan.

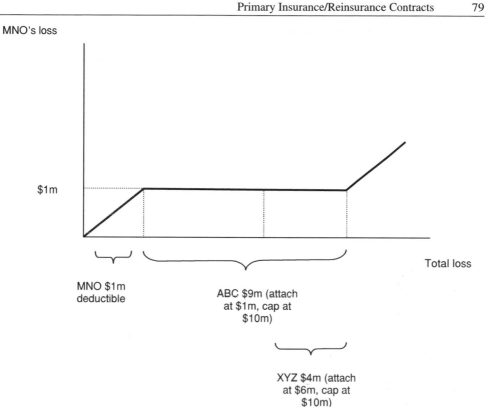

MNO's loss

$1m

Total loss

MNO $1m
deductible

ABC $9m (attach
at $1m, cap at
$10m)

XYZ $4m (attach
at $6m, cap at
$10m)

Figure 4.9   Layered coverage: Example 3

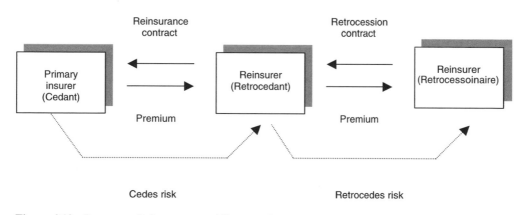

Reinsurance
contract

Retrocession
contract

Primary
insurer
(Cedant)

Reinsurer
(Retrocedant)

Reinsurer
(Retrocessoinaire)

Premium

Premium

Cedes risk

Retrocedes risk

Figure 4.10   Insurance, Reinsurance, and Retrocession

reinsurance is insurance cover written by a reinsurer for a primary insurer, while **retrocession** is insurance cover written by a reinsurer for another reinsurer. A primary insurer seeking to lower its risk will pass the exposure on to a reinsurer, obtaining a cover known as a cession. The reinsurer, as **retrocedant**, will pass any unwanted exposure to the retrocessionaire in the form of a retrocession. These relationships are depicted in Figure 4.10.

Reinsurance achieves several important goals. It permits portfolio diversification, creates profit stability and increases underwriting capacity; it also protects ceding insurers against low-frequency/high-severity events and provides some amount of financing relief (particularly when structured as a finite contract). In the first instance, an insurer transferring selective risks by entering into a reinsurance contract diversifies its own portfolio of exposures and achieves better balance. For example, an insurer might have certain constraints related to **large line capacity** (a large loss exposure on a single policy) or **premium capacity** (a large volume of policies written on the same line of cover). By using reinsurance, either concentration (or both) can be reduced, giving the insurer a portfolio with better diversification and balance (of course, this is not pure risk mitigation, as the insurer assumes the credit risk of the reinsurer(s) in the process). Reinsurance cover can also create profit stability (and reduce the probability of financial distress) by ensuring that the insurer is not exposed to an excess of losses that might damage its underwriting results. It also permits more insurance to be written in a particular sector, since reinsurance cover allows insurers to reduce their unearned premium reserves. A reduction of reserves increases the insurer's capital/surplus position, permitting more insurance to be written (in this sense reinsurance acts as a *de facto* equity infusion).

Reinsurance contracts can be ceded and accepted in a variety of ways. In the first instance an insurer must decide between facultative and treaty reinsurance. It can then select between quota share, surplus share, and excess of loss, or it may decide to form part of a reinsurance pool. We consider each mechanism, summarized in Figure 4.11, in the following section.

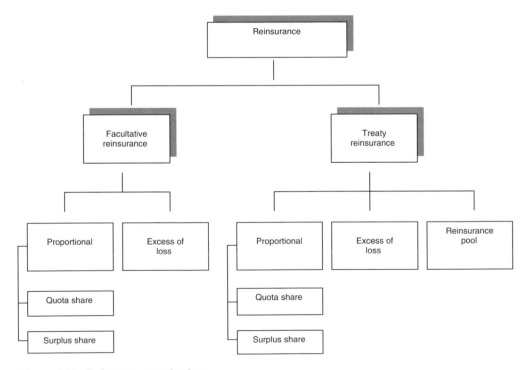

Figure 4.11   Reinsurance mechanisms

4.4.1   Facultative and treaty reinsurance

Reinsurance contracts can be written on a facultative or treaty basis. **Facultative reinsurance** is the term applied to any reinsurance transaction that involves a case-by-case review of under-writing risks. Under a facultative contract, which is highly customizable, the primary insurer is not obligated to cede a particular risk and the reinsurer is not obligated to accept it. Each risk that is ceded and accepted is analyzed on its own merits and governed by a separately negotiated contract (reflecting the bespoke nature of the process). Not surprisingly, a faculta-tive agreement is often used when risks are very large and unique, or require special attention and consideration. Facultative reinsurance is widely used to cover various risks in the P&C sector. For instance, standard insurance lines in the property sector may be reinsured through a facultative agreement on a proportional or excess basis based on analysis related to probable maximum loss and maximum foreseeable loss. In the casualty sector, general liability, auto-mobile, workers' compensation, excess liability, and umbrella covers can be reinsured through a facultative agreement, as excess transactions.

Though facultative business gives both parties greater ability to specifically examine risks prior to commitment, it also means that there is no *ex-ante* guarantee of cession or coverage. Thus, if the reinsurer believes that a particular exposure generated by the primary insurer is inconsistent with its own risk tolerance, it can decline to write the cover. Or, if an insurer generates an especially attractive and profitable risk, it may choose to retain the entire exposure. In general terms, the ceding insurer gives the reinsurer information on the specific exposure it seeks to cover. If the reinsurer agrees to accept the risk it provides a quote and written confirmation; if the insurer accepts the quote, the reinsurer then forwards confirmation of binder and receives a policy from the insurer, which it uses to prepare the final certificate of reinsurance.

Treaty reinsurance, in contrast, is a contract where risks are automatically ceded and accepted (for that reason it is sometimes referred to as an obligatory reinsurance contract). The primary insurer agrees to cede a portion of all risks conforming to pre-agreed guidelines under a treaty agreement. The reinsurer is similarly bound to accept all conforming risks. Underwriting criteria in the treaty must be delineated in enough detail to eliminate any doubt about the nature of risks to be ceded and accepted. Those that do not conform fall outside the scope of the treaty and would need to be considered on a facultative basis; those that conform are automatically transferred. While the treaty process is efficient and economical (e.g., less expensive on a "per risk" basis than facultative cover), and provides comfort that coverage will be available, it also reduces a certain amount of the reinsurer's 'underwriting power'; that is, the reinsurer agrees to take all risks that conform, up to a limit, without being able to inspect each one individually. In addition, some of the risks assumed by the reinsurer through the treaty may ultimately be unprofitable (though in the long run the reinsurer expects the relationship to be profitable). Equally, while the ceding insurer gains comfort from having automatic capacity for conforming risks, it can no longer choose to retain certain exposures for its own book (e.g., very profitable ones).

4.4.2   Quota share, surplus share, excess of loss, and reinsurance pools

Reinsurance risks, returns, and losses can be divided between the primary insurer and the reinsurer on a proportional (or pro rata) basis or an excess of loss basis. This is true for both facultative and treaty risks.

Proportional agreements, such as the quota share and surplus share arrangements discussed immediately following, call for the insurer and reinsurer to share premiums, exposures, losses, and loss adjustment expenses (LAEs), on the basis of some predefined formula, such as a fixed or variable percentage of the policy limits. Proportional treaty agreements always result in some amount of cession and allocation of losses, while proportional facultative agreements always result in cession and allocation of losses once an exposure has been agreed and accepted. The advantages to the insurer of using a proportional agreement include recovery on small losses, protection of net retentions on a "first dollar lost" basis, and protection against frequent and severe events. **Excess of loss (XOL) agreements**, in contrast, call for the insurer and reinsurer to allocate risks and returns in specific horizontal or vertical layers (as noted in the simple example earlier); depending on the magnitude of losses and the sequence and level of attachment, a reinsurer may or may not have some cession and allocation of losses. The advantages to the insurer in using an XOL mechanism include greater protection against frequency or severity (though this depends on retention), increased retention of net premiums, and improved efficiencies in administration and premium allocation.

Under the **quota share** (QS) structure the insurer and reinsurer agree to split premiums, risk, losses, and LAEs as a fixed percentage of the policy limit, rather than in specific dollar terms. The reinsurer thus pays the primary insurer a ceding commission for a share of the exposure and premium. A QS permits the ceding insurer to reduce its unearned premium reserves (through premiums ceded to the reinsurer) and increase its surplus (through commissions received from the reinsurer). The assets of the ceding insurer are reduced by the premium paid to the reinsurer, while liabilities (reserves) are reduced by the lower unearned premium reserve. Since the decrease in liabilities is greater than the decrease in assets (by the amount of ceding commission received) the ceding insurer's surplus increases. A QS can also strengthen other financial ratios, such as premium to surplus; the more capital an insurer has on hand to support the premiums it is writing, the stronger is its financial condition (i.e., the insurer has greater capital strength to absorb losses that are greater than expected). A QS written with a creditworthy reinsurer provides the insurer with credit for reinsurance ceded, helping to decrease the premium to surplus ratio.

Consider the following example: Insurer ABC and Reinsurer XYZ negotiate a 20% QS on a treaty basis that requires XYZ to accept 20% of all policies underwritten and ceded by ABC and receive 20% of premiums earned; XYZ pays ABC a 10% ceding commission on all business ceded. If Policy 1 has a limit of $1m and a premium of $100 000, XYZ accepts $200 000 of risk and receives $20 000 of premium; it also pays ABC a $2000 ceding commission. If Policy 2 has a limit of $5m, XYZ accepts $1m of risk and $200 000 of premium, and pays $20 000 in ceding commissions; and so forth. If losses occur on Policies 1 and 2, ABC covers 80% and XYZ 20%, after the original cedant has paid any deductible.

Risks retained and ceded across a portfolio of policies governed by a QS are depicted in Figure 4.12.

Through a **surplus share** (SS) structure the reinsurer agrees to accept risk on a variable percentage basis above the insurer's retention limit, up to some defined maximum, and pays the insurer a ceding commission for a share in the premium; the amount the ceding insurer retains is referred to as a 'line' and is expressed in dollar terms. Once the insurer's retention limit has been exceeded, the reinsurer takes the additional exposure on its books and premiums, losses, and LAEs are shared between the two on a fractional basis. Since separate dollar retention is set for each policy (or certain groups of policies) the sharing is variable in percentage terms across an entire portfolio. An SS can help an insurance company to improve its surplus account,

Limits

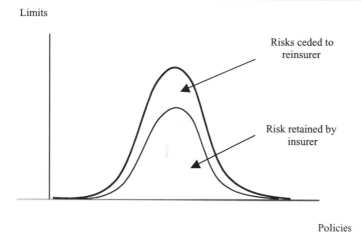

Risks ceded to
reinsurer

Risk retained by
insurer

Policies

Figure 4.12   Quota share: risks retained and ceded

Limits

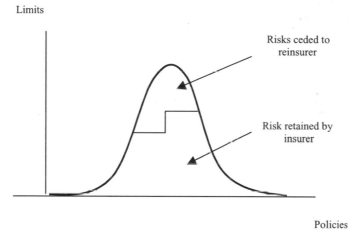

Risks ceded to
reinsurer

Risk retained by
insurer

Policies

Figure 4.13   Surplus share: risks retained and ceded

reduce the possibility of large losses from catastrophic events, and provide an increased level of underwriting capacity. It is worth noting that even though the ceding insurer must pass on a portion of risk and premium to the reinsurer, it has flexibility in selecting the retention level on each policy (or group of policies); this means that adverse selection can occur. For instance, the insurer might choose higher retention (lower cession) on all of the low-risk policies and lower retention (higher cession) on the high-risk policies.

Consider the following example: Insurer ABC and Reinsurer XYZ structure an SS where ABC has a retention limit of $2m and cession of $8m, meaning that it can underwrite $10m of insurance for its end-use clients. If ABC writes $5m of cover, it retains $2m of exposure and cedes $3m to XYZ. The split of premiums, losses, and LAEs is thus two-fifths for ABC and three-fifths for XYZ.

Risks retained and ceded across a portfolio of policies governed by an SS are shown in Figure 4.13.

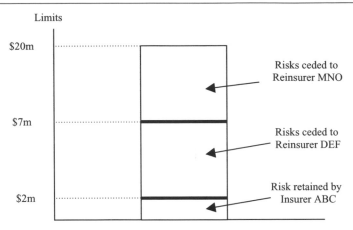

Figure 4.14   Excess of loss agreement with vertical layering

While QSs and SSs share risks and returns on a fixed/variable basis, the XOL agreement allocates exposure through non-proportional layers, based on actual claims received. Through an XOL the reinsurer agrees to pay any losses above a specified retention level (i.e., the attachment point), up to a maximum limit. Coverage can be set for a single exposure/occurrence, or cumulative losses over a defined time period. For example, a reinsurer might agree to '$10m XOL $5m' meaning that it will cover losses above $5m (e.g., it attaches at $5m) up to a maximum loss level of $10m (e.g., it caps out at $10m), implying net loss coverage of $5m (e.g. $10m − $5m). Since there is no longer any equal sharing of risk (as under the proportional QS and SS agreements), the premium charged by the reinsurer is no longer based on a fractional portion of the amount charged by the primary insurer to its own clients. Rather, it becomes a function of general underwriting factors, including the nature of the risks, concentrations, prior loss experience, portfolio composition, and so forth. The XOL gives the primary insurer capacity to write large lines and protects against high-severity/low-frequency events; in fact, while XOL cover is typically associated with protection against catastrophic exposures, it is also widely used in a range of P&C covers, including those with a greater likelihood of occurrence.

In some cases several reinsurers might participate in an XOL agreement, each taking a preferred layer of exposure; this is known as **vertical layering** (and extends the concept we introduced in the layering example earlier). For instance, Insurer ABC might retain $2m of a $20m P&C cover and cede $5m to Reinsurer DEF (who attaches at $2m and caps at $7m), and cede $13m to Reinsurer MNO (who attaches at $7m and caps at $20m); this layering is depicted in Figure 4.14. If an $8m loss occurs under this scenario, ABC bears the first $2m, DEF assumes responsibility for the next $5m and MNO the last $1m. XOLs may also be structured with **horizontal layering**, where different reinsurers take pieces of the same loss layer. For instance, in the last example MNO might only take 50% of the vertical layer between $7m and $20m, while new Reinsurer TUV might take the other 50%. This scenario is shown in Figure 4.15.

As noted, layering works in practice because different reinsurers often have different risk/geographic expertise and portfolios; one might that find a 'closer to the mean' first loss layer is better for its business, while a second might find that a 'farther from the mean' second loss layer is better, and so forth. Willingness to participate in different layers can change over time, as the composition of a given reinsurer's portfolio changes.

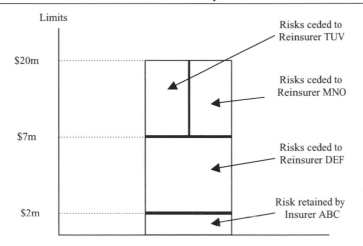

Figure 4.15   Excess of loss agreement with horizontal layering

Variations of XOL cover exist, including:

- **Catastrophe per occurrence XOL**   An agreement providing the primary insurer with cover for adverse loss experience from an accumulation of catastrophic events. Such agreements may have an incremental deductible and coinsurance.
- **Property per risk XOL**   An agreement providing the primary insurer with cover for any loss in excess of the specified retention on each type of risk.
- **Stop loss XOL**   An agreement designed to protect overall underwriting results after accounting for other forms of reinsurance by providing indemnification for incurred losses in excess of a specified loss ratio or dollar amount.
- **Aggregate XOL**   An agreement providing the primary insurer with cover for a large number of small losses arising from multiple policies (all occurring in the same year).

In practice, XOL policies – particularly those related to catastrophic risk – may feature deductibles and coinsurance at the upper layers. Thus, the ceding insurer might have an initial deductible, several layers of reinsurance coverage, then a second deductible (and/or coinsurance obligation) before the highest catastrophic XOL layer comes into effect. Figure 4.16 illustrates this structure, where ABC has an initial deductible of $5m, a $25m cession to DEF (to a limit of $30m), a further $5m deductible, and then a 75%/25% upper layer XOL with TUV to a limit of $75m ($40m of coverage, with TUV responsible for $30m of losses).

In some cases reinsurance coverage is provided through a **reinsurance pool**, a mechanism that groups together a number of reinsurers who agree to underwrite risks on a joint basis. Under a typical pool each pool member agrees to pay a set percentage of each loss (or a percentage of each loss above some retention level). In fact, a reinsurance pool is similar to a QS arrangement, but the pool provides a maximum loss limit to each participating insurer from any single loss; once a pool member suffers a loss in excess of the specified amount, pool members share the balance. This mechanism is used when a single reinsurer is unable to provide an insurer with sufficient risk coverage.

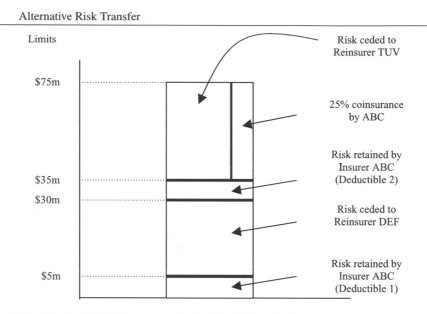

Figure 4.16   Catastrophic XOL agreement with deductible and coinsurance

4.4.3   Finite reinsurance

As noted earlier in the chapter, finite programs can be written between a primary insurer and a reinsurer. **Finite reinsurance**, commonly referred to as financial reinsurance, is a financing facility with limited risk transfer that a reinsurer makes available to an insurer. The insurer pays premiums into an experience account (upfront or over time) and receives cover for losses once they exceed the funded amount (up to certain predetermined maximum limits). The same element of profit-sharing found in finite risk policies exists in finite reinsurance. Benefits accrue to the insurer in the form of cheaper coverage, and to the reinsurer through exposure to a lower level of losses. Finite reinsurance is available in various retrospective and prospective forms, including spread loss, financial quota share, LPTs, ADCs, funded XOL, and aggregate stop loss, among others. Since many of these are variations on what we have discussed above, we shall only consider two prospective finite reinsurance products: the spread loss and finite quota share.

A **spread loss** is an agreement where the cedant pays a premium into an experience account every year of a multi-year contract period; the experience account generates an agreed rate and is used to pay any losses that occur. If a deficit arises in the account at the end of any year, the cedant covers the shortfall through an additional contribution; if a surplus results, the excess is returned. The cedant and reinsurer share profits on a pre-agreed basis if the spread loss account is in surplus at the end of the contract tenor. During any given year the reinsurer makes loss payments on behalf of the cedant as they occur – indicating that this is a prospective, rather than retrospective, cover. In fact, the reinsurer is pre-funding losses (up to an annual and total limit) so that the cedant can spread the losses over a longer period of time (rather than funding them as they occur). Although the amount of risk transfer is relatively small, it is sufficient in most jurisdictions to allow the spread loss to qualify as a reinsurance contract for tax purposes.

Through the **finite quota share (FQS)** a reinsurer pays a fixed or variable proportion of claims and LAEs on behalf of the ceding insurer as they occur, again making this a prospective structure. Ceding commissions and investment income from reserves typically cover actual claims but, if they do not, the reinsurer funds the shortfall and recoups the difference from the insurer over the life of the contract. Under a typical FQS, liabilities are explicitly limited, whether or not underlying insurance contracts have caps.

While this discussion is intended to serve as a primer on insurance and reinsurance contracts, we shall note in subsequent chapters how corporate risk managers use some of these instruments as part of a broader package of ART solutions. While some instruments, such as finite programs, are generally considered to be ART products on a standalone basis, others, such as full and partial insurance, must generally be packaged with other products or channels to be considered part of the ART market.

5
Captives

We have noted in Chapter 1 that risk retention is an important element of the broad risk management class of loss financing. Retention can be achieved through self-retention programs on the corporate balance sheet and certain insurance contracts (i.e., those with very large deductibles or small policy caps), as well as captives. In fact, captives are a central component of the ART market and remain the single most actively used channel for ART-related activity; they are a popular and efficient way of retaining primary layer risks that have a certain amount of predictability. In this chapter we consider the motivations, costs, and benefits of using captives, and discuss the general characteristics of the most common structures, including pure captives, group captives, sister captives, rent-a-captives, protected cell companies, and risk retention groups.

5.1 USING CAPTIVES TO RETAIN RISKS

5.1.1 Background and function

A **captive** is a closely held risk channel that is used to facilitate a company's insurance/reinsurance program and retention/transfer activities. It is generally formed as a licensed insurance/reinsurance company, controlled either by a single owner or multiple owners (often referred to as the sponsor(s)). The owner/sponsor(s) provide upfront capital to commence the operation (initial capital levels of approximately $250 000 are common, but this has to be increased in relation to the amount of business written); in exchange for the provision of capital, the captive generally pays the owner(s) periodic interest and/or dividends.

The captive insures the sponsor or third-party user(s) directly by accepting a transfer of risk in exchange for premium, or it can act as a reinsurer by dealing through a fronting insurer. The latter structure allows it to avoid many of the regulations that are applied to primary insurance companies and participate freely in the professional reinsurance market, where it can often obtain better pricing and terms. Captives are generally not licensed to do business outside of their domiciles and must make use of an admitted insurer if they choose to do so (e.g., offshore captives can only do business in the US through the admitted insurer). Figures 5.1 and 5.2 illustrate the simple pure captive as insurer and reinsurer.

Captives were originally developed in the 1960s as a "check" on the cost-efficiency of risk retention and transfer via traditional insurance contracts. They became popular in the 1970s as large corporations realized the cost advantages that could be obtained by managing their own risks and insurance coverage, particularly during hard market cycles. Hundreds of captives were formed during this period, including some by the world's large corporations. Popularity declined for a period in the 1980s as certain tax benefits were eliminated and insurance/reinsurance markets softened; companies found, once again, that they could obtain cheaper cover through traditional risk transfer and risk-financing mechanisms. However, with harder markets and a growing focus on enterprise risk management developing in the 1990s, use of captives accelerated again – a trend that continues to gather momentum into the early part

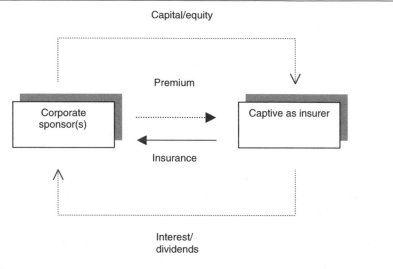

Figure 5.1   Captive as insurer

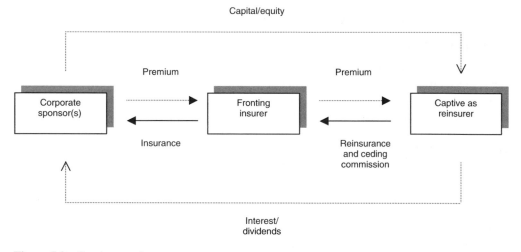

Figure 5.2   Captive as reinsurer

of the millennium. In fact, a number of new offshore captive jurisdictions have been created in recent years, proving that the demand for properly structured self-insurance vehicles remains strong.

Although there was some concern by industry participants that the corporate failures and scandals of the millennium (some involving offshore subsidiaries) would intensify scrutiny of offshore captives and dampen activity, this does not appear to have occurred. By 2003 approximately 5000 captives had been established globally; these companies held assets of $130bn and took in approximately $25bn in gross premium, equal to nearly 10% of global commercial insurance premiums. Although Bermuda remains the single largest captive center (i.e., 20% share by number, 50% share by premium), captive-friendly legislation has appeared in numerous other locations in recent years. Indeed, regional centers appear to attract companies from specific countries. For instance, US companies (which own 60% of all captives) tend to establish entities in Bermuda, Cayman Islands, British Virgin Islands, and Vermont; UK firms use Guernsey, Bermuda, and the Isle of Man; German, Swiss, and French companies (which collectively own 25% of all captives) use Luxembourg and Ireland; Canadian companies use Barbados, Bermuda, and British Columbia; Asian companies use Singapore and Labuan; and so forth. The selection of an appropriate locale for the establishment of a captive is dependent on a number of factors, including insurance/reinsurance restrictions, capital and tax requirements, regulatory requirements, reserve requirements, premium taxes, political and regulatory stability, and infrastructure.

Captives are generally subject to some level of regulatory oversight, which helps to ensure that the sponsors are aware of the captive's activities and exposures, and that the entity is operating prudently with regard to liquidity and solvency. Although rules vary by jurisdiction, regulators typically specify minimum reporting requirements, capital/surplus levels, and investment restrictions. Operationally, captives manage their activities in the same way as any other insurance or reinsurance company, establishing unearned premium reserves and loss reserves, adhering to minimum capital/surplus levels, actively managing the risk portfolio through diversification and cessions to the reinsurance market, managing the investment portfolio, and so on. Although the nature and operation of captives varies by company, the focus is often on high-frequency/low-severity risks – the highly predictable exposures for which self-insurance is a cost-effective alternative. This means that less predictable risks, e.g., high-severity/low-frequency exposures, are still transferred to the reinsurance market, which is more readily equipped to handle them. In fact, captives generally protect their own operations through the purchase of "excess insurance".

5.1.2 Benefits and costs

Captives have proven popular and enduring because they provide users with a number of benefits, including:

- appropriate and flexible risk cover, particularly for exposures that might otherwise be hard to insure (or are, in fact, uninsurable);
- lower costs, primarily by avoiding agent and broker commissions and insurance overhead/profit loadings;
- possible tax advantages related to investment income, premiums, and/or incurred losses (depending on the structure and location of the captive);
- incentives to implement loss control measures;
- decreased earnings volatility as a result of increased cost predictability (i.e., not subject to the same hard/soft market cycles discussed in Chapter 2);
- easier access to the professional, and often more cost-competitive, reinsurance market;
- incremental profit potential if third-party business is written;
- increased investment income from the reserve fund, payable to sponsor/user rather than a third-party insurer.

All of these benefits are important, but perhaps the single most compelling fact is that a captive often allows a company to retain and manage its high-frequency risks in a very cost-effective manner. A captive can actually be viewed as an internal retention fund with a distinct corporate structure and organization. Also, like a retention fund, it adds enterprise value if assets yield a return that is greater than the cost of capital. Since insurance premiums normally cover the present value of expected losses, *plus* insurance acquisitions costs, overhead expenses, and profit loading, the non-claims portion of the premium can be as high as 30–40% of the total; if a company has highly predictable risks, there is little economic justification for paying away such a large sum to a third-party insurer. In addition, since premiums are paid in advance but claims occur over time, a company can lose benefits derived from the time value of money; in fact, it is much more sensible for a firm to preserve these underwriting cash flows. Naturally, captives cannot be viewed as short-term risk solutions to be implemented, used, and then shut down over a short time frame. In fact, open claims and losses incurred but not reported under any of the covers being managed result in tail risk, meaning that a longer horizon must factor into the initial decision-making process.

Of course, some costs/disadvantages also exist. In particular, captives:

- require payment of upfront fees for initial establishment;
- reduce capital management flexibility by 'locking-up' capital in the entity for an extended period of time (i.e., capital cannot be withdrawn at will by the sponsor(s), but in some jurisdictions, such as Vermont and Hawaii, the sponsor(s) can borrow against the capital contribution);
- must adhere to regulatory rules/reporting, suggesting an incremental level of costs;
- may not always be tax-advantaged (depending on the structure and jurisdiction).

Despite these potential costs, the benefits that can be obtained are often much greater, hence a key reason for their popularity.

To understand the economics that drive the development and use of a captive, we consider a simple case study that traces initial and ongoing cash flows that impact the risk management decision process.

CASE STUDY

A captive program

Company ABC faces a fairly predictable level of expected losses in its workers' compensation program and is comfortable retaining a certain amount of risk. Historically, ABC has paid $2m per year in premiums for a standard insurance policy that transfers its workers' compensation exposure, but has estimated that it can save $250 000 in premiums initially, and annually thereafter, by retaining the risk and reinsuring through a captive. Accordingly, it wants to create a pure captive as a licensed reinsurer. Establishing the captive will involve a one-time fee of $200 000 and annual captive management fees of $50 000. Since the entity will be created as a reinsurer, ABC will need to use a fronting insurer, which will require the payment of $75 000 in fronting fees (upfront and at the end of every year in which the program remains active).

Since ABC is planning to create a pure captive that will write no other third-party business, it obtains no premium tax deductibility. The firm does not intend to alter its investment policy on retained funds (we thus ignore any impact in the decision framework), and assumes that it will face a 5% cost of capital and a 34% tax rate during the three-year planning horizon (the three-year time horizon is simply for initial planning purposes; if successful, ABC would intend to use the captive for many years).

Given these assumptions, ABC's risk managers use a standard NPV evaluation to determine whether the cost/benefit tradeoffs justify the creation and use of the captive. Over the three-year period, ABC notes that it will face the following initial and ongoing *costs*:

- Start up fee (initial)
- Administration fee (initial and ongoing)
- Fronting fee (initial and ongoing)
- Taxes (initial and ongoing).

However, it will also *benefit* from:

- Insurance premium savings (initial and ongoing).

Table 5.1 summarizes ABC's cash flows over the three-year period.

Table 5.1 Cash flows for ABC's pure captive program

	Start of program	Year 1	Year 2	Year 3
Captive start-up costs	−$200 000	−	−	−
Captive admin. fee	−$50 000	−$50 000	$50 000	$50 000
Fronting fee	−$75 000	−$75 000	−$75 000	−$75 000
Insurance savings	+$250 000	+$250 000	+$250 000	+$250 000
Pre-tax cash flow	−$75 000	+$125 000	+$125 000	+$125 000
Taxes (34%)	+$25 500	−$42 500	−$42 500	−$42 500
After-tax cash flow	−$49 500	+$82 500	+$82 500	+$82 500

Using the annual cash flows, and applying the 5% cost of capital, ABC's risk managers obtain an NPV of:

$$\$175\,166 = -\$49\,500 + (\$82\,500/1.05^1) + (\$82\,500/1.05^2) + (\$82\,500/1.05^3)$$

Since the NPV is positive $175 000, ABC can increase its own enterprise value by creating the captive and retaining its workers' compensation exposures. Although it faces certain upfront and ongoing costs, these are ultimately outweighed by its ability to access the reinsurance market on a cost-effective basis. This example is simplified, but it illustrates the advantages that a firm might obtain in creating a captive to cover particular risk exposures.

The actual establishment of a captive is relatively simple and inexpensive, making it appealing even for small and medium enterprises. Consider, as an example, a summary of the process used to establish a captive in Bermuda, the largest center of captive activity:

- The sponsor contracts with necessary professional advisers (insurance manager, lawyer, auditor) to obtain assistance with technical details.
- The sponsor and advisers complete pre-incorporation documents.
- Application is made to the Ministry of Finance as an exempt Bermuda company (which need not adhere to the 60% local ownership rule, making it suitable for international firms).
- Application is made to the Bermuda Monetary Authority as a registered insurer.
- Assuming that all materials are in order, approval is obtained.
- The sponsor pays in the minimum capital requirement ($120 000 for a Class 1 pure captive, $250 000 for a Class 2 group captive, $1m for a Class 3 commercial insurer/reinsurer writing at least 20% unrelated business) and elects a board of directors.

- The sponsor submits the approved insurance application to the Bermuda Monetary Authority.
- The Supervisor of Insurance grants a Certificate of Registration.
- Operations commence.

Similar processes exist in other jurisdictions. Like Bermuda, their procedures are quite efficient (e.g., an average turnaround of 3–6 weeks), and reasonably priced (e.g., $50 000 to $100 000 in start-up costs, plus initial capitalization (generally $250 000)).

5.2 FORMS OF CAPTIVES

Captives can be structured in a variety of forms, and selection of the proper one is generally a function of a company's specific financial and risk management goals (e.g., retentions, costs, benefits, taxes). In general terms, captives may have single or multiple owners/sponsors, and single or multiple users that are either related or unrelated to the owners/sponsors. On one extreme is the related single owner/user structure (e.g., the pure captive), and on the other are various unrelated single/multiple owner and multiple user structures (e.g., the protected cell company and agency captive); various other combinations exist between these extremes, as noted below. Figure 5.3 summarizes the general universe of captives. (Note that in the discussion and illustrations that follow we ignore the interposition of fronting insurers for ease; in reality many captives are established as reinsurers and make use of the additional fronting "layer".)

5.2.1 Pure captives

A **pure captive** (sometimes known as a single-parent captive) is a licensed insurer/reinsurer that is wholly owned by a single sponsor and writes insurance cover solely or primarily for that firm; a pure captive may thus be regarded as an insurer covering risks from restricted origins. It is, in fact, the single most popular type of structure; approximately 70% of the

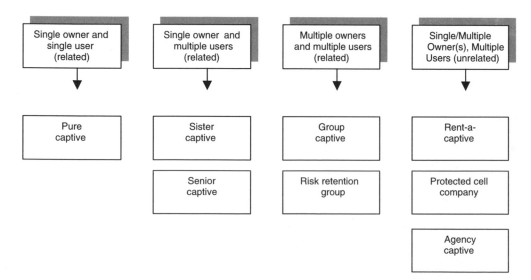

Figure 5.3   The universe of captives

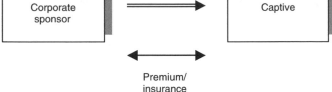

Figure 5.4   Pure captive

5000 captives in use during the early part of the millennium were established as single-parent entities. A pure captive can be capitalized by the sponsor with internal or external funds, which are invested in low-risk securities on behalf of the parent to generate periodic returns; capital levels must be increased as business levels expand. Since the sponsor is in sole control of the captive, it has direct operational authority over the entity, specifying underwriting, claims, and investment criteria. As in any insurance relationship, the parent sponsor pays the captive premiums in order to transfer risk. In the event of a loss the sponsor forwards a claim to the captive and receives the relevant compensatory payment (as dictated by the terms of the coverage).

Pure captives can also be established with multiple branches in different locations/regulatory regimes in order to accommodate the business of a parent company's individual subsidiaries. Companies using a fronting insurer can direct their local subsidiaries to the local branches of the fronting insurer, which then cedes all risks to the captive. Although many of the earliest entities were formed as pure captives (and a majority retain that form), there has been a gradual migration toward a related structure known as the **senior captive**, a wholly owned subsidiary of the sponsor that writes a greater amount of external business; this often permits more favorable tax treatment, as discussed below.

Figure 5.4 – which can be contrasted with the group captive and sister captive figures below – illustrates the insurance relationship between the corporate sponsor and the pure captive.

5.2.2   Sister captives

A **sister captive** is an extension of the pure captive structure. The entity is typically solely owned by the sponsor company, but writes cover for other companies that form part of the same 'economic family', i.e., subsidiaries or affiliates of the parent or holding company sponsor. Accordingly, there is a greater diversification of risk across entities, but the risk is still contained within an overarching corporate group. The sister captive is summarized in Figure 5.5.

5.2.3   Group captives

A **group captive** (also known as a multi-parent captive or an association captive) is an insurer that is owned by a number of companies and writes insurance cover for all of them (indeed, a mutual insurance company might be considered a type of group captive). Ownership is often diverse and business is not confined to a single company or economic family. Indeed, in addition to writing cover for the group sponsors, a group captive generally writes third-party business

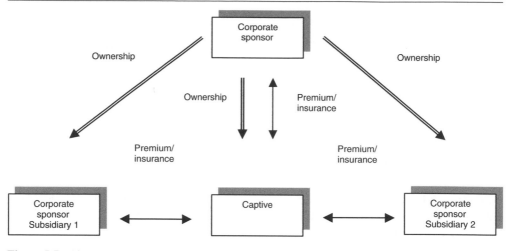

Figure 5.5   Sister captive

(i.e., insurance cover for companies that have no owner relationship with either the captive or the sponsor companies). Since risks assumed by the captive from the sponsors and third parties can be unique and independent, there is a greater amount of portfolio diversification and risk transfer than under a pure or sister captive (though in the specific subclass of association captives, the risks covered may be more uniform and specific to a particular industry – e.g., energy captive, airline captive, medical malpractice captive, and so on). Loss coverage in the group structure is often set in proportion to the premiums paid by each individual sponsor, meaning that losses are not necessarily reduced, but expenses and cash flow risks are lowered. Although participating companies do not exercise the same degree of operational authority over the captive as the sponsors of pure or sister captives, they face lower costs; in most cases they also receive more favorable tax treatment. Figure 5.6 summarizes the relationship between the group sponsors, external clients and the captive.

Other types of captive structures exist, including **agency captives** (entities owned and operated by insurance agents that share in underwriting profits and investment income on cover placed through agency members), branch captives (established as onshore branch offices of offshore captives), and so on. Although these variations are actively used, we shall not consider them in further detail.

5.2.4   Rent-a-captives and protected cell companies

In addition to the standard dedicated owner/user captives mentioned above, a broader group of 'for hire' captives – including rent-a-captives and protected cell companies – has emerged in recent years. These vehicles are often owned by one or more parties, are managed by independent agents, and write business with a large number of unrelated parties through unique structural mechanisms.

A **rent-a-captive** (RAC) is a reinsurer that offers captive capabilities through a structure that is very similar to the group captive, but without direct ownership by the sponsor/user(s). A company wishing to use a captive for purposes of administering a self-insurance program,

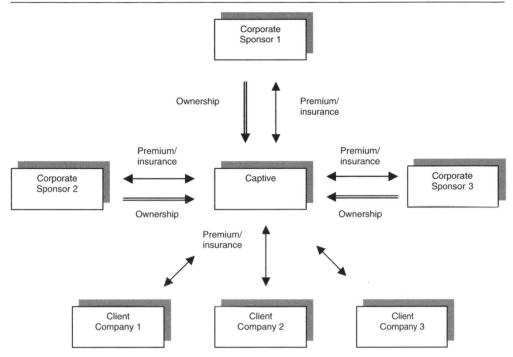

Figure 5.6 Group captive

but not wanting to own the entity (wholly or partly) or bear the costs and time of establishing an entity, can use a RAC to achieve the same end goals. RACs are typically maintained and managed by a reinsurer or broker on behalf of an unrelated, third-party owner (e.g., the provider of debt and equity capital, who earns a yield and fees). Under a typical transaction, a client company cedes risks to a fronting insurer, which reinsures to the RAC. Individual customer accounts are established within the RAC to track premiums and risks. Although risks are independent across customer accounts (being segregated by contract and a shareholders' agreement), commingling of assets is possible, meaning that a severe loss in one of the accounts can theoretically impact on other customer coverage levels. RACs have been used successfully without incident and have emerged as a quick and convenient retention mechanism (they are also used as special-purpose issuance vehicles for the capital markets instruments we consider in the next part of the book). Figure 5.7 illustrates the structure of a RAC.

Since RACs permit commingling of assets, **protected cell companies** (PCCs, also known as segregated account companies) were created in 1997 as 'ring-fenced' entities providing greater customer account protection. While RAC cells are separated by contract, with a shareholders' agreement designed to avoid "cross contamination", PCC cells are separated by statute – making the segregation much more robust. Through specific legislation, the assets and liabilities of individual cells (client accounts) are isolated and untouchable, meaning that commingling is not permitted. The first PCC legislation appeared in Guernsey and was soon followed by similar changes in Cayman, Bermuda, Singapore, Malta, and other locales.

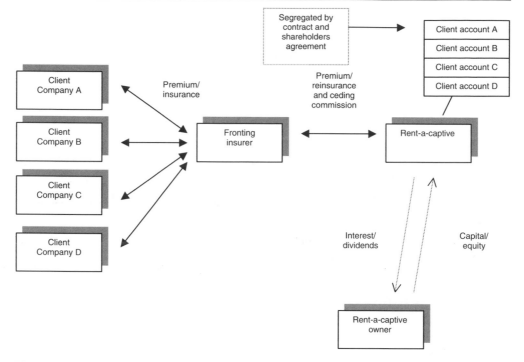

Figure 5.7   Rent-a-captive

A typical PCC is structured with two components: the core and the cells. An independent third party, such as a financial institution[1] or insurer, often owns the core (and may also act as manager). Alternatively, management duties may be subcontracted to a professional management party. Each PCC client contracts to use one or more cells, paying for costs and a share of the equity provided by the core; cell users thus pay only for the equity they actually use. Under terms of enabling legislation, creditors of a cell can only access the assets of that cell, and not the assets of other cells. If assets are insufficient creditors have recourse to the non-cell assets owned by the PCC's sponsor. Most cell owners are required to collateralize the risk in their cells, so the sponsor has access to the collateral on an "as needed" basis. PCCs have proven to be quite popular as a result of their security and flexibility. In addition to providing standard insurance cover for a client company, PCCs are used to provide insurance cover for joint ventures, catastrophe cover, and segregated risk management programs for individual client subsidiaries; they are also adapted for use as special-purpose vehicles for dealing in derivative transformations and structured note tranches. Figure 5.8 illustrates the general structure of a PCC.

Since RACs and PCCs are an efficient form of accessing the benefits of captives, many industry professionals believe that they will become even more prevalent in the future. Additional growth may also come from new market players, including small and middle-market companies, which might use these vehicles as part of a cost-efficient risk management program.

---

[1] For instance, Lehman Brothers/Arrow Re, CSFB/Boston Re, ACE Insurance/ACE PCC, Royal Bank of Scotland/Drummond Insurance PCC, and so forth.

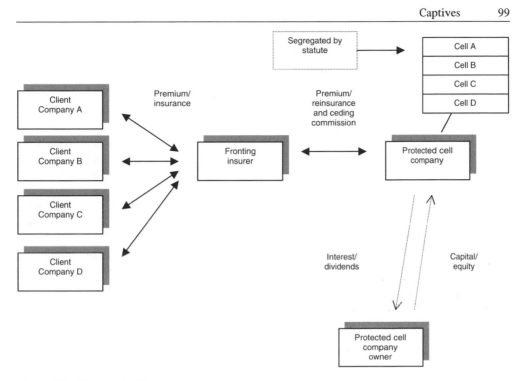

Figure 5.8 Protected cell company

5.2.5 Risk retention groups

Risk retention groups (RRGs) are retention vehicles that are conceptually similar to group captives, but are organized in a unique fashion and subject to different regulations. The RRG acts as a group captive insurer and is primarily involved in assuming and spreading the liability risks of its members via retention or pooling. They have become especially popular in the US, where the Risk Retention Act of 1986 permitted the establishment of "special liability mutual insurance companies" in order to give participating companies access to liability insurance; the process commenced in the professional services and healthcare industries, and has since expanded to many other sectors.

RRGs are effectively exempted captives formed by groups that represent a "community of interest" – those with similar business and homogeneous risk exposures – for the express purpose of sharing liability risks. RRGs can provide protection for members through self-funding of specific risks or joint purchasing of third-party insurance. They are typically licensed in the US state (or other jurisdiction) in which the RRG policyholders are resident; once licensed, they can offer similar coverage in other states or jurisdictions. Unlike other captives, RRGs do not require the use of a fronting carrier. Risk pools are similar, if less formal, risk transfer arrangements established between companies or insurers to mobilize enough capacity to cover large exposures; they can be considered a type of mutual, with participating companies/insurers acting as policyholders. Risk pools are often established on a national or risk basis, and may be formed as insurance pools or reinsurance pools. Examples of risk pools include the US workers' compensation pool, the UK terrorism risk pool, the Japanese auto pool, the German nuclear risk pool, and so on.

CASE STUDY

Reinsuring mortgage insurance through a captive

US banks granting mortgage loans to residential homeowners typically require a 20% down payment on the purchase of a single family home; they then provide the remaining 80% of financing in fixed or floating rate terms, taking the underlying property as security against the loan. In some instances banks are willing to extend financing above the typical 80% loan-to-value (LTV), i.e., to 90% or even 95%. In such cases, however, they require borrowers to purchase mortgage insurance to cover the value of the property. In practice, banks arrange for the mortgage insurance through a third-party insurer and charge the premium back to the borrower. Although this may seem somewhat inefficient, regulations prohibit banks from writing the mortgage insurance in-house, and mortgage insurers are not allowed to make payments to banks. However, in 1996 federal regulators permitted banks to assume risk on mortgage insurance through captives; this cleared the way for banks to reinsure mortgage insurance, assuming a portion of the premium and underwriting risk in the process.

Bank LMN is an active mortgage lender and periodically originates loans with an LTV in excess of 80%. In order to capture a share of the premium that would normally be paid by the borrower to a third-party insurer for the mortgage insurance, LMN establishes a reinsurance captive, LMN Re. LMN Re is capitalized with enough funds to meet regulatory requirements, as well as those imposed by the primary mortgage insurer, Insurance Company QRS. LMN continues to originate loans; those with an LTV greater than 80% are insured via QRS. Through an XOL reinsurance treaty QRS then cedes a portion of the mortgage insurance to LMN Re; LMN Re pays QRS a ceding commission in exchange for its share of the risks and premium. Thus, on $500m of high LTV loans requiring mortgage insurance (with an expected loss of $5m), LMN Re assumes upper layer risk from $10m to $13m, receiving its share of premium in return. Through this process the captive helps the bank to achieve its goal of generating income from the mortgage insurance business. LMN Re earns premiums from the underlying high LTV borrowers and, though the bank assumes additional risk in the process, it calibrates the expected losses and premiums so that it remains profitable.

5.3   TAX CONSEQUENCES

An integral component of the cost/benefit framework for captives relates to tax treatment. In order to maximize cost efficiencies and reduce the cost of risk, the sponsor or user wants to take advantage of favorable tax treatment. Tax rules vary by country and jurisdiction, but we can make certain general statements to illustrate the main points. As we have noted before, insurance-based risk transfer solutions generally receive better tax treatment than risk retention programs (e.g., deductibility of premiums when paid and/or deductibility of losses when incurred). Non-insurance companies can only deduct losses paid during the year, while insurers (including approved captives) can deduct the discounted value of incurred losses. In addition, the tax benefit from premium deductibility is normally more valuable than the deduction of uninsured losses, since the premium is generally greater than the expected value of loss, and deduction occurs earlier.

In general, captives established by UK, German, French, and Canadian companies permit premium deductibility under a broad range of scenarios. The US, however, is more restrictive. Throughout the 1970s, premiums paid by US sponsors to captives were generally deductible, even if the captive only wrote sponsor-related covers (e.g., a pure captive). In the late 1970s and early 1980s the Internal Revenue Service (IRS) began to challenge premium deductibility, claiming that pure captives were self-insurance rather than true insurance, and therefore not entitled to deductibility. It successfully prosecuted that view in many cases, noting that when risk is retained within an economic group, the premium must be viewed as a form of capital contribution and claims payments from the captive to the sponsor as a dividend distribution. Since there is no substantive transfer of risk, premiums paid by the sponsor company to a pure captive are not tax deductible (indeed, the IRS has argued that paying premiums to a pure captive is essentially equivalent to funding a self-insurance reserve, which is not generally a tax-deductible scheme).

There are, however, some exceptions to the rule. Premiums can be deducted when some amount of third-party business is written (as a more diversified risk portfolio is created). When a group captive writes risk cover that is distributed broadly, premiums paid by each cedant (as cosponsor) are deductible. The same is true for captives that write unrelated, third-party risk business. For instance, in 1991 the US courts allowed premium tax deductibility for pure captives doing a "significant amount" of unaffiliated insurance business (e.g., making the pure captive appear more like a senior captive). The decision was based on risk pooling: any reduction in the variance of average losses means that shifting of the risk is legitimate and favorable tax treatment is applicable. In 1992 the courts indicated that approximately 30% of business from unrelated parties would help to qualify a pure captive for tax benefits (and the 'rule of thumb' appears to have held). In 2001 the IRS abandoned a long-standing "economic family theory" that prevented tax deductibility for sister captives. In addition to premium and incurred loss tax issues, captives can also attract favorable investment tax treatment. For instance, if a captive's income does not have to be recognized by the sponsor as taxable income, then it will only have to pay taxes in the local jurisdiction (which is almost certain to carry a lower offshore tax rate). The general rule for US tax treatment therefore suggests that pure captives writing less than 30% of business with unaffiliated parties do not benefit from premium deductibility, while pure captives writing more than 30% in third-party business, group captives, sister captives, association captives, RACs, PCCs, and RRGs all gain from tax benefits.

Despite certain tax complexities and ambiguities, it is clear that captives, RACs, retention groups, and similar structures are part of the mainstream of the risk management markets, and should continue to convey relevant benefits for those seeking particular risk retention options.

6

Multi-risk Products

Multi-risk products represent an innovative, flexible, and gradually expanding segment of the ART market. As the name suggests, a **multi-risk product** is an instrument that combines various exposures into a single contract, giving a firm an efficient and cost-effective risk solution. Since multi-risk products provide post-loss financing based on the occurrence of one of several events or perils, the effects of correlation and joint probabilities typically result in risk protection that is cheaper than the sum of the individual parts. Multi-risk products can be regarded as a subclass of enterprise risk management or integrated programs (which we consider at greater length in Chapter 10); though an integrated program often features multiple instruments, programs, or structures covering multiple risk exposures, multi-risk products typically embed risk transfer features into a single contract. Nevertheless, the concept and logic behind the two are very similar.

In this chapter we consider two broad classes of insurance-based multi-risk products:

- **Multiple peril products**   contracts that provide coverage for multiple classes of related or unrelated perils.
- **Multiple trigger products**   contracts that provide coverage only if multiple events occur.

Each class can be subdivided further: multiple peril products include multi-line policies, commercial general liability policies, and commercial umbrella policies, while multiple trigger products include dual and triple trigger instruments with fixed, variable, or switching trigger references. We consider each contract in greater detail below.

The general class of multi-risk products is summarized in Figure 6.1.

6.1   MULTIPLE PERIL PRODUCTS

We know from our discussion in Chapter 4 that traditional insurance often provides coverage on a per-peril basis, with each element of coverage negotiated, documented, and managed separately – that is, each policy features its own deductible, cap, terms, and premium, such as illustrated in Figure 6.2. This process tends to occur when covers are added incrementally as exposures appear or grow, different units within a firm are granted responsibility for particular risks, and/or a firm purchases unique forms of protection from distinct insurers. As a result of this 'piecemeal' approach to insurance cover, a company seeking insurance risk protection across many perils may not actually be creating an efficient, or cost-effective, program.

Multiple peril products (sometimes also known as multiline or blended products) act as risk consolidation programs, gathering all designated exposures within a firm's portfolio and combining them into a single, multi-year policy with an aggregate premium, deductible, and cap. Since considerable time and effort go into creating the initial coverage, most contracts feature maturities of 3 to 7 years. Multiple peril contracts effectively eliminate the individual "slices" created for specific perils, amalgamating them into one comprehensive contract (as illustrated

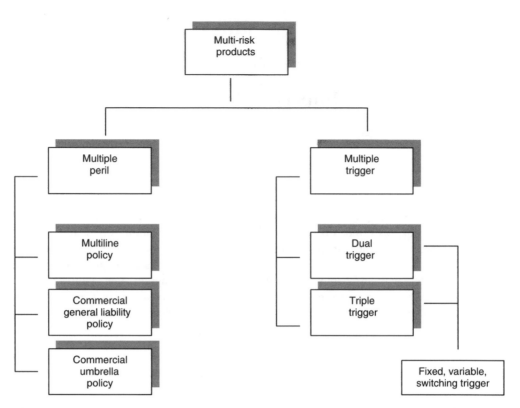

Figure 6.1   Multi-risk products

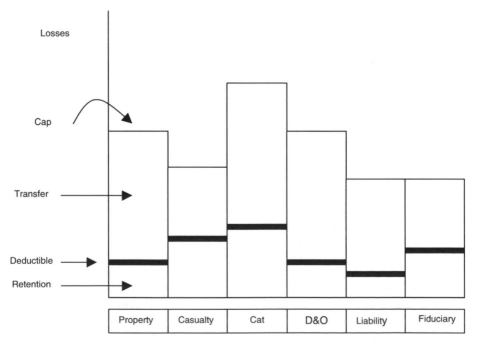

Figure 6.2   Individual coverage of specific perils

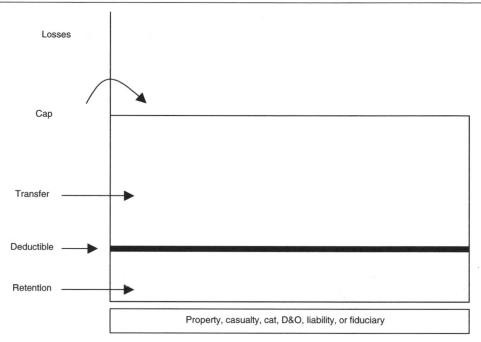

Figure 6.3 Combined coverage of perils

in Figure 6.3). Rather than insuring each exposure individually (e.g., P&C, catastrophic business interruption, workers' compensation), a company contracts to have all exposures covered in unison. In doing so, it no longer needs to worry about the specific source of a loss, and as long as it is a named peril, the policy provides appropriate indemnification. In practice it is most common for multiple peril products to provide coverage of "like" risks rather than those spanning a broader spectrum. For example, a multiple peril policy might provide coverage of professional, D&O, and fiduciary liabilities, rather than health or environmental liability. Broader coverage tends to be the domain of much more bespoke enterprise risk management programs.

Multiple peril contracts have several beneficial characteristics, including:

- lower transaction costs, since negotiation and contracting for each individual piece of protection is eliminated;
- lower premium, since the exposures included in such policies are often uncorrelated (e.g., recalling that a diversified portfolio has less risk);
- less chance of overinsurance, since it is unlikely that, in the normal course of business, a firm will suffer simultaneous losses from each of its named exposures.

Although a company can reduce instances of overinsurance, it must take care that it does not underinsure its operations through a tight, single policy cap. To help to guard against this, combined policies often include a provision for reinstatement, which allows limits to be "refreshed" in the event they are fully used prior to maturity. The reinstatement provision provides specific details on new limits that will be granted and the premium that is payable.

The insurance market has featured multiple peril products for many years,[1] including the multi-line policy, commercial general liability policy, and commercial umbrella policy. Companies seeking to cover multiple perils often use the **multi-line policy** (sometimes also known as a commercial package policy). The standard multi-line policy contains common policy declarations and conditions, and specific coverages (with their own declarations, coverage forms and causes of loss forms). A package might include commercial property, business interruption, general liability, equipment, inland marine, and automobile. If a loss occurs in any of the mentioned perils, the cedant is covered up to a net amount that reflects the deductible and cap.

The **commercial general liability** (CGL) **policy** is used by firms seeking to cover exposure related only to liabilities, including liability exposure from premises, products, contracts, contingencies, environmental damage,[2] and director and officer fiduciary breaches. The **commercial umbrella policy** provides protections for very large amounts – well in excess of those that might be obtained through a standard P&C policy or a CGL policy. The umbrella policy covers a broad range of insurable risks (and is thus multi-peril), but serves primarily as an excess layer facility rather than a first loss cover. For instance, a typical umbrella policy only provides loss coverage after certain minimum liability covers have already paid out; in addition, it may feature some exclusions, and is therefore unlikely to be truly comprehensive in scope. An umbrella policy is generally designed to pay out the ultimate net loss in excess of a retained limit (where ultimate net loss is the amount the insured must legally pay and the retained limit is the total amount of insurance plus self-insurance/retention if the loss is not covered by a policy).

To obtain the desired multi-risk coverage, a firm can select from the attachment method or the single text method. Under the **attachment method** several monoline policies (e.g., separate covers for P&C, general liability, and so on) are grouped together under a new master agreement. Through the **single text method**, existing covers are redrafted into a new policy so that all named perils are included under a single agreement. In general, the attachment method is easier to create but is susceptible to overlaps, gaps, or conflicts. In order to establish an aggregate deductible and cap to cover all named perils (e.g., as illustrated in Figure 6.4), a company (working, perhaps, with an insurance broker) will identify its retained risk appetite on a portfolio basis and, through various cost/benefit modeling scenarios, determine how much of a deductible and maximum limit might be optimal; not surprisingly, the modeling relies heavily on correlations and joint event probabilities.

6.2   MULTIPLE TRIGGER PRODUCTS

The second major class of multiple peril products we consider centers on multiple trigger instruments. Unlike multiple peril products, which provide restitution if a loss from *any* named peril occurs (e.g., either P&C event *or* a liability event *or* a catastrophe event), multiple triggers are only effective if various events occur (e.g., a P&C event *and* a financial event, or a catastrophe event *and* a financial event). If only one of two (or three) named events occurs, and

---

[1] Numerous global insurers write multiple peril products as a standard line of business; though they may specialize in particular segments of the market, the general approach they take is reasonably consistent. For instance, Swiss Re offers the Multiline Aggregate and Combined Risk Option, which is a multi-line, multi-year policy with a single annual aggregate deductible and single aggregate exposure limit; AIG offers Commodity Embedded Insurance, which covers all named risks once a specified deductible is exceeded. Cigna and XL offer the TwinPack, a multiple peril policy with a somewhat narrower scope (e.g., excess layer P&C risks), and so on.

[2] Only basic liability protections are provided under CGLs for environmental damage. In most instances far more detailed and comprehensive covers are arranged, since environmental issues are particularly complex; the same is true for workers' compensation.

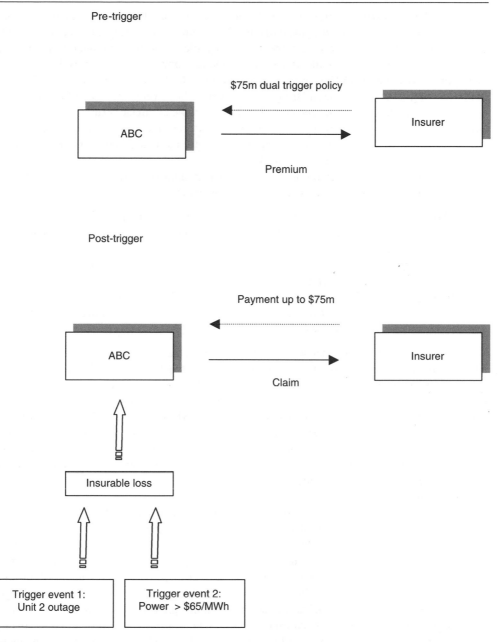

Figure 6.4   Dual trigger structure

the cedant still suffers a loss, no payout is made. This suggests that multiple peril policies can be considered single, rather than multiple, trigger products (i.e., once aggregate losses exceed the deductible, indemnification occurs).

Dual triggers are contracts that require the onset of two events before payout occurs, while **triple triggers** are contracts requiring three breaches. Since multiple triggers provide payment only when the second (dual) or third (triple) events occur, the likelihood of a payout is lower than for similar multiple peril contracts, meaning that the cedant obtains cheaper protection (though, as noted below, there is likely to be some margin payable for bespoke product development). For instance, if there is a 10% likelihood of damage to a power plant and 10% likelihood of power prices rising above $100 per megawatt hour (MWh), there is only a 1% probability of both occurring at the same time and triggering a payout. The lower probability of payoff means that risks that might have once been considered uninsurable are made insurable, a key benefit and important to the ART market in general. Indeed, insurers and reinsurers are often eager to write such cover, as the resulting joint exposure is unique and manageable, and permits better diversification within their own risk portfolios.

In general, multiple trigger products are created as multi-year insurance contracts with annual trigger resets. Triggers come in several forms, including:

- **Fixed trigger**   A trigger that is simply a barrier determining whether or not an event occurs; fixed triggers do not usually impact the value of the contract, they simply indicate whether a contract will pay out.
- **Variable trigger**   A trigger where the value of the payout is determined by the level of the trigger in relation to some defined event.
- **Switching trigger**   A trigger that varies on the basis of how individual risk exposures in the cedant's portfolio are performing (i.e., if one part of the firm is doing well it can bear more risk on one trigger, and vice versa).

Structures may be created on a per occurrence or aggregate basis. Per occurrence triggers permit a reset of the trigger each time an event occurs, while aggregate triggers allows accumulation over multiple events. To create a multiple trigger contract a firm must first analyze the causal relationships between specific events and losses. In particular, it must focus on events that can create losses, and how such losses "behave" (e.g., whether they get larger with time or the severity of an event, whether they remain relatively static once they occur, and so on). Reverting to our discussion from Chapter 1, this means that a company must be very rigorous in its identification and quantification processes. Once causal relationships are understood, triggers can be structured to provide an appropriate level of protection at a price that reflects a lower probability of payout.

Though the nature and level of the trigger is specifically negotiated between cedant and insurer, one of the triggers is usually based on an outside metric in order to avoid instances of moral hazard (and thus lower the cedant's costs); however, the outside trigger must still be sufficiently well correlated to the cedant's underlying exposure to ensure adequate restitution (e.g., basis risk cannot be too large). In fact, one trigger might reference a financial, or non-insurance, event, while another might reflect a specific insurance hazard: the financial trigger might be an equity index level, an interest rate, an economic growth rate, a temperature index, or a power price, while an insurance hazard trigger could be a business interruption loss, property damage loss, workers' compensation loss, environmental liability, and so on. Two financial and two non-financial triggers can also be considered. In all cases, however, the cedant must demonstrate an insurable interest in order for the multiple trigger structure to be considered insurance.

Consider the following simple examples:

A power company supplying electricity to industrial and retail customers might be financially impacted when its generators suffer business interruption as a result of mechanical failure (first trigger) and the price of electricity rises dramatically (second trigger) – the higher the power price, the greater the loss. While either event may be financially manageable, the combination of the two might produce very large losses, and though each could be insured or hedged separately (e.g., protecting against business interruption losses through a standard insurance contract and protecting against higher electricity prices through derivatives), cheaper protection can be obtained by combining the two. (We shall consider a more detailed example of this in the case study that follows.)

A commodity-producing company might be impacted by high workers' compensation claims (first trigger) and a decline in the price of the commodity it produces (second trigger) – the larger the price decline the more difficult it is for the company to meet the high claims. Again, either event on its own might be financially acceptable, but the two together might be too great a threat for the company, so a dual trigger might be an appropriate and cost-effective scheme.

The insurance industry is particularly interested in making sure that its two primary sources of income – underwriting and investment – are not in jeopardy at the same time. If an insurer has a poor underwriting season, it must turn to its investment portfolio to remain profitable, and vice versa. Accordingly, a P&C insurer might be concerned with maintaining an appropriate surplus in the face of a difficult underwriting environment and a poor investment market; if both occur at the same time it will suffer losses that will erode its capital surplus and creditworthiness. It can arrange a multiple trigger that provides an economic payment if losses in the P&C portfolio exceed a particular amount (first trigger) and the performance of its equity portfolio begins to deteriorate (second trigger) – the worse the equity markets perform, the greater the payment to the insurer.[3]

An industrial company might be concerned about business interruption losses, but only if it is doing poorly in its core businesses (i.e., it is already in a weakened financial state). It might arrange a dual trigger that provides restitution if key financial indicators (e.g., leverage, liquidity and cash flows) are faring poorly against industry averages (first trigger) and business interruption losses exceed a particular amount (second trigger) – the worse the business interruption losses the greater the restitution, but only when it is triggered into effect by the weakened financial state.

While the theoretical coverage of events is broad, in practice most transactions still occur in the energy sector, where a combination of **volumetric risk** (the risk of loss from volume imbalances, due to demand forces or a supply constraint arising from production problems) extremely high or low temperatures, and very high power prices can lead to significant losses. In fact, several major insurance companies have established dedicated energy risk teams to focus on just such loss eventualities.

CASE STUDY

Contingent power outage

Utility ABC supplies power to industrial and retail customers in its district. It operates two base load power generators, both coal-fired, as well as a natural gas-peaking unit that can come online quickly to meet any excess demand. The peaker and one of the coal generators (Unit 1) are both relatively new, having been put in place within the past 10 years; both have strong maintenance records and have been trouble-free. The second coal generator

---

[3] For instance, CLM Insurance Fund and the California State Auto Association have used a trigger providing a payout if catastrophic losses impact underwriting performance and equity indexes fall and damage investment performance.

(Unit 2) is considerably older and has had some scheduled maintenance downtime, though it has never been offline for unscheduled reasons. ABC has contracts to deliver specified quantities of power to various industrial customers in its district during peak hours. Since the industrial customers require the power to produce goods in their factories, they cannot suffer any interruption. The contracts therefore specify that the power delivery from ABC is non-interruptible (in fact, the industrial customers are paying a slight premium for the non-interruptible feature). The retail customers are interruptible, at least for a period of up to several hours.

ABC has a standard fixed premium insurance contract that provides P&C coverage (including business interruption) on all three units; the policy has a $5m deductible and $25m cap and is renewable on an annual basis. In reviewing the financial status of the utility, ABC's managers express some concern about a potential 'disaster scenario' – one generating losses in excess of its $25m cap that could lead to financial distress. Specifically, they are worried that unscheduled maintenance on Unit 2 could lead to the interruption of power delivery to the industrial customers. In normal circumstances – that is, under normal market price conditions – the scenario is unlikely to present difficulties: if Unit 2 goes down for several hours, or even days, ABC can simply purchase power in the spot market and continue transmitting to its industrial customers. More serious concerns arise when power prices spike above 'normal' market prices. Over the past year power has traded in the 'normal' range of $30–50 per MWh (which, again, is of no concern to ABC). However, if power trades above $75 per MWh for an extended period of time, ABC's managers believe financial pressures could set in. Accordingly, the management team consults with its broker on possible solutions, which draws up the following solutions:

- Alternative 1: *Excess umbrella coverage*. Under this alternative, ABC can simply contract with its insurer to obtain excess umbrella coverage up to $75m. It can be tailored specifically to meet concerns about Unit 2, which is older and less reliable than Units 1 and 3.
- Alternative 2: *Dual trigger*: Business interruption plus power price. Under this alternative, ABC can arrange a dual trigger structure that covers outage on Unit 2 (fixed trigger) and the price of power (variable trigger). Specifically, the structure provides restitution if Unit 2 goes down for unscheduled maintenance and is offline for at least 6-hours (the 6-hour period acts as a *de facto* deductible, lowering the cost of the structure). Once this occurs (e.g., the fixed trigger is breached), the amount of loss coverage for ABC will depend on the price of power: if power trades above $65 per MWh, ABC will receive coverage of $10 000 per MWh, up to a maximum payout of $75m. If power trades below $65 per MWh after a unit outage, the second trigger will not be in breach and ABC will not be able to claim a loss.
- Alternative 3: *Triple trigger*: Business interruption plus power price plus temperature. Under this option ABC can arrange a trigger that is similar to Alternative 2, but includes an extra trigger related to temperature. Specifically, if temperatures exceed 95 degrees on any day that unit outage has occurred, and power trades above $65 per MWh, ABC will receive a loss payment based on the formula above. The fixed temperature trigger thus serves as another contingent event that must occur in order for a claim to be made; although temperature and high power prices are strongly correlated, the addition of the third event results in slightly cheaper protection for ABC.

- Alternative 4: *Electricity call options*: Under this alternative ABC purchases electricity call options, struck at $65 per MWh, exercisable on an American basis. The company thus has an optionable interest, meaning it can generate a gain even if no unit outage occurs – as long as power prices spike above the strike price of $65 per MWh (e.g., such as might occur during a heat wave or during a supply/demand imbalance induced by transmission problems). ABC can purchase enough contracts to give it coverage to $75m under extreme market price scenarios.

Each of these alternatives has relative costs and benefits that ABC's management team must weigh. The purchase of excess cover is simplest, as it involves an incremental cost over an existing policy, and ABC's management is already very familiar with insurance-based risk management; however, the premium for the excess layer is greater than ABC wants to pay, given its expected loss scenarios. The purchase of electricity call options is a new alternative for the company. As a traditional utility, it lacks experience in purchasing options and some managers are uncomfortable with the idea of buying an instrument with an optionable interest that can generate a gain even if Unit 2 suffers no outage. In fact, the managers believe that some of ABC's shareholders will view the transaction as speculative, since a gain can occur even if the company sustains no loss. The trigger structures are also new to ABC's managers. Unlike the electricity call, however, they are more comfortable with the insurable interest characteristics of the triggers; knowing that the firm can only make a claim if it sustains a loss through Unit 2 outage obviates the "optical" concerns embedded in the call options. After reviewing the pricing and structure of the two triggers in isolation, and in comparison with the excess umbrella coverage, ABC opts for Alternative 2, the purchase of a dual trigger on outage and power prices. The ABC team believes that the structure is competitively priced since it requires two separate events to occur before generating a payout. In addition, the correlation between power prices and temperature is high enough that the price savings from the triple trigger structure does not outweigh the potential cost of losing a great deal of money with Unit 2 outage, soaring power prices, but a maximum temperature that stays just slightly below 95 degrees. Accordingly, ABC instructs its insurance broker to arrange a 1-year dual trigger structure providing protection up to $75m on a variable basis. Figure 6.4 illustrates the pre- and post-trigger scenarios for Alternative 2.

Although multiple triggers have various advantages, they do have certain drawbacks. For instance, most transactions include a charge that reflects the cost of product development. Since multiple trigger products are, by definition, highly customized structures, insurers and reinsurers must spend time and resources developing them for each client; while some aspects can be replicated, others cannot, meaning that they cannot then be reoffered to others as a 'standard' product. To the extent that some standardization occurs, there may be an excess of basis risk inherent in a given transaction, which may remove the coverage benefits a client is seeking. In addition, there is a 'gray area' regarding the accounting and legal treatment of multiple trigger structures; although most users treat the instrument as insurance, there remains some ambiguity. While the non-financial insurance trigger (e.g., the P&C hazard) is clearly an insurance component, a contract that hedges a price tied to a financial index can be viewed as a derivative, requiring mark-to-market treatment and generating less benefits related to tax deductibility. The treatment of the entire package is thus subject to some interpretation.

End-users that actively deal in the product tend to treat the entire contract as insurance for financial and tax purposes by demonstrating very explicitly that they have an insurable interest and are transferring risk exposure. In fact, those using a multiple trigger rather than a derivative to mitigate the exposure note clearly one of the key differences: while a multiple trigger, properly structured, guarantees post-loss financing should the events occur, the same is not necessarily true of a derivative contract (e.g., it is possible for a loss to occur but the derivative to remain slightly out-of-the-money, providing no restitution).

Multi-risk products are an integral element of the risk management sectors and offer companies a range of flexible alternatives. Although the bespoke nature of the contracts means that a fair amount of quantification work is necessary in order to package the right types and sequencing of exposures, the cost and efficiency benefits that can be obtained often make the effort worth while.

Part III
Capital Markets

7

Capital Markets Issues and Securitization

As we noted in Chapter 3, the global capital markets, which represent the financial aspect of funding, risk management, and investment management, form a significant component of the ART market. Indeed, when capital markets instruments and strategies are applied to insurable risks, the ART market gains its unique breadth and depth. Although there are various ways of defining and categorizing capital markets products and services, we divide them into three segments, including capital markets issues and securitization (considered in this chapter), contingent capital structures (Chapter 8), and insurance derivatives (Chapter 9). We shall also revisit these components in our discussion on enterprise risk management in Chapter 10.

7.1 OVERVIEW OF SECURITIZATION

Securitization – the process of removing assets, liabilities, or cash flows from the corporate balance sheet and conveying them to third parties through tradable securities – has been a feature of the financial markets for several decades. During the late 1970s and early 1980s Wall Street investment banks became active in pooling assets and placing them in trust vehicles that issued multiple tranches of securities, each with its own risk and return characteristics. According to the portfolio theory concepts we summarized in Chapter 2, pooling assets in portfolios results in a reduction in the variance of returns to investors – a considerable benefit to those providing risk capital. Securitization efforts started with mortgage-backed securities (MBS, pools of residential mortgages), collateralized mortgage obligations (CMOs, pools of MBS), commercial MBS, and asset-backed securities (ABS, pools of receivables, leases, and virtually any other kind of asset).

During the early- to mid-1990s securitization technology was extended to the credit markets, leading to the creation of collateralized loan obligations (CLOs, pools of loans), and collateralized bond obligations (CBOs, pools of corporate bonds) – together comprising the broad class of CDOs, to which we have referenced earlier in the book.[1] While CDOs and other financial securitizations are not generally considered to be part of the ART market (and, apart from the basic concepts in the notes, shall not be considered in this book in further detail), the same structures have been successfully applied in the insurance sector, providing another link between the financial and insurance markets.

---

[1] Broadly speaking, CDOs are structured either as balance sheet CDOs (also known as cash flow CDOs) or synthetic CDOs (also known as arbitrage CDOs). **Balance sheet CDOs** are based on assets physically held in an investment or loan portfolio that an institution *sells* into a conduit; **synthetic CDOs** are based on assets that an investment portfolio manager *purchases* and actively manages in order to achieve desired results. Funded synthetic CDOs involve the actual purchase of assets in the portfolio through proceeds raised from note issuance, while unfunded synthetic CDOs involve the use of credit derivatives, including total return swaps (swaps that transfer the economics of the reference asset), basket options or basket swaps. Most balance sheet and synthetic CDOs allocate funds through the cash flow method, where specific interest and principal flows from underlying securities (or derivatives) are used to pay investors as they are received by the trust. If the flows are insufficient to service all investors sequentially, they are redirected to the senior-most investors. There has been a shift, in recent years, from funded to unfunded structures, which require less rated tranches and can be assembled more inexpensively. In insurance terms CDOs can be viewed as a form of credit reinsurance, where the more subordinated investors are reinsuring the more senior investors, at a price (e.g., the increased yield spread).

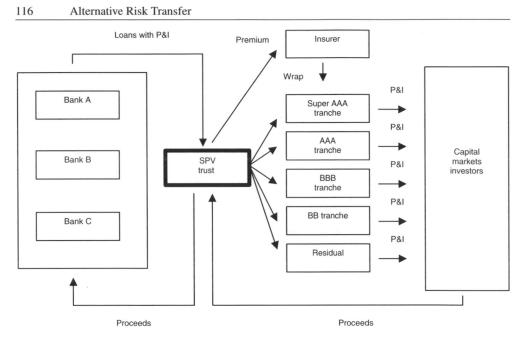

Figure 7.1 Structural cash flows of a CLO

Under a generic financial securitization, an issuing trust is structured as an independent, bankruptcy-remote entity, responsible for managing cash flows, administering receivables and payables, arranging swap hedges, and so on. In order to generate the desired risk and return profiles for each tranche, the trust redirects cash flows from the underlying assets, repaying investors principal and interest (P&I) in order of priority. Thus, the most senior (i.e., lowest return, lowest risk) investors are repaid first, and the most junior (i.e., highest return, highest risk) investors last. In most instances the issues are supported by a highly subordinated "equity-like" tranche, known as the residual, that carries equity returns and risks. In some instances, the arrangers also credit-enhance certain tranches through letters of credit, overcollateralization, financial guarantees, or insurance wraps, thus creating a higher rating (including so-called 'super AAA' tranches, where the risk of default is infinitesimal). The intent behind any securitization is two-fold: to remove assets or liabilities from the balance sheet, and transfer risk to investors (by giving them the precise instrument they want through the tranching mechanism).[2] To summarize the securitization process, Figure 7.1 depicts basic cash flows related to the purchase of pools of corporate loans from various banks and the creation of a CLO (the same process applies to MBS, CMOs, and so on).

7.2 INSURANCE-LINKED SECURITIES

7.2.1 Overview

Given past success with financial securitization, banks took their asset-driven securitization technologies to the insurance market in the 1990s, creating notes and bonds based on

[2] For instance, financial institutions are active asset managers (e.g., they have a strong asset focus on loan origination and investments), while insurers are active liability managers (e.g., they have a strong focus on liability repayment schedules, loss reserves, and unearned premiums) – and although each has a unique focus on the securitization process, both seek ultimately to transfer risks through securitization.

insurance-related events. Although the first issue did not appear until the mid-1990s, the actual groundwork was laid several years earlier.[3] The concept behind insurance-based capital markets issues, or **insurance-linked securities** (ILSs – we use the terms interchangeably) is similar to other securitizations: issuing securities that reference insurance risks in order to transfer exposures and create additional risk capacity. Early efforts were based on securitizing catastrophic risks related to hurricanes and earthquakes. Although this remains the focus of activity, other insurance-related risk securitizations have appeared in recent years, including those based on exposure to temperature, residual value, life insurance policy acquisitions costs, auto insurance, workers' compensation, and so on. Activity in this area remains modest compared to catastrophic risk securitizations, but growth possibilities exist.

While ILS structures have been refined and customized in recent years, the basic architecture has remained relatively unchanged: an insurance or reinsurance company issues securities through an SPE and bases repayment of interest and/or principal on losses arising from defined insurance events. If losses exceed a predetermined threshold, the insurer/reinsurer is no longer required to pay investors interest; if structured with a non-principal protected tranche all, or a portion, of the principal can also be deferred or eliminated.[4] Through this elemental structure new risk supply is created: the issuer passes a defined exposure to capital markets investors, lowering its risk profile; this provides capital and reserve relief and allows new business to be written. Importantly, the mechanism bridges the insurance and capital markets, permitting the insurance sector to tap into the tremendous supply of capital held by investors. While the reinsurance sector features approximately $25bn in capital, the capital markets are over $14tr in size – and thus an excellent source of capacity. Indeed, as a result of investment opportunities, a dedicated base of 100–150 institutional ILS investors[5] has developed over the past few years, helping to drive the market (of course, in order to remain interested and committed, these investors demand steady issuance to enable them to fulfill their own portfolio requirements). In fact, a portion of the issuance that now occurs is demand-driven, with issuers tailoring tranches of deals to the requirements of certain institutional investors.[6] The market is still concentrated primarily on institutional clients and retail participation is very modest. Certain dedicated mutual funds have, however, begun to offer ILS exposure to small investors in recent years.[7]

Not surprisingly, most ILS issuers are insurers and reinsurers that are eager to use another tool to manage their risk portfolios. Direct corporate issuance has been very small, with only a handful of issues appearing in recent years[8]; in fact, most companies with catastrophic exposures find it simpler and more efficient to use standard insurance products to cover risks to hurricanes, earthquakes, and so on. Although ILS activity is somewhat cyclical, issuance levels have been relatively steady since the late 1990s and into the early part of the millennium,

---

[3] Indeed, a property catastrophe bond was due to be launched by Merrill Lynch on behalf of AIG in 1992, but was postponed in light of Hurricane Andrew.

[4] For instance, as a result of the devastating French windstorms of 1999 the Reliance IV bond resulted in investors receiving a coupon that was 500 basis points lower than originally expected; similarly, an issue by Georgetown Re resulted in investors losing all of the 1999 coupon and 2% of principal.

[5] This group includes major US fund managers such as TIAA/CREF and PIMCO, along with a large number of onshore and offshore hedge funds.

[6] For instance, while early ILS deals featured maturities extending to 10 years, investors have come to favor 5- to 7-year securities, and issuers have responded accordingly. Investors also have a predilection for single peril deals.

[7] For instance, Bank Leu has created a dedicated catastrophic bond mutual fund that is aimed strictly at retail investors.

[8] For instance, Oriental Land/Tokyo Disneyland launched a bond in 1999 (see the case study on page 128). Vivendi Universal issued a transaction in late 2002 to hedge against California earthquake in the vicinity of its Universal Studios theme park. The Vivendi transaction is a combination of a note and preferred share issue that provides coverage capped at $175m. The preferred investors take the first loss at 100%, after which note investors have their principal at risk as well.

with $750m to $1.25bn of new issues launched annually. As more than 50 issues have been floated since 1994, growth may be characterized as steady.

Since ILSs are a substitute (but not permanent replacement) for insurance/reinsurance, the price differential between reinsurance and capital markets issues has an influence on overall activity.[9] When a hard market develops, ILS issuance can accelerate (but remains within a relatively tight boundary, i.e., there is no evidence of a large spike in issuance). Since creating the ILS structure can be relatively expensive – based on costs associated with forming SPEs, preparing documentation, engaging investment banks to underwrite the issue, and so on – it is only justifiable in the cost/benefit framework when other loss-financing alternatives are more expensive. While an insurer/reinsurer's decision to proceed with an ILS will depend on price, it must also take account of other issues, such as the amount of overall risk it wishes to retain and reinsure, the amount of credit exposure it wants outstanding to various reinsurers, and so on.

Most ILS issuance has occurred in the catastrophic risk sector, through securitization of earthquake, hurricane, and windstorm risks; these are collectively known as **catastrophe (cat) bonds**. The standard cat bond structure is quite similar to other securitized capital markets structures, except that a special-purpose reinsurer (SPR), rather than an SPE trust, acts as the issuance vehicle; we consider this point below. Notes are issued to investors and the trustee invests proceeds to generate a return (which might be fixed by a swap); the return is supplemented by payment of premium from the ceding company. The collateral in the trust account is used to repay principal at maturity, unless a catastrophic event triggers a reduced payout; if this occurs, investors may not receive interest and/or principal on a timely basis, if at all (in some cases they will only receive recompense after all claims and contingent liabilities arising from the insurable event have been paid). By reducing or eliminating the payout to investors in the event a defined catastrophic event strikes, the ceding company mitigates its exposure to that event.

Investment banks remain the primary arrangers of ILSs given their experience in other types of securitizations and their ability to place bonds through large distribution networks; with a few exceptions, insurance intermediaries are still largely absent from the intermediation process. Most issues in the market are based on analytics generated by specialist providers, such as RMS and AIR. Such firms have sophisticated modeling capabilities that permit them to generate probability scenarios for different types of catastrophic events. These analytics help investment banks to price the issues and investors to understand the relative risk/return they are facing in purchasing individual tranches of a given issue. The rating agencies play an active role in evaluating the risks associated with individual deals and tranches, but they take different approaches: for instance, Moody's rates issues and tranches on the basis of expected loss estimates, while Standard and Poor's bases their assessment on the probability of first dollar loss.

7.2.2   Costs and benefits

Securitization of insurance risks benefits various parties, including ceding companies, investors, and intermediaries. For instance, the ceding company (generally an insurer, as noted) can make use of another loss-financing mechanism to manage risk. During a hard reinsurance

---

[9] For instance, a 2001 issue by Residential Re providing $450m of coverage at $L + 499$ bps was equivalent to paying $22.5m in premium for $5.6bn of loss coverage. A cost/benefit tradeoff between the two options can thus be made.

market this might be an attractive alternative in the cost/benefit framework. It also reduces its credit exposure to individual reinsurers; since the risk is repackaged into notes and sold to investors via the SPR, the ceding insurer no longer needs to be concerned about specific performance by the reinsurer. In addition, since the marketplace is highly bespoke, the insurer can design its preferred note structure: assuming greater basis risk but eliminating moral hazard; bearing the incremental cost of moral hazard but reducing basis risk; issuing single-year or multi-year cover; protecting against single or multiple perils; and so on. Investors also gain by purchasing securities that are likely to have little, or no, correlation with other risk assets in their portfolios. This is very appealing for investment managers, who are eager to find opportunities to earn extra yield without compounding the risk effects of the portfolio (e.g., a hurricane or earthquake event is not correlated with the movement of bond yields or the stock market, meaning that diversification possibilities exist). Investors are also able to capture good returns. Most deals of the late 1990s and early part of the millennium featured a 'novelty premium' of 50–100 basis points in excess of what could be earned on similarly rated corporate bonds as an inducement to participate; although margins have compressed as investors have grown more familiar with potential risks, they remain attractive. Intermediaries benefit from new sources of business in both issuance and placement business; they can earn fees from helping to structure the securities and commissions/spreads from selling the bonds. There are, of course, certain costs and disadvantages, including the expenses involved in establishing issuance vehicles/programs and floating securities, the analytic work that must be performed in assessing and pricing the securities, the general illiquidity of the marketplace (e.g., it is largely 'buy and hold'), and the lack of good hedging instruments for intermediaries that might otherwise be willing to make markets and add liquidity.

The market for ILS can be segregated into catastrophic and non-catastrophic risk issues based on index, indemnity, or parametric triggers. Catastrophic bonds can be subdivided into securities that reference hurricane, earthquake, windstorm, and other low-frequency/high-severity natural disasters; they may be created to cover single or multiple perils per bond or tranche. Non-catastrophic ILS can be classed into temperature, residual value, mortgage default, trade credit, and life acquisition costs. We consider each in the sections that follow. Figure 7.2 summarizes the universe of ILS. (Note once again that, although aspects of credit risk fall under the class of insurable risks, we consider the CDO market to be a separate financially driven marketplace and will not consider the structures in further detail.[10])

7.3 STRUCTURAL FEATURES

Since the ILS market has been in existence for several years, a number of structural features have emerged and become standard operating practice for those issuing securities. In this section we consider common features related to issuing vehicles, triggers, and tranching.

7.3.1 Issuing vehicles

A pure securitization of risk does not help a ceding insurer to meet its statutory capital surplus requirements; thus, some amount of risk must be reinsured to the SPR. This permits the

---

[10] Exceptions to the rule might center on bonds issued by insurance companies seeking to hedge portfolios of credit investments/exposures by transferring risks back to capital markets investors through index triggers rather than indemnity triggers. Transactions of this type, such as a $500m, 3-year deal assembled in 1999 by Gerling (and linked to a general credit index), are still quite rare.

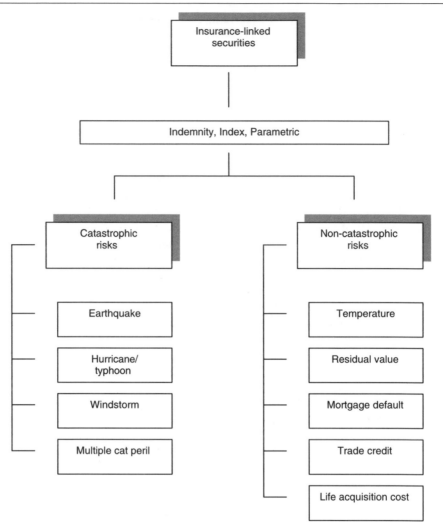

Figure 7.2   Universe of insurance-linked securities

risk to be first reinsured, and then securitized, which allows for the necessary capital relief. Accordingly, it is common for an ILS to be issued through a vehicle that is established as a reinsurer rather than simple trust SPE. The bankruptcy-remote SPR is responsible for writing a reinsurance contract to the cedant in exchange for premium. Since the protection provided to the cedant is in the form of a reinsurance contract rather than a derivative, the SPR must be established as a licensed reinsurance company. Naturally, in order for the insurer to receive the benefit of ceded exposure, risk must be transferred, meaning that the ceding insurer cannot directly own the SPR. In fact, charitable foundations sponsor most SPRs in order to fulfill this "independence" requirement. In addition to writing the reinsurance cover, the SPR also issues notes to investors, channels proceeds of the premium to the trustee for further investment, and arranges any swaps that might be necessary to fix coupon payments to investors. The general SPR structure is summarized in Figure 7.3.

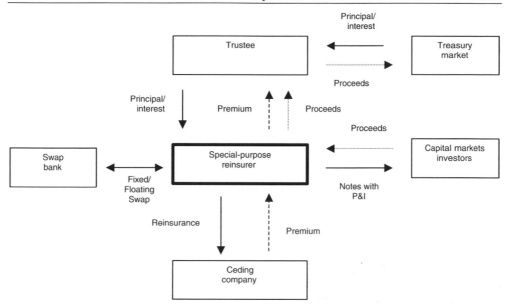

Figure 7.3   ILS with SPR as issuance vehicle

In some instances another reinsurer is interposed between the ceding company and the SPR, meaning that the contract becomes retrocession instead of reinsurance; this structure, depicted in Figure 7.4, permits the reinsurer to accept indemnity risk and hedge with index contracts to avoid the ceding company having to bear basis risk.

Since ILSs are theoretically subject to double taxation (on income generated and interest disbursed), many SPRs are located in offshore, tax-friendly locations where they issue securities in the form of debt (rather than equity or an equity hybrid). Debt securities may be issued as private placement or public securities. The private placement market is a professional market for institutional investors, characterized by larger unit denominations (to dissuade retail participation) and lower liquidity (restrictions exist on who can trade on a secondary basis, and how much)[11]; issues need not necessarily be rated by a credit-rating agency, although they often are.

7.3.2   Triggers

Every ILS has a trigger that determines the conditions under which the ceding company can suspend interest and/or principal payments (either temporarily or permanently). In general, a trigger may be based on single or multiple events (occurrences) and becomes effective after a cedant's losses exceed a particular amount (e.g., a *de facto* deductible). Triggers can take one of the following forms:

- **Indemnity trigger**   The suspension of interest and/or principal occurs when actual losses sustained by the issuer in a predefined segment of business reach a certain level (e.g., an actual book of business).

---

[11] For instance, in the US under Rule 144A, participants must be "qualified institutional buyers" (QIBs), an issue must be limited to a certain number of investors, and secondary trading is typically confined to the group of QIBs and dealers.

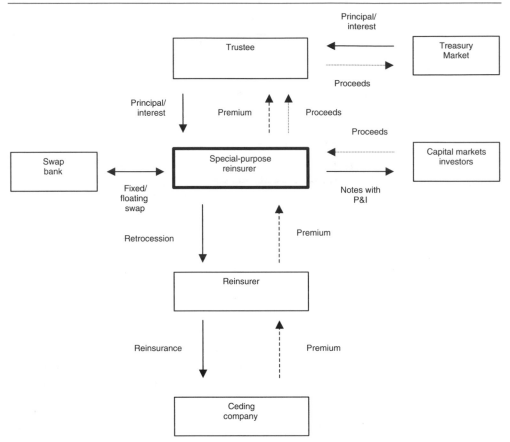

Figure 7.4   ILS with intermediate reinsurer

- **Index trigger**   The suspension of interest and/or principal occurs when the value of a recognized third-party index reaches a certain threshold.
- **Parametric trigger**   The suspension of interest and/or principal occurs when a specific loss metric reaches a certain value (e.g., a disaster of a particular magnitude/location).

Since indemnity bonds are based on a ceding insurer's actual book of business, they give rise to the moral hazard risks we have discussed earlier; the cedant knows that the ILS trigger (and, therefore, restitution) is based on actual loss experience and might not be as diligent in underwriting risks or enforcing loss control behaviors. However, since the loss experience is perfectly matched, basis risk is eliminated. In practice, indemnity deals require the cedant to reveal the nature of risk exposures and/or underwriting standards, and share in a portion of the losses; this helps to obviate some of the moral hazard that might otherwise appear.

Index and parametric bonds remove the specter of moral hazard, since suspension of principal and interest is based on external events or values that are tabulated by third parties. The tradeoff, naturally, is an increase in basis risk for the issuer, as it is very unlikely that actual exposure matches the trigger; indeed, the ceding company must determine whether there is an index or parametric gauge that is sufficiently correlated to actual exposures to make the transaction viable. When a firm uses a parametric or index trigger it faces lower costs (because it is assuming more basis risk) and is not required to divulge the actual details of the business being secured (in fact, investors are often indifferent as to whether the cedant has particular exposures – they can simply review the analytics and index construction rather than the cedant's portfolio). Index and parametric securities may also be somewhat more liquid and tradable, as they are based on transparent metrics that all investors can evaluate (that said, the securities are still considered illiquid, certainly as compared with similarly rated corporate securities). Most early transactions in the market were based on indemnity and index triggers, and only a small number on parametric triggers. In recent years the market has shifted from a majority of indemnity deals (e.g., 70%+ in the late 1990s) to a majority of index transactions (e.g., 70%+ in the millennium by both dollar and volume). This is consistent with investor preferences; many investors favor index transactions because they add transparency and do not require a full evaluation of the cedant's underlying risk portfolio.

7.3.3 Tranches

ILSs are issued with multiple tranches that allow investors to select the level of risk and return participation they deem most suitable. For instance, hedge funds may purchase low-rated/high-risk tranches, while investment funds and bank/insurance company investment accounts prefer higher rated pieces. Tranches can be structured in combinations that reflect different levels of interest and/or principal delay or forfeiture. Although every unsecured tranche is at risk (i.e., there are no principal and interest-protected securities unless specifically enhanced by a third party), potential loss can range from modest to extreme. As we have noted, some tranches might be credit enhanced by a highly rated guarantor in order to boost the credit rating and broaden distribution; since some investors cannot purchase sub-investment grade securities, there are occasions when distribution requires the issuer to bear the cost of a credit wrap. Table 7.1 illustrates a sample of tranches that might be encountered on a typical ILS. Tranche A, credit-enhanced through a credit guarantee from an insurer or a letter of credit from a bank, might be rated AAA or AA; Tranche B, featuring possible loss of interest payments, is often rated in the A/BBB category; Tranche E, with the potential for complete loss of principal and interest, is akin to a BB-rated security. Note that, apart from credit-enhanced tranches, bonds need not be 'explicitly' rated by the rating agencies and may only be 'shadow-rated'.

Table 7.1 Sample ILS tranches

Tranche	Risk	Credit rating
A	Credit enhanced: No loss of interest payments or principal repayments	Highest
B	Loss of interest payments	High
C	Loss of interest payments Delay in principal repayments	Middle
D	Loss of interest payments Partial loss of principal repayments	Low
E	Loss of interest payments Loss of principal repayments	Lowest
Residual	Residual equity risk Loss of interest and principal payments	Not rated: equity

Tranches that feature a delay mechanism might return some principal as scheduled, and the balance over a period of time, through a funded zero-coupon position. Although individual tranches carry stated final maturities, actual maturity can be lengthened after an insurable event occurs because claims may be slow to develop; thus, stated and actual maturity may differ. In practice, cedants prefer long loss development periods as they permit the accumulation of a greater amount of claims, which can help to reduce principal/interest repayments. Investors, not surprisingly, prefer shorter periods, which allow them to receive and reinvest their principal/interest. Note that while many ILS transactions are multi-tranche and multi-year (given the desire to take advantage of the one-time expenses needed to establish the program) they are still governed by caps that can be breached before the final maturity. Thus, if a 5-year Japanese earthquake bond has a $250m cap, and a $300m loss event occurs in Year 2, the issue is effectively extinguished with 3 years remaining until final maturity (the loss development period may cover 6 months to 1 year).

7.4 CATASTROPHE BONDS

To help to illustrate the practical ART applications of ILSs, we consider several types of catastrophe bonds that have appeared in recent years. The focus on cat bonds is appropriate since they remain the dominant form of ILS issuance in the marketplace (in the section immediately following we consider other ILS structures that have appeared in recent years and may exhibit additional growth in the future). Although growth in cat bonds has been relatively consistent since 1998 – with approximately $1bn in new issuance per year – the scope of coverage has expanded steadily, with new covers available on Hawaiian hurricanes, Monaco earthquakes, French storms, French earthquakes, and so forth. The cat ILS market commonly references 11 major catastrophe risk classes, summarized in Table 7.2.

7.4.1 Hurricane

Hurricane destruction can be devastating, so it is not surprising that firms seek appropriate coverage in the insurance market, and insurers seek cover of their own through reinsurance or alternative mechanisms such as hurricane bonds. The financial losses accumulated over the years from hurricane destruction have been considerable. (The aggregate losses of Hurricanes

Table 7.2 Catastrophic risk classes for ILSs

Risk class	Territory
Earthquake	California
	US Midwest
	Japan
	France and Monaco
Hurricane	US Northeast/Atlantic
	US Gulf
	Puerto Rico
	Hawaii
	Japan
Windstorm	Europe
Hailstorm	Europe

Hugo, 1989, Andrew, 1992,[12] Amber and Iniki, 1992, were so large that they left 15 P&C insurers insolvent.) In addition, some analytic simulations suggest that a $75bn hurricane could occur in the future, which would seriously impact reinsurance capital and severely constrict risk capacity. Hurricane-based cat bonds were the first to enter the market, in the mid-1990s, and have proven to be enduring, with steady to increasing annual issuance since that time. Most hurricane peril covers are written on the US Northeast/Atlantic, Gulf Coast, and Hawaii, as well as typhoon equivalents in Japan. These areas feature important commercial and residential developments, many in center-of-hurricane trajectories. Deals are structured with indemnity, parametric, and index triggers. We consider a pioneering transaction for insurer USAA in the case study.

CASE STUDY

USAA's hurricane bond

USAA, a mutually owned insurance company providing auto, homeowners, dwelling, and personal liability risk coverage to US military personnel and their families, had been interested in alternative forms of risk exposure coverage since the early 1990s. Although most of its risk management had occurred through retention, diversification, and reinsurance, it began to think about catastrophe-linked securities as early as 1992. This became a greater priority in the aftermath of Hurricane Andrew, which resulted in $17.9bn of damage. USAA itself experienced a disproportionate loss of $620m from Andrew due to its risk concentrations in Florida. In fact, as a result of its business insuring military personnel, USAA had an undue concentration of exposures in various 'high-risk' states, including California, Texas, Florida, and North Carolina. Accordingly, the insurer was eager to eliminate a portion of the excess layer risk arising from P&C damage in these 'catastrophe-prone' states. After preliminary work on a structure during 1994, USAA sent out requests for proposals in 1995 to nine investment banks and, by early 1996, had narrowed the selection down to three. Working with analytics firm AIR, the insurer evaluated the proposals and awarded the mandate to Merrill Lynch.

The groundwork was difficult, since the idea of a hurricane-linked bond was novel. Much of 1996 was spent resolving structural, legal, and regulatory issues, and addressing the concerns and questions of potential investors and the credit-rating agencies. The insurer remained uncommitted on the deal at this point, given the uncertainties, complexities, and costs, and continued to evaluate its alternatives (e.g., conventional reinsurance, self-insurance, the Chicago Board of Trade's PCS options, and surplus notes). The realizable benefits of a cat bond were still uncertain and this was an important transaction, not only for USAA, but for the marketplace as a whole: failure to successfully structure and place the bonds was bound to create nervousness about USAA's financial position and broader concerns about the validity of securitizing catastrophic risk. However, by early 1997 transaction details began to solidify; USAA added Goldman Sachs and Lehman Brothers to the underwriting syndicate and the team prepared for launch.

The bond was structured to give the insurer coverage of the XOL layer above $1bn, to a maximum of $500m at an 80% rate (e.g., 20% coinsurance) – this was equal to

---

[12] Hurricanes Hugo and Andrew alone caused $22bn of damage.

$400m of reinsurance cover. An issuance vehicle, Residential Re, was established as an independent Cayman SPR to write the reinsurance contract to USAA and issue notes to investors in two classes of three tranches: Class A-1, rated AAA, featuring a $77m tranche of principal protected notes and $87m of principal variable notes; and Class A-2, rated BB, featuring $313m of principal variable notes. Figure 7.5 and 7.6 summarize the Class A-1 and A-2 tranches. The transaction was based on a single occurrence of a Class 3, 4 or 5 hurricane, with ultimate net loss as defined under USAA's portfolio parameters (e.g., cover under existing policies/renewals and new policies, in 21 listed states). The bond was thus a multi-tranche, single-event bond with an indemnity trigger. One of the important elements of this pioneering transaction was convincing regulatory authorities that investors were actually purchasing bonds and not writing reinsurance contracts (which was not permitted); regulators finally agreed to give investors capital markets treatment. With details resolved and pre-marketing completed, the three-bank syndicate issued the bonds on a 'best-efforts' basis and placed the entire targeted amount. In fact, pricing was purposely made attractive (e.g., priced at a wide spread) to induce a larger number of investors to participate and to ensure successful placement. This inaugural hurricane bond thus set the stage for many others to follow (some using the same mechanics). USAA, convinced of the efficacy of the structure as a risk management tool, has been a relatively frequent issuer of cat bonds.

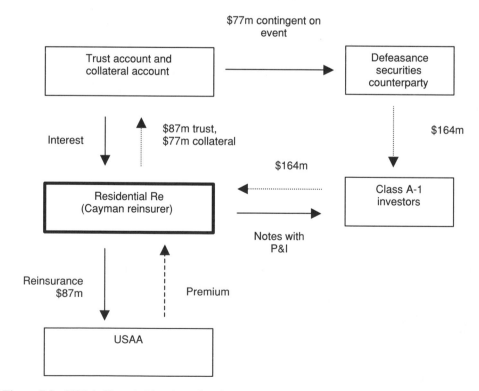

Figure 7.5   USAA Class A-1 hurricane bond

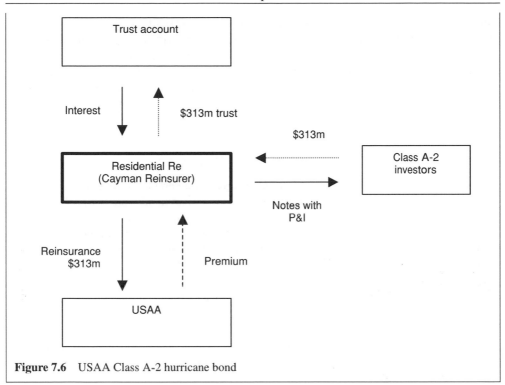

Figure 7.6   USAA Class A-2 hurricane bond

7.4.2   Earthquake

Like hurricanes, earthquakes are another source of concern for companies and insurers attempting to manage P&C risks, meaning that the earthquake-based ILS is an important corporate risk management tools. Experience has shown that the financial damage wrought by earthquakes can be considerable (e.g., Northridge 1994, Kobe 1995) and the possibility of even greater losses exists; in fact, some analytic projections estimate that an 8.5 Richter earthquake on the US New Madrid fault line could lead to direct and indirect losses of $115bn (from P&C, business interruption, and so on). It is no surprise, therefore, that issuance of earthquake ILS has been reasonably active over the past few years. Deals have been structured to cover earthquakes in California, Midwestern US, and Japan, with indemnity, index, and parametric triggers. Several examples are considered in the following case study.

CASE STUDY

Earthquake bonds

Swiss Re SR Earthquake Fund: index trigger

In 1997 Swiss Re created the SR Earthquake Fund, a $137m multi-tranche bond with repayments linked to California earthquake. The deal was designed as a hedge for a retrocession cover the insurer had already written, and was based on the largest insurable losses sustained from California earthquake over a two-year period (with a one-year loss development period), as determined by the Property Claims Service (PCS) index. Principal on the tranches was reduced according to the size of the loss reflected in the PCS index. The first two tranches (one fixed, one floating and both rated investment grade) had 60% of principal at risk. The third tranche, subinvestment grade, had 100% principal at risk; the fourth tranche, which was unrated, resulted in complete loss of principal if the PCS index losses exceeded $12bn.

Tokio Marine/Parametric Re: Parametric trigger

In 1997 Tokio Marine, one of Japan's largest insurers, and Parametric Re created a unique risk protection mechanism for the insurer's exposure to earthquake-related P&C damage in the Tokyo area. Specifically, the two firms designed a parametric security with multiple tranches related to the size and location of an earthquake in the Tokyo district. Inner and outer grids surrounding the city were created to define the location of a potential event; this, coupled with the magnitude of an earthquake (determined by the scale produced by the Japan Meteorological Agency (JMA)), was deemed an appropriate parametric index that would eliminate any instance of moral hazard and obviate the need for a loss development period; it did, of course, introduce an element of basis risk. Under the terms of the deal a 7.4 earthquake on the JMA scale led to 44% deferral of principal on notes in the outer grid, and 70% deferral of principal on the outer grid. The ILS was issued as a package of securities, including notes with 100% exposure and units of two types: those with no exposure and those with 100% exposure.

Oriental Land/Tokyo Disneyland: Parametric trigger

Tokyo Disneyland was developed in 1983 on the outskirts of Tokyo as the Disney's first overseas theme park. When the theme park commenced operations, Oriental Land, the owner/operator, chose not to seek specific insurance cover for possible P&C damage from earthquake as it was primarily interested in the economic impact of an earthquake on its business rather than the specific P&C damage it might sustain; no such coverage, however, was available. Not until 1999 did the company find a solution through the ILS market, becoming the first corporate issuer to launch an earthquake-related deal. In May 1999, with the help of Goldman Sachs, Oriental Land launched a $200m, two-tranche parametric deal: the first tranche was intended to protect the company against economic losses caused by business interruption from an earthquake in the vicinity of Tokyo Disneyland, and the second was designed to supply post-loss reconstruction financing. The first tranche, $100m, of 5-year floating rate notes issued by the Concentric Re SPR and paying L + 310, featured a parametric trigger: regardless of the amount of specific damage to the theme park, the payout was dependent on parameters related to earthquake magnitude, location and depth; the closer and larger the earthquake to the vicinity of the park, the greater the effective payout to Oriental Land. The second tranche, $100m, 5-year floating rate notes issued through the Circle Maihana SPV at L + 75, was designed to provide reconstruction funding in the aftermath of a defined event. The bond was successfully placed, giving Oriental Land the cover it had long sought.

7.4.3   Windstorm

Windstorm risk is a third class of catastrophic exposure and relates specifically to the P&C damage arising from very strong winds and rain. Several windstorm-based ILSs have been floated in recent years. Such covers are written primarily on European references (either the entire European continent (including the UK) or individual countries, particularly France); some transactions have also included wind peril in Florida and other US states, but these are relatively rare. As noted earlier in the chapter, certain bonds referencing French windstorm have resulted in reduced interest and/or principal payments on select issues, demonstrating in practice the risk-shifting capabilities of ILSs.

7.4.4   Multiple cat peril ILS and peril by tranche ILS

In some cases ILSs are structured to handle multiple cat perils, such as losses from earthquake and hurricane occurring in different regions of the world. Such multiple peril ILSs are intended to give the ceding company maximum flexibility and efficiency by eliminating the need to launch separate transactions for each named peril (in fact, while the structure can be appealing to cedants, some investors find the evaluation of such a complex package of risks daunting). Multiple peril ILSs can be issued with indemnity, index or parametric triggers, and with single or multiple tranches (related to overall interest/principal protection rather than peril exposure, as all named perils are covered in each tranche). The number of multiple cat peril ILSs appears to be on the rise. Starting with the earliest multiple peril issues in 1999,[13] issuance has grown in terms of size and creativity. For instance, Swiss Re launched the SR Wind bond, covering French windstorm and Florida and Puerto Rico hurricane via two separate, but contingently linked, notes: if one peril attached then the limit on the other could be transferred to cover losses from the peril already triggered. In the same year French insurer AGF launched the Med Re bond covering both European windstorm and French earthquake. Securities were floated in dollars but covered losses in euro for both events (with 65% quota share reinsurance) and the first wind event (35% quota share reinsurance). Various other multiple peril bonds have been launched, and the prospect of further issuance appears strong.

Multiple peril ILSs are distinct from multiple tranche bonds that cover distinct perils. As noted above, an investor in the former buys a single security whose value can be affected by one of several perils. An investor in the latter purchases a security that references a specific peril, but securities are issued under an "umbrella" that allows for multiple tranche issuance (i.e., peril by tranche); there is thus no commingling of risks and investors need not deal with the valuation and risk complexities characteristics of a multiple peril security. For instance, in 2002 Swiss Re created the $2bn Pioneer "catsec" program allowing for issuance of specific tranches of securities covering P&C risks attributable to North Atlantic windstorm, European windstorm, California and Midwestern US earthquake, and Japanese earthquake. In 2003 Swiss Re issued the three-tranche Phoenix Quake bond for Zenkyoren (the Japanese National Mutual Insurance Federation of Agricultural Cooperatives). The $470m issue covered Zenkyoren's exposure to earthquake and typhoon, and investors were able to select from among the three parametric bonds (Quake Ltd, Quake Wind and Quake Wind II), each with its own peril,

---

[13] 1999 marked a key year for the issuance of innovative multiple peril ILSs, including Halyard, Juno, Gold Eagle, Atlas and Domestic, among others. The successful placement of securities was important in helping to demonstrate that even complex multi-risk exposures could be transferred through securitization.

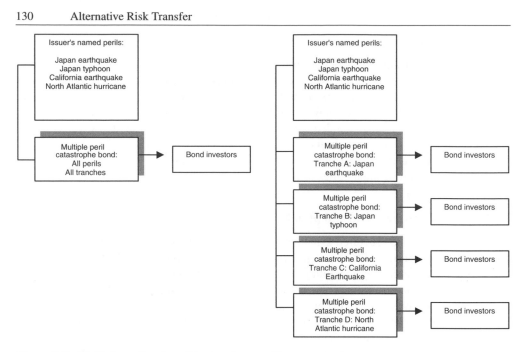

Figure 7.7   Multiple peril and peril by tranche securities

trigger, payout, and coupon. The differences between the two structures are summarized in Figure 7.7.

7.4.5   Bond/derivative variations

Certain variations on the standard cat ILS structure can be designed to meet specific issuer or investor goals. In some instances insurers float bonds that do not actually securitize risks and take them off balance sheet or transfer them, but generate a payoff related to an index; this can be likened to issuing a bond with embedded derivatives. In particular, a select number of bond deals have been floated that provide investors with an enhanced coupon if the index value of a named peril remains below some threshold, or no coupon if it rises above it. This is simply equal to a bond with strip of embedded digital options that provide an enhanced coupon or zero at each evaluation date. For instance, in 2002 Winterthur issued subordinated convertibles with hail-based catastrophe coupons. Investors received a coupon that was one-third greater than standard convertibles as long as the number of auto claims from hail/storm damage remained below 6000, and no coupon if claims exceeded 6000; the deal was thus a package of a subordinated bond, an equity option, and a strip of digital options referencing hail damage.

Synthetic cat bonds

Synthetic cat bonds – a package that effectively comprises an option on a cat bond – can be created to cap future reinsurance costs arising from a market hardening. The optionable bond permits protection should the cycle turn against standard reinsurance cover, but does not obligate the insurer/reinsurer to commit to a specific ILS transaction until the cycle turns. For instance, Allianz Risk Transfer created an option on an ILS (which it purchased from investors through Gemini Re) that gave it the right to issue a 3-year ILS with principal and interest repayments tied to European windstorm and hailstorm if losses reached a pre-specified trigger amount. If loss experience rose above the threshold, Allianz exercised the option, issuing $150m in standard cat bonds that were purchased by the investors/option sellers (the 'forward' nature of the commitment obviously entailed a dimension of credit risk, e.g., being certain that the option seller (investor) would be financially willing and able to provide funds when (if) exercise occurred). If loss experience never breached the threshold, the insurer would not launch the ILS.

7.5   OTHER INSURANCE-LINKED SECURITIES

Some firms have begun using cat ILS securitization techniques to securitize some of the non-cat insurance risks affecting their operations. Although the market for these bonds is nascent, prospects appear quite strong, particularly as the base of investors begins to understand the risk/return characteristics of individual categories of perils, and as companies can be induced to produce a steady supply of bonds with enough uniformity to build a critical investment mass. We consider several simple examples of issues that have been arranged to transfer the risks arising from temperature, residual value, mortgage pool default, trade credit, and life insurance acquisition costs; various others exist, but tend to follow similar lines.

The concept of a **temperature-linked bond** – an ILS with principal/interest redemption that is tied to the level of cumulative temperatures in a particular city, group of cities, or region – has been mooted for several years, ever since activity in the weather risk management began to accelerate in the late 1990s. While the underlying market for temperature derivatives has grown rapidly since the turn of the millennium (as we discuss in Chapter 9), the same has not yet occurred with temperature-based ILSs. Indeed, the inaugural issue by trading firm Koch Industries in 1999 represents the only weather securitization completed through the early years of the millennium.[14] Koch issued its $54m, 3-year Kelvin bond to create risk capacity by paying reduced principal in the event that temperatures in 19 US cities breached predefined levels; if they remained within the trading band, investors earned an enhanced coupon. Apart from the unique reference, the Kelvin issue had various structural complexities, including two separate tranches governed by 'events': under terms of the transaction, the second tranche (event) was activated only if the first tranche (event) had been previously attached (but not necessarily exhausted); the second tranche would not attach, however, until the first tranche was exhausted (in addition, coverage was confined to predefined days).[15] Although activity in temperature bonds has been minimal, market participants expect further issuance over time.

Residual value securitizations are ILS structures designed to protect firms against the residual value risks embedded in a variety of hard asset leases by shifting exposure to capital markets investors. Companies with assets such as airplanes and automobile fleets often retain risk if they have provided a residual value guarantee. The fundamental risk embedded in such deals is that the original estimate of terminal value will be greater than the fair market value of the asset at the end of the lease. By transferring the future value (and/or credit) of the leased assets to the financial markets balance sheet risk can be reduced; mechanically, the lessor sells the

---

[14] A planned temperature issue by now-bankrupt energy firm, Enron, was cancelled in 2000.

[15] As a result of the complexities and the novelty of the temperature indexes, a planned $200m issue was scaled down considerably. Goldman Sachs, as placement agent, was unable to find sufficient demand to absorb the full issue.

lease receivable to investors. This provides protection against future residual value at the end of the lease term or protection against the expected earnings of the asset (where relevant it can lead to the release of balance sheet reserves). Residual value ILSs can be executed for leasing companies, financial institutions with lease portfolios, and original equipment manufacturers. Insurance companies writing residual value insurance (and financial risk insurance, which includes risk to residual value and the credit of the lessee) can similarly securitize their risks.

The structure debuted in 1998 through an issue by Toyota Motors. Others, including BAE, Saab, and Rolls Royce, followed with similar structures of their own. Each one of these firms faces the risk that the residual value of assets (cars, jet engines, aircraft) that they have leased to customers will fall below market value. Leases generally give lessees the right to purchase the underlying asset at the conclusion of the lease period, which they will do if the market price is below the residual value. Accordingly, the companies as lessors are exposed to a loss equal to the difference between the residual and resale values, and transfer the risk through the ILS market. For instance, Toyota, in a note issue arranged through the Grammercy Place Insurance SPV, launched a $566m three-tranche securitization covering 260 000 vehicle leases serviced by Toyota's financing arm, Toyota Motors Credit Corporation (TMCC). Under the terms of this residual value ILS, Grammercy provided three years of annual protection against residual value losses (with TMCC bearing a 10% copayment and approximately 9% deductible). Every year TMCC submitted its residual value claims (e.g., losses above the deductible, less the coinsurance) to Grammercy. Initial investor proceeds held by the trustee in a collateral account were used to repay TMCC's claims, and any remaining balance was then used to repay investors. If TMCC had no residual value claims in a given year, investors received full principal and enhanced coupons; if, however, there was a shortfall, they absorbed a fractional portion of the loss. (This is not unlike a CDO investor; in fact the only difference between a CDO and a residual value ILS is that the trigger event shifts from a pure credit claim to an asset value claim.) Saab's transaction, conceptually similar to Toyota's, provided for $1.17bn of 15-year lease risk protection. Although residual value ILSs represent something of a niche market, they are gradually becoming more popular with firms facing such lease value claims.

A variation on the residual value securitization is the **mortgage default securitization**, which permits mortgage purchasers to obtain default insurance through securities rather than a standard insurance policy. For instance, Morgan Stanley structured a deal providing Freddie Mac with mortgage protection through an issue of mortgage default recourse notes floated through the G3 Mortgage Reinsurer SPR. G3 issued five classes of securities paying principal and interest based on mortgage pool defaults and wrote the corresponding insurance contract to Freddie Mac. Proceeds raised through the issuance of notes were used to purchase collateral, which was liquidated as needed to cover defaults in the pools. After coverage of defaults, investors were paid principal and interest according to the seniority terms embedded in their securities.

Trade credit securitizations – structures that provide for the transfer of trade credit insurance to the securities markets – have been structured by insurance companies that actively guarantee trade credit facilities. Companies implicitly or explicitly extend trade credit to suppliers and vendors when services or products are delivered prior to payment. The accounts receivable that are generated through this activity are valuable, if credit risky, assets on the corporate balance sheet. To protect against risk of loss, companies can purchase trade credit insurance from an insurer, who covers any credit defaults by the trade debtors. Some insurers have then securitized their pools of trade credit insurance through the ILS mechanism, effectively creating capacity to underwrite more credit insurance or otherwise diversify and rebalance their portfolios. For instance, in 1999 German insurer Gerling issued several tranches of SECTRS (Synthetic European Credit Tracking Securities) to transfer risks in pools of European corporate trade credits that it had insured; the portfolio included 92 000 randomly selected businesses. Under terms of the transaction Gerling launched €450m of ILS in three tranches through the SECTRS 1999 SPR (with Goldman Sachs as placement agent). Namur Re, interposed between Gerling and SECTRS, provided Gerling with reinsurance cover on an XOL basis (in three different portfolios, i.e., one for each tranche). The trigger under the issue was based on annual and cumulative default counts in each of the three portfolios. Retrocession was activated when the annual count exceeded an annual attachment point, or the cumulative count (starting in Year 2) exceeded the cumulative attachment point. When triggered, the payment due from SECTRS to Namur Re was obtained by multiplying the excess over the attachment times a recovery rate. Principal repayments to investors were reduced according to claims from Namur Re (which were based on claims from Gerling). Through this ILS structure, Gerling obtained extra capacity to write more credit risk business. Like other non-cat ILSs, trade credit transactions are still relatively uncommon in the marketplace.

A number of **life acquisition cost securitizations** – i.e., mechanisms that permit transfer to the capital markets of the costs associated with writing life insurance policies – have been structured since the mid-1990s. The intent behind these unique issues is to transfer a portion of the costs associated with originating and servicing life insurance business, which often includes front-loaded expenses for the insurer (e.g., broker fees, sales distribution fees, and so on). In some instances securitization is driven by specific regulatory requirements; for instance, German regulations do not permit acquisition costs to appear as assets on the balance sheet, creating pressures on the financial position of any large underwriter of life policies. Under a life acquisition cost securitization, the insurer grants another insurer (or parent company, joint venture partner, or financial institution) the right to receive future profits from a particular pool or portfolio of life policies in exchange for the present value of future cash inflows, which can then be used to cover upfront costs (and reduce the impact on the income statement and balance sheet). In fact these securitizations can be viewed as versions of risk financing rather than pure risk transfer (although much ultimately depends on the specific structure). For instance, in 1996 and 1997 American Skandia Life sold its parent company the rights to future mortality and expense charges for a present value payment of expected future claims. The parent company securitized future fees via an SPV collateralized by the receivables. National Provident, a UK insurer, securitized future profits on its life policies through the Mutual Securitization SPV, which issued two tranches of bonds (featuring final maturities in 2012 and 2022), with principal and interest tied to the surplus on the insurer's life policies. This permitted the insurer to crystallize, on a present value basis, the surplus embedded in life policies that would otherwise only be realizable over a long period of time. Others, including Hannover Re, have structured similar deals.

Other ILS variations have appeared, and will continue to appear. For instance, FIFA, the world football governing body, arranged a bond to cover cancellation or postponement of its world cup finals. It was forced to turn to the ILS market after its traditional insurer cancelled a previously existing policy because FIFA refused to drop terms related to earthquake and political instability. The ILS became a mechanism for FIFA to obtain the precise cover it wanted (one that an insurance company was unwilling to write, demonstrating one of the advantages of the ART market).

Issuance in some sectors of the ILS market has been steady; a dedicated investor base has developed and spreads have tightened (making them an even more compelling alternative to traditional reinsurance mechanisms during some market cycles). Activity in other segments, however, is still relatively quiet and will take time to develop. Secondary liquidity in all ILS sectors is still extremely thin; the securities must essentially be viewed as "buy and hold" investments. ILSs are often challenging to structure and value, particularly those related to multi-peril catastrophe. In all cases, however, growing investors/issuer experience and advances in analytics are helping to build market activity. Thus, capital markets issues referencing specific elements of insurable risk can be regarded as a legitimate mechanism and an important, growing, dimension of ART.

8

Contingent Capital Structures

In Chapter 7 we introduced the concept of capital markets structures and ILSs. We continue with a similar theme in this chapter, discussing the general category of post-loss financing products known as **contingent capital,** contractually agreed financing facilities that are made available to a company in the aftermath of a loss event. As with other capital markets products, the contingent capital structure helps to link the insurance and financial markets by raising funds from capital markets providers/investors upon the trigger of an insurance-related event. Unlike ILSs, which contain aspects of insurance/reinsurance and securities, contingent capital facilities are structured strictly as funding/banking facilities or securities transactions, with no element of insurance contracting. Accordingly, users must take account of a different set of regulatory, tax, and capital treatment issues.

Although the contingent capital facility is not yet as prevalent in the ART marketplace as the ILS,[1] companies developing broad risk management programs must consider its use as an element of post-loss funding. In this chapter we discuss the motivations for creating post-loss financing products and analyze some of the most popular contingent capital structures, including:

- **Contingent debt** Any post-loss debt financing made available when specific events are triggered.
- **Contingent equity** Any post-loss equity financing made available when specific events are triggered.

Within these broad classes we can subdivide contingent debt into committed capital facilities, contingent surplus notes, contingency loans, and guarantees, and contingent equity into loss equity puts and put protected equity. We consider each of these products, summarized in Figure 8.1, below.

8.1 CREATING POST-LOSS FINANCING PRODUCTS

In Part I we discussed the need for companies to minimize the possibility of financial distress in order to help to maximize enterprise value. Insufficient capital in the aftermath of a loss can lead to financial distress and is a key driver in the development and use of risk management products that provide post-loss indemnification. Contingent capital allows a firm to raise capital during a defined commitment period if a specific loss-making event occurs. Importantly, since these facilities are arranged in *advance* of any loss leading to financial distress, their cost does not reflect the risk *premium* that would be apparent in the aftermath of distress (i.e., lower creditworthiness and less access to liquidity, leading to a higher cost of capital). This makes the facilities cost-efficient across a range of financial scenarios. A firm that attempts to arrange funding after a disaster has weakened its financial condition will pay a higher cost of funds;

---

[1] Approximately $6bn in deals were arranged between 1995 and 2002.

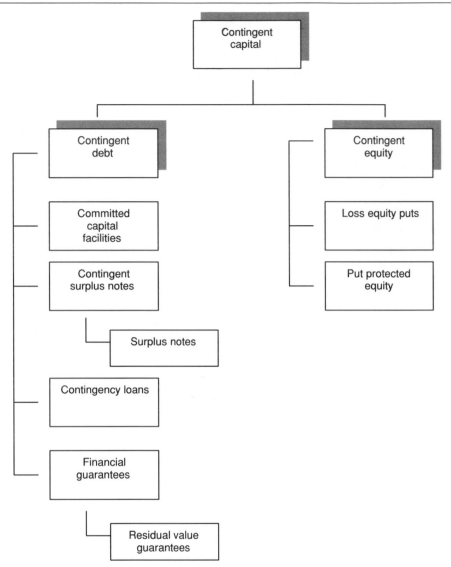

Figure 8.1   Contingent capital structures

this is especially true if its credit condition has been lowered to sub-investment grade levels. A firm that has been impacted by the same disaster but arranged its capital access *ex-ante* will be indemnified and recapitalized at the cost of capital agreed pre-loss.

Through a generic contingent capital structure (illustrated in Figure 8.2 as a securities issue, although it can easily be adapted for a banking facility) a company identifies an amount of capital that it wishes to raise in the event it suffers a loss, determines the events that can trigger the loss, and the specific form of securities it will issue in order to raise capital. If the event occurs, the capital provider supplies funds by taking up securities issued by the company at the *ex-ante* price. In return, the company pays the capital provider a periodic (or upfront),

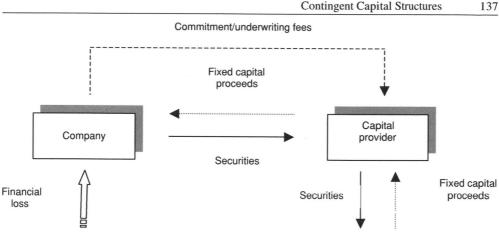

Figure 8.2   Generic contingent capital structure

non-refundable commitment fee (payable whether or not securities are ever issued) plus an underwriting fee (payable only if securities are floated). Although the legal commitment to provide funds rests with the capital provider, in practice it will almost certainly distribute the securities to a base of institutional investors. However, if the provider cannot place the securities with investors, it must still supply the company with funds (which leads to certain counterparty credit risk issues, as we note below). Therefore, the capital-raising effort, in underwriting parlance, is considered a 'firm commitment' or 'bought deal' (contingent on the triggering event), rather than a 'best efforts' or 'agented' transaction. We can also view the generic structure in terms of an option, where the company is effectively purchasing a put option from the capital provider; the strike price and notional size equate to the issue price and proceeds that will be raised in the event of exercise. If exercise occurs, the company invokes its right to sell the capital provider securities in exchange for capital proceeds. The exercise of the option is, of course, dependent on the occurrence of the trigger event; it cannot be exercised at will or at maturity, as would be common under an American option or European option. The commitment fee payable by the company can be viewed as the premium any option buyer would pay a seller.

Contingent capital products are based on triggers that are activated by a stated level of loss. The triggers can be created on a customized basis in order to match a company's exposure to a specific loss-making event, or they can based on market indexes that are widely tracked; this is similar to the various triggers found on ILSs. When triggers are indemnity-based a company reduces its basis risk but increases the specter of moral hazard, and will generally face a higher cost in securing contingent financing. If triggers are parametric or index-based, moral hazard and associated costs decline, but basis risk increases. The terms of the resulting securities, negotiated in advance between the company and the capital provider, can vary widely. Securities can be issued as common equity, debt or preferreds. If equity, dilution issues must be considered, and if debt or preferreds, specific details related to leverage, subordination, maturity, coupon (or dividend), callability, and dividend treatment must be resolved. The most flexible transactions permit any number of structural options to be embedded in the securities, including maturity extensions, funding deferral, conversion, and so on. If debt funding occurs via bank lines rather than securities, similar issues must be addressed, along with drawdown features, material adverse change clauses and covenants, and so on.

Although the marketplace sometimes has a negative view on accessing capital in the event of a financial loss, no such perception appears to attach to the use of a contingent capital facility. While companies suffering losses and needing to access liquidity to ease financial pressures are often loathe to access bank lines (fearing the negative message that is sends to the marketplace and the resulting impact it can have on other sources of liquidity and cost of funds) the same stigma does not seem to exist with a contingent capital facility. Indeed, a company that publicly declares that is has accessed post-loss financing through a facility arranged in advance might be viewed as an astute risk manager.

Post-loss financing products such as contingent capital can be used in conjunction with traditional insurance or financial hedges. Since contingent capital is focused primarily on low-frequency disaster events rather than high-frequency/low-severity insurance events, it is meant to supplement, and not replace, other forms of risk transfer and financing (e.g., a firm would use an insurance policy to cover close to the mean risks, and a contingent capital facility to cover upper layers). Contingent capital products also have the advantage of giving a company the ability to manage risks that might not be possible through other traded instruments (e.g., losses arising from a particular catastrophe that does not lend itself to reference monitoring via a standard contract, losses emanating from certain forms of credit risk, and so on). In practice, companies in many industries can use them. For instance, a bank might arrange a facility that is triggered by unexpectedly large credit losses; the infusion of capital arising from the breach of the trigger can be used to replenish capital and reserves. An insurer or reinsurer might use contingent capital to provide additional funding in the event of a large catastrophic loss; this can serve as a complement to any other ILS or XOL coverage the insurer/reinsurer might have. The structure can also be applied to broader events. For instance, if a company is highly sensitive to economic growth – perhaps it fears it will be downgraded to sub-investment grade if a recession strikes and causes production and sales to decline sharply – it might arrange for a contingent capital facility that will allow it to borrow at rates determined today, before any recession hits. If economic growth slows and impacts revenues, causing the downgrade, the firm will not be exposed to higher borrowing costs associated with its weaker credit status; the trigger in this example is based on a macroeconomic indicator, such as gross domestic product.

Ultimately, of course, a company will use contingent capital if the cost/benefit analysis suggests that value can be added. Benefits center on the reduction in the cost of financial distress, along with potential tax deductibility from ongoing interest payments, should debt funding occur. Costs are based on payment of an upfront, non-refundable fee to secure financing that may never be required (along with additional underwriting/arranging fees should financing actually occur). In addition, it is important to remember that contingent capital is not insurance, but a balance sheet and cash flow arrangement (that actually shares structural similarities with various finite risk programs) and does not therefore provide earnings protection or feature the same tax deductibility characteristics of insurance policies. Furthermore, a company arranging an issue of contingent financing relies on the provider of capital to supply funds when called upon to do so. The company thus assumes the capital provider's credit risk on a contingent basis. We can imagine an extreme scenario, where a company and a bank (as capital provider) agree to a $500m capital infusion in the event the company suffers a severe loss. If the trigger is breached and the company loses more than $500m, it expects the compensatory equity infusion from the bank. However, if the bank fails to perform (e.g., perhaps it has encountered financial distress of its own or has actually defaulted on its obligations), the company is left without the vital capital injection it expects, which may be enough to create financial distress or insolvency. Credit risk issues are thus central to any contingent capital structure. Although most transactions are arranged and funded by top-rated counterparties, some may be arranged by medium-rated entities (or higher-rated entities that deteriorate over time); corporate risk managers must therefore exercise appropriate care.

8.2   CONTINGENT DEBT

Within the general category of contingent debt we consider several structures, including committed capital facilities, contingent surplus notes, contingency loans, and guarantees. Although each features slightly unique characteristics, all have the same end goal: providing the company with pre-negotiated post-loss debt financing.

8.2.1   Committed capital facilities

The **committed capital facility** (CCF) – funded capital arranged prior to a loss and typically accessed when two trigger events are breached – is one of the most common forms of contingent capital. Under a typical CCF a company creates a financing program, defining the specific debt it intends to issue upon triggering, e.g., seniority/subordination, maturity, repayment schedule, and coupon. The insurer/reinsurer arranging the facility acts as the capital supplier, providing funds in the event of exercise, which only occurs if the triggers are breached. The first trigger is often implicit – that is, the option will not be exercised unless it has value, and it will only have value if a loss occurs and the company cannot obtain cheaper funding from another source. The second trigger is generally related to the exposure that the company is seeking to fund (in order to minimize basis risk), but the specific trigger event is unlikely to be under the company's control (in order to eliminate moral hazard).

As with other contingent capital structures, the CCF generally has a fixed maturity date and is intended as a form of financing rather than risk transfer. The price of a CCF will be approximately equal to option premium and loading, but a portion of the premium can be returned if the option is not exercised. The CCF may contain covenants that can be used to protect one or both parties. These could include material adverse change clauses, change of control, financial strength/ratios, and so on. The intent it to ensure that if the facility is triggered, the insurer/reinsurer providing funding does not become structurally subordinate to other bank lenders. In more complex structures the insurer/reinsurer writing the contingent option might join with a bank (or syndicate of banks) to provide funding; this eases the financing burden on the insurer/reinsurer and places the funding in the financial sector where it more appropriately belongs. The bank syndicate might then choose to hold the funding instruments or sell them to end institutional investors.

Consider the following example. A bank seeks to protect its reserve levels from low-probability/high-severity credit losses in its loan portfolio and arranges a CCF with an insurer. Under the facility the bank can trigger additional funding through the issuance of up to $750m of preferred stock (qualifying as debt rather than equity) if its loan portfolio suffers exceptional credit losses. This mechanism allows the bank to replenish its reserves when needed, but also to manage its balance sheet more efficiently by not having to hold greater reserves than necessary. Since the bank's credit portfolio is sufficiently well diversified, an external loan index comprising cross-industry and country credits is selected as the reference trigger; this helps to eliminate the possibility of moral hazard.

8.2.2   Contingent surplus notes

Contingent surplus notes (CSNs) – another form of contingent debt financing – are often issued by insurance and reinsurance companies seeking protection against exceptional losses in their portfolios. Under a typical CSN structure an insurer contracts with a financial intermediary to establish an investment trust, which is capitalized by outside investors through trust-issued notes paying an enhanced yield. The trust invests proceeds in high-grade investments (e.g., AAA-rated bonds) until (if) the contingent capital is required. If the insurer breaches a predefined loss trigger, it issues CSNs to the trust. The trust liquidates the AAA-rated bonds and delivers cash to the insurer. In exchange for providing the initial commitment and contingent capital, the investor achieves an all-in yield that is greater than similarly rated corporate securities. The insurer obtains a post-loss funding commitment in advance at a price that, in a hard reinsurance market, might prove advantageous. The commitment fee the insurer pays to the trust can be viewed in the same light as the option premium in the CCF. Figure 8.3 summarizes a generic CSN structure.

Consider the following example. An insurance company arranges a $500m 5-year CSN issue that will be triggered in the event that losses in its P&C portfolio exceed $500m over the next two years. The arranging bank identifies several institutional investors that 'pre-fund'

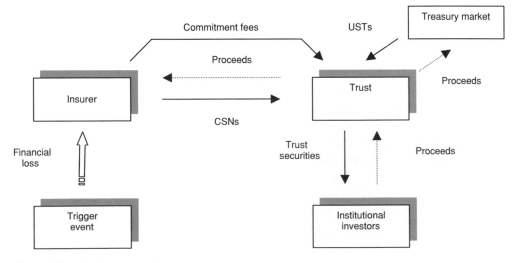

Figure 8.3   Contingent surplus note structure

a trust in the full amount of $500m in exchange for an all-in yield equal to the commitment fee plus the return on 5-year US Treasury notes. The $500m in pre-funding proceeds are used to purchase US Treasuries; and the investors receive notes in the trust reflecting an enhanced coupon. Assume that one year from now loss experience is greater than expected and causes the trigger to be breached. The insurance company issues $500m of 5-year notes to the trust, and the trust liquidates its Treasury position and uses the proceeds to acquire the CSNs. The trust now holds the insurance company's CSNs, the insurance company receives $500m of cash to help to manage its financial position, and end-investors continue to receive the enhanced yield on their trust-issued notes.

The first CSN, a $400m 10-year note, was issued by National Mutual in 1995. Under terms of the transaction, National Mutual was able to access up to $400m in fresh capital through a trust, which issued surplus notes to investors as needed. In a variation on the standard structure, the insurer was able to raise funds whenever it wanted, and not just in the event of a loss. The risk to investors (for which they received an above-market coupon) was the possibility that the state insurance commissioner would instruct National Mutual to cease paying principal and/or interest if policyholders were deemed to be disadvantaged or prejudiced by such payments.

In addition to standard CSNs, insurers may also issue **surplus notes**, which are subordinated securities that function much like the CSN, except that they are issued directly by the company rather than through a trust. Surplus notes typically have maturities of 10 to 30 years and must be approved by insurance regulators. Importantly, these notes increase statutory capital, but not financial accounting capital.

8.2.3 Contingency loans

The **contingency loan** – a variation of the CCF – is a bank of line of credit that is arranged in advance of a loss and invoked when a trigger event occurs. Unlike a traditional line of credit, which can be used for any purpose and accessed at will, the contingency loan is only available to cover losses arising from a defined event and can only be drawn when that event occurs. Since the company has less flexibility in drawdown (and the probability of drawdown is much lower), it pays less than it would for a standard bank line. In addition, since the probability of drawdown is lower, a company can often negotiate a larger borrowing amount, giving it greater comfort that financial flexibility will not be impaired in the event of a trigger-induced loss. As with the CCF above, key terms of the contingency loan are defined in advance, including maximum amount, fixed or floating rate, maturity, repayment schedule, trigger(s), and so on. From the funding bank's perspective it can retain the loan commitment or syndicate it to other institutions.

Consider the following example. An auto manufacturer that produces and sells primarily in the Americas wants to arrange contingent financing that it can access in the event of a slowdown in economic growth. Through intensive factor analysis, the company understands its revenue sensitivity to each basis point decline in economic growth and is aware that the resulting loss of revenues is likely to lead to financial pressures, a credit rating downgrade, and a rise in its cost of funding. The company discusses the matter with its bankers and they develop a contingency loan that allows the auto firm to draw down up to $500m of a multi-year loan facility in the event economic growth rates in North America and Latin America fall below certain average levels. Since the average growth rates that serve as the trigger reference external indexes, there is no possibility of moral hazard. The contingency loan is structured with an appropriate rate, maturity and repayment schedule. If the drawdown occurs as revenues slow and the rating agencies downgrade the firm's credit rating, the company remains indifferent as it has secured access to debt capital and locked in its cost of funding.

8.2.4 Financial guarantees

Financial guarantees, which have existed for many decades, are most commonly used to transfer risk; however, by virtue of their construction, they also represent a form of contingent financing. In its most basic form a company and a financial guarantor (e.g., an insurer or reinsurer) agree to a loss trigger that, if breached, allows the company to access funds from the guarantor. Guarantees of this type are commonly used to protect companies and SPEs against credit losses or residual value claims. They are also used by exchanges and clearinghouses, who want to ensure the availability of sufficient capital in the event of a low probability, loss-making event (e.g., a massive counterparty default).[2] Bond insurance issued by monoline insurers for the benefit of SPEs that issue CDOs or other credit-sensitive asset-backed transactions, is essentially a financial guarantee. In exchange for a fee, the insurer 'wraps' the SPE's CDO with a guarantee so that it can achieve a higher credit rating (and thus be saleable to a broader range of investors). If credit loss experience is greater than expected – thus breaching the trigger embedded in the guarantee – the SPE receives a capital infusion from the insurer which it passes on to investors holding the guaranteed tranches (e.g., the original super-AAA or AAA tranches; the holders of subordinated tranches or residual equity will not receive the benefit of the capital infusion).

Residual value guarantees perform a similar function by giving a company minimum protection against the residual value inherent in leased assets (e.g., airplanes or aircraft engines). If a company finds that the residual value at the end of a lease is much less than originally anticipated it might suffer a capital shortfall and become vulnerable to financial distress. The residual value guarantee ensures some minimum value for the assets, meaning that the company receives a capital inflow if a shortfall occurs. This again represents a contingency, as if the residual value remains at, or above, the scheduled value, no infusion is required. As noted in the last chapter, residual value guarantees (and insurance) can be securitized through the ILS market.

8.3 CONTINGENT EQUITY

Not all contingent capital structures are debt-based. In some instances a company prefers, or requires, incremental funding in the form of either common or preferred equity. This helps to ensure that the post-loss recapitalization effort does not increase the debt burden and negatively impact leverage ratios; since the infusion comes in the form of equity, leverage is preserved or lowered. However, any contingent equity structure that involves the issuance of new common shares results in earnings dilution; in addition, since equity capital is generally more expensive than debt capital, the pure economics of the post-loss capital-raising exercise might not be as compelling. We consider two different forms of contingent equity: the loss equity put and put protected equity.

---

[2] For instance, pan-European clearinghouse Clearnet has a financial guarantee for €170m that is intended to cover counterparty default in excess of its capital cushion.

8.3.1 Loss equity puts

The **loss equity put** (LEP) – sometimes known as the catastrophe equity put[3] when related specifically to a natural disaster trigger – is a contingent capital structure that results in the issuance of new shares in the event that a predefined trigger is breached. The structure and mechanics of the typical LEP are similar to the committed facilities noted above, except that equity, rather than debt, is issued if a trigger is breached. In a typical structure a company purchases a put option from an intermediary that gives it the right to sell a fixed amount of shares (often on a private placement basis) if a particular loss trigger occurs during the life of the contract. In exchange, the company pays the intermediary an option premium. Since the terms of the put option are fixed (e.g., number of shares to be issued and strike price), the post-loss financing is arranged and committed in advance of any loss. If the option becomes exercisable, the company issues new shares to the intermediary, pays any additional underwriting fees, and receives agreed proceeds. In order to avoid dilution issues that arise from the issuance of new common shares, LEPs often result in the issuance of preferred, rather than common, equity. They may also be issued as convertible preferred shares, with an implicit understanding between the two parties that the preferreds will be repurchased by the company at a future date, prior to any conversion (thus avoiding dilution).

Each LEP transaction is characterized by standard terms and conditions, including exercise event, form of securities, minimum amount of securities to be issued on exercise, the time period of coverage, the maximum time allotted for issuance of securities, strike price, and specific warranties (e.g., minimum net worth (or statutory capital) on exercise, change in control, minimum financial ratios, and so on). To reduce the possibility of moral hazard arising from an indemnity structure, LEPs often have two triggers. The first trigger is the company's stock price, which must fall below the strike price in order to become effective; this is consistent with any option framework, where the derivative will only be exercised if it moves in-the-money. The second trigger relates to specific loss levels that must be breached in order for exercise to occur. Thus, it is not sufficient for a company's stock price to decline, it must also be accompanied by a loss event. In fact, the two triggers are likely to be quite related if losses are large enough; that is, the company's stock price is more likely to fall through the strike price if the marketplace becomes aware that the firm has sustained large losses. LEPs can be structured with an index or parametric trigger instead of an indemnity trigger.

In addition to the obvious benefit of "locking in" post-loss funding at predetermined levels, LEPs feature at least two other advantages. First, unlike debt facilities that often contain material adverse change clauses that limit or prohibit funding in the event of disruption (either in the market or with the ceding company), LEPs have no such limitations (except for maintenance of minimum net worth), meaning that they are certain to be available when needed. Second, the cost of an LEP can compare quite favorably to a standard reinsurance contract because the option purchaser must remain financially viable in order to claim access to funding (the same is not true in a standard reinsurance contract, where the cedant can become insolvent and the reinsurer must still perform on its reinsurance obligation). Specifically, to ensure that the option writer is not forced to invest in a financially distressed company, transactions generally include minimum net worth covenants; if the option buyer's net worth falls below a predetermined threshold it cannot exercise the option and raise new proceeds. For instance, if a cedant has net

---

[3] Insurance broker AON, which developed the original structure in 1996, has coined (and registered) the product name CatEPut®, which seems to have entered the financial vernacular.

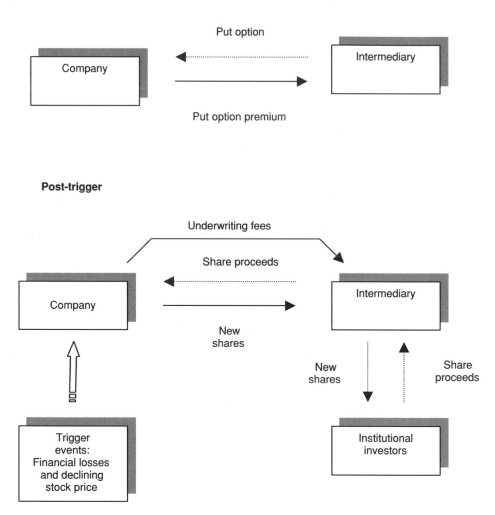

Pre-trigger

Put option

Company

Intermediary

Put option premium

Post-trigger

Underwriting fees

Share proceeds

Company

Intermediary

New
shares

New
shares

Share
proceeds

Trigger
events:
Financial losses
and declining
stock price

Institutional
investors

Figure 8.4   Loss equity put structure

equity of $100m and a loss equity put that will give it access to a further $50m on exercise, a loss leading to net equity of only $10m would place the put seller in a dire situation by having to invest $50m in a company that only has a current net worth of $10m. The mechanism avoids this situation.

Figure 8.4 illustrates the flows of an LEP pre- and post-trigger. Note that as in the contingent debt structures above, the intermediary is ultimately responsible for taking up new shares and delivering proceeds if the LEP is exercised. In practice it might turn to its base of institutional investors to distribute the shares.

Consider the following example. Insurer ABC, whose stock is currently trading at $32 per share, is concerned about risk concentrations in its catastrophe portfolio and wants to be protected in the event that total losses over the next underwriting season exceed $500m; it this occurs, ABC will issue new common stock in order to replenish its capital base and remain comfortably within regulatory capital requirements (its current equity level is $1.5bn). It purchases a $500m LEP from Reinsurer XYZ struck at $30 per share (e.g. 16.6 million shares), with an indemnity trigger of $500m and a maturity of 12 months. In order to exercise the option ABC must preserve a statutory equity base of at least $850m. Assume the following scenarios:

- *Scenario 1* Within the next 12 months ABC's catastrophic risk portfolio continues to perform reasonably well; though the firm sustains losses of approximately $75m, these are entirely manageable within its loss reserves and the insurer has no need for new equity; indeed, ABC's stock price trades at $36 per share. The LEP expires worthless.
- *Scenario 2* A bad hurricane season leaves ABC with $600m of losses in its portfolio; the market, concerned with the news, pushes the stock price down to $20 per share. However, ABC exercises its LEP against XYZ, delivering 16.6 million new shares at the strike price of $30, for gross proceeds of $500m. The increase in capital helps to stabilize ABC's financial condition and the stock price eventually rebounds.

CASE STUDY

RLI's catastrophe equity put

RLI Corporation, a specialty property liability subsidiary of USA Insurance Company writing excess layer earthquake coverage, had traditionally reinsured portions of its risk portfolio in the reinsurance market. This risk management process worked to good effect until the Northridge, California, earthquake struck in 1994, causing $13bn in insurance industry losses. Following the event, RLI's access to reinsurance was effectively exhausted (i.e., its lines with various reinsurers were fully utilized), leaving it financially exposed in the event of another earthquake. Realizing that it needed a solution to this problem, the company and its broker, AON (working in conjunction with Centre Re, the reinsurance subsidiary of the Zurich Insurance Group), developed a novel ART mechanism. Specifically, in 1996 AON and Centre Re designed the first catastrophe equity put, an option designed to give RLI additional capital in the event that it exhausted its reinsurance lines in the future.

Under the terms of the transaction, RLI bought a put option from Centre Re, giving it the right to put up to $50m of cumulative convertible preferred shares to Centre if the company's reinsurance lines were to be fully used in the aftermath of another disaster. The 3-year transaction featured two blocks of shares: one that Centre Re could convert from preferred into common stock in 3 years (50% of the total) and another enabling it to convert into common stock after another 4 years (50%). Implicit in the structure was an understanding that, in the event of exercise, RLI would repurchase the convertible preferreds from Centre Re within the 3- and 7-year time frames, so that they would never be converted into RLI common shares. This effectively meant the new issuance of capital upon exercise could be treated as debt for internal and tax purposes, but equity for regulatory purposes. Although the put was more expensive for RLI than standard reinsurance coverage, the firm was not in a position to negotiate a full amount of reinsurance coverage and the new instrument emerged as a viable alternative. Other firms have also arranged contingent equity puts (e.g., Horace Mann, La Salle Re/Trenwick[4]). Figure 8.5 illustrates the put arrangement between RLI and Centre Re in the event of a hypothetical exercise.

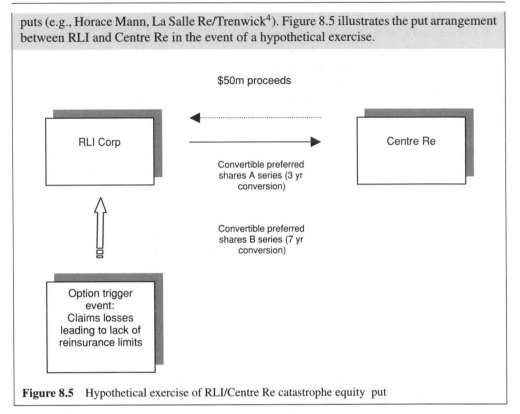

Figure 8.5   Hypothetical exercise of RLI/Centre Re catastrophe equity put

8.3.2   Put protected equity

A second form of contingent equity is **put protected equity** (PPE), where a company buys a put on its own stock in order to generate an economic gain should the value of its stock decline in the aftermath of a loss. Under a typical PPE a company purchases a put from an intermediary, defining the number of shares, strike price and maturity (as in any option). If the company suffers a major loss (e.g., the event it is seeking to protect itself against), there is a significant chance that its stock price will decline. The company then exercises against the put seller for an economic gain. The economic gain can be used to increase retained earnings alone, or to provide a price hedge against the issuance of a new tranche of stock. If the PPE is only used to generate an economic gain based on a decline in the company's stock price (e.g., the company is delivering to the intermediary shares that it purchases in the open market), the addition to equity capital is indirect, rather than direct; that is, it accrues to the retained earnings account rather than the paid-in capital account, meaning that the after-tax proceeds will be lower and there will be no share dilution. If the PPE is used to protect the company's issuance of new shares, then the gain on the put serves to offset the increased number of shares that will occur when the stock is issued at the new lower price. As with the LEP, if new common shares are

---

[4] The La Salle Re/Trenwick transaction became the center of legal dispute in 2002. Trenwick assumed La Salle Re's position to issue up to $55m to European Reinsurance Company on trigger. Following the September 11, 2001 terrorist acts Trenwick suffered $140m of losses and attempted to exercise the put in March 2002. The put writer declined to provide coverage, indicating remaining capital did not meet contract terms. The matter went to arbitration for further resolution.

issued, dilution is a factor; if preferreds are involved, no dilution concerns arise. Unlike the LEP, the PPE does not need to be governed by a specific loss trigger; that is, the company might simply purchase a put on its own stock under the assumption that any sizeable loss will be sufficient to cause downward pressure on the stock price. However, PPEs can be viewed negatively in the market. If investors become aware that a firm is buying puts on its own stock, they might be concerned that there is bad news ahead; the share price may thus be forced down as investors sell their shares – and not because of any specific loss.

In addition to the contingent equity structures described above, a company can achieve similar results by issuing a reverse convertible bond. While a standard convertible bond gives the investor the right to convert a bond into shares of the issuer, a **reverse convertible bond** grants the issuer the right to convert the bonds into shares at a specified strike price. The issuer will only exercise the conversion right when the stock price falls below the price where shares offered are worth less than the debt. In fact, optimal exercise occurs when debt is worth more than equity; equity becomes a cheaper source of capital and reduces leverage.

It should be apparent that a company has available a number of options when it comes to arranging post-loss financing in advance of any instance of financial distress. The time to consider and arrange such facilities is obviously before any potential problem, when the best possible terms can be negotiated. As such, prudent risk management program must focus on the range of structures and options that are available. Ultimately, however, contingent capital products must still be accommodated within a rational cost/benefit framework, and they must only be considered one part of a financial solution rather than a complete risk management tool.

9

Insurance Derivatives

Derivatives, which we have defined broadly as financial contracts that derive their value from a market reference, comprise the third major type of financial instrument used in the ART markets. Since derivatives permit users to transfer the economics of specific risk references, including variables that can cause corporate losses, it is natural that they have been adapted for use in the ART market. The underlying derivative markets have, of course, existed for many years. In fact, some exchange-traded (listed) derivatives date back several hundred years – although in practice most contracts entered the "mainstream" financial markets with the rise in inflation and volatility of the 1970s. The listed market now features some of the most liquid risk management instruments in the financial system. The market for over-the-counter (OTC) derivatives is a more recent creation, having been developed in the early 1980s; despite a relatively short history, OTC derivatives have assumed a dominant role in financial engineering as a result of their flexibility. Since the scope of derivatives is broad, we limit our discussion in this chapter to general types of derivatives and mechanisms used to manage insurance-related risks.[1] Before considering specific instruments, however, we begin with a review of derivatives and ART, and a general discussion of the characteristics of derivatives.

9.1 DERIVATIVES AND ART

Listed and OTC derivatives convey an optionable interest and can be used by institutions either to hedge or speculate. This, as we have noted, distinguishes them from insurance contracts, which are based on an insurable interest and cannot be used to generate speculative profit. Thus, an OTC catastrophe option is not considered an insurance contract, as the purchaser of the option does not need to prove a loss to obtain the economic benefit of an in-the-money position, while an XOL catastrophe contract providing the same economic protection is considered insurance as the buyer needs to prove an insurable interest and sustain a loss in order to receive a claim payment.[2] Though derivatives can be used to speculate, many companies use them to hedge their risks, making them an important loss-financing mechanism. Derivatives can be used to neutralize the downside effects of a single risk, diversify a portfolio of exposures (and, in so doing, reduce risk), and provide capacity to engage in additional risky business. Any of these can be accomplished when a company identifies the exposure it intends to protect or the portfolio it wants to diversify, and arranges a transaction that provides a compensatory payment when (if) the underlying exposure generates a loss. Since derivatives are not indemnity contracts, a company generally accepts some amount of basis risk. While certain financial risks can be matched quite precisely via derivatives (e.g., specific exposure to exchange rates or interest

---

[1] Those interested in a comprehensive treatment of financial derivatives may wish to consult Banks (2004).

[2] The New York Insurance Department (NYID) ruled in June 1998 that instruments such as catastrophe options are not insurance, as neither payments nor triggering events bear any relationship to the purchaser's loss or gain. The NYID applied the same rationale to weather derivatives in February 2000.

rates), insurance-related risks often cannot (e.g., specific exposure to catastrophe or weather). The tradeoff in accepting more basis risk is a reduction in the specter of moral hazard and the creation of a cheaper risk management tool.

Derivatives have certain benefits and characteristics that can make them an important part of an ART solution:

- Some derivative contracts are quite liquid and can yield a cost-effective risk solution.
- Transactions arranged through the listed market eliminate credit risk.
- Transactions structured through the OTC market are highly customizable and flexible.
- Insurable interest and proof of loss do not have to be demonstrated.
- Delays in receiving payment in the event a contract pays off are minimal (e.g., there is no loss development period or claims adjustment process).
- Financial payments to the party holding the in-the-money contract are generally not capped (e.g., no policy limits).

Derivatives have certain costs/disadvantages, including:

- Exposures that can be covered in the listed market, particularly in non-financial asset classes, are somewhat limited.
- Greater basis risks are assumed, resulting in imperfect risk hedges.
- Credit risks for OTC transactions can be significant (similar to those that might be encountered in the insurance/reinsurance market).
- Spreads are wide and liquidity is limited for certain "exotic" risks.
- Bilateral contracts (e.g., swaps and forwards) expose a firm to downside payments.

We shall consider these advantages and disadvantages when we discuss specific types of insurance derivatives later in the chapter.

9.2   GENERAL CHARACTERISTICS OF DERIVATIVES[3]

In Chapter 1 we summarized the broad classes of derivatives that companies might consider using as part of their risk management programs. As a reminder, these include listed futures, options[4] and futures options, and OTC forwards, swaps, and options. There are, of course, various subclasses of exotic derivatives (e.g., complex swaps and options, structured notes), but these are beyond the scope of our discussion in this chapter. General classes of derivatives are summarized in Figure 9.1.

A *future* is a contract that represents an obligation to buy or sell a specific quantity of an underlying reference asset, at a price agreed but not exchanged on trade date, for settlement at a future time. It can thus be considered a contract for deferred payment and delivery. All futures (and other listed contracts) are traded through physical or electronic exchanges and cleared through centralized clearinghouses, which mitigate credit risk by requiring buyers and sellers

---

[3] Some portions of this section draw on the discussion presented in Banks (2003), adapted for the specific requirements of this text.

[4] Variations on the standard listed option structure have appeared over the past few years in response to competition from the OTC market. For instance, some exchanges have introduced flexible options (e.g., options that permit users to define key parameters such as strike price and maturity), overnight options, long-term options (e.g. 3 to 5 years), low-exercise price options (e.g., which mimic a futures or underlying position), and so on. Some innovation has also occurred in futures, including the introduction of "mini" contracts, intended to appeal to the retail client base.

Table 9.1   Long/short futures relationships

Position	Reference asset ↑	Reference asset ↓
Long futures	Gains value	Loses value
Short futures	Loses value	Gains value

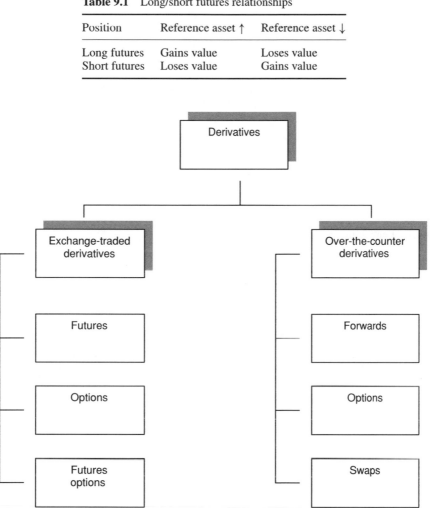

Figure 9.1   General classes of derivatives

to post initial margin; positions are revalued daily and those in deficit (a loss position) generate variation margin calls, which must be met if the position is to be preserved. A futures contract may feature financial settlement (i.e., cash exchange) or physical settlement (i.e., underlying commodity/asset exchange), and a fixed maturity extending from one day to several quarters. A long futures position – one that is purchased or owned – increases in value as the reference price rises and loses value when the price falls. A short futures position – one that is borrowed or sold – increases in value as the price falls, and decreases in value as the price rises. Futures profit and loss (P&L) relationships are summarized in Table 9.1; the payoff profiles are illustrated in Figures 9.2 and 9.3.

An *option* is a contract that gives the purchaser the right, but not the obligation, to buy (call option) or sell (put option) the underlying reference asset, at a level known as a strike price,

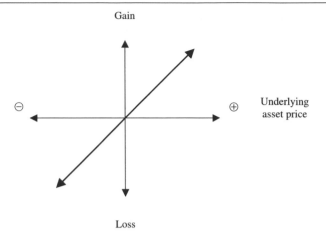

Figure 9.2   Long futures payoff profile

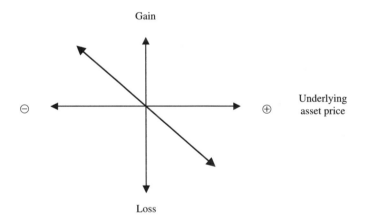

Figure 9.3   Short futures payoff profile

at any time until an agreed expiry date (American option) or on the expiry date (European option). In exchange for this right the buyer pays the seller a premium payment (one, it should be stressed, that is different from the premium we have discussed for insurance contracts). By accepting the premium the option seller has an obligation to buy or sell the underlying asset at the strike price if the option is exercised. The maximum downside of any long-option position is limited to the premium paid to secure the option (just as a cedant's maximum downside on an insurance contract is limited to the cost of premium paid). As with futures, options may be settled in financial or physical terms. Options P&L relationships are summarized in Table 9.2, and the payoff profiles of long and short puts and calls are reflected in Figures 9.4 through 9.7.

A *futures option* is an option giving the purchaser the right to enter into an underlying futures transaction in exchange for a premium. A futures put gives the purchaser the right to sell a futures contract at a set strike price, while a futures call gives the purchaser the right to buy a

Table 9.2 Long/short options relationships

Position	Reference asset value ↑	Reference asset value ↓
Long call	Gains value	Loses value (but loss limited to premium paid)
Short call	Loses value	Gains value (but gain limited to premium earned)
Long put	Loses value (but loss limited to premium paid)	Gains value
Short put	Gains value (but gain limited to premium earned)	Loses value

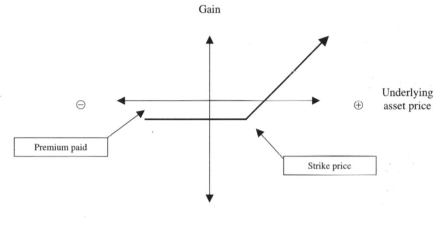

Figure 9.4 Long call payoff profile

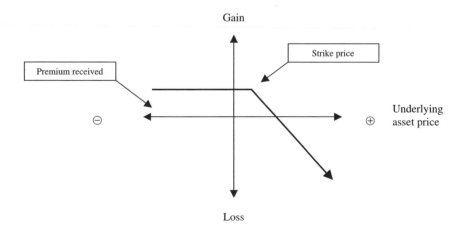

Figure 9.5 Short call payoff profile

Table 9.3   Long/short futures options

Position	Right/obligation
Long futures call	Right to buy a futures contract at the strike price
Short futures call	Obligation to sell a futures contract at the strike price, if exercised
Long futures put	Right to sell a futures contract at the strike price
Short futures put	Obligation to buy a futures contract at the strike price, if exercised

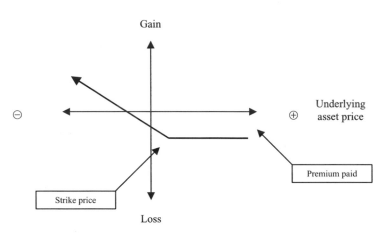

Figure 9.6   Long put payoff profile

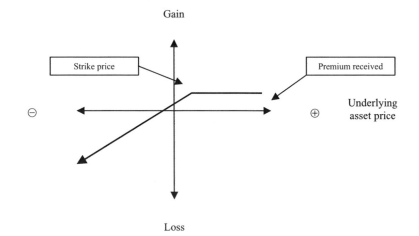

Figure 9.7   Short put payoff profile

futures contract at a set strike price; the reverse occurs for the seller. Long and short futures options are summarized in Table 9.3.

All exchange-traded contracts – whether futures, options, or futures options – are characterized by standard terms, including:

- trading units
- delivery date
- deliverable grades
- delivery points
- contract months
- last trading day
- other terms and conditions as applicable, including price limits
- strike price/exercise style (for options/futures options).

OTC options have similar definitional parameters but can include more unique and complex payout terms and conditions.

A *forward* is a customized, bilateral, single period contract referencing a specific market/asset reference. Like a futures contract, it represents an obligation to buy or sell a specific quantity of an underlying reference asset at a price agreed but not exchanged on trade date, for settlement at a future time. Unlike a futures contract, no intervening cash flows are exchanged (i.e., there is no daily revaluation of the position). Since the forward trades in the OTC market, without the benefit of a centralized clearinghouse, it exposes both parties to potential credit risk (unless collateral is specifically negotiated). The P&L relationships of long/short forwards and reference asset prices are the same as those depicted in Table 9.1 and Figures 9.2 and 9.3 above.

A *swap* is a bilateral transaction calling for periodic (e.g., annual, semi-annual, quarterly) exchange of payments between two parties based on a defined reference index, and can be regarded as a package of forward contracts. Swaps are generally denominated in notional terms and can have maturities extending out for many years (e.g., 10–30 years, although transactions with such long maturities are reserved for counterparties with the best credit ratings or those willing to post collateral). Since swaps are bilateral OTC contracts, they can expose either party to credit risk (unless exposures are collateralized).

Swaps and forwards are defined by various terms, including:

- notional amount
- underlying reference index
- maturity
- payment frequency (for swaps only)
- settlement terms
- forward (fixed) reference price
- floating reference price.

OTC derivatives are often managed on a "net" basis, which reduces the exposure generated by the individual components comprising a portfolio. Netting, which is accomplished through the use of a master netting agreement in a jurisdiction that accepts the legal basis of net exposures, allows parties to lower their counterparty credit exposures from a gross to a net basis.

Exchange-traded and OTC derivatives are important to the efficient functioning of the financial markets, and provide ample opportunity for risk management and investment strategies to be arranged on cost-effective terms. The key differences between listed and OTC derivatives are summarized in Table 9.4. In the sections that follow we shall consider these contracts in light of specific insurance risks.

Table 9.4   Primary differences between exchange-traded and OTC derivatives

	Exchange-traded	OTC
Terms	Standardized	Customized
Trading forum	Central exchange (physical or electronic)	OTC (telephonic or electronic)
Price transparency	Good	Poor/fair
Liquidity	Reasonable/strong	Limited/fair
Credit exposure	Negligible	Significant unless collateralized
Margins	Required	None unless negotiated
Settlement	Generally closed-out	Generally held until maturity
Regulation	Full	Partial to full

9.3   EXCHANGE-TRADED INSURANCE DERIVATIVES

Exchange-traded derivatives are characterized by standard contract terms, meaning that all participants trade the same underlying instruments. This helps to generate a greater critical mass of liquidity, leading to tighter bid–offer spreads and more cost-effective risk management solutions. The world's most liquid-listed contracts reference various important financial indicators, such as short-term and long-term interest rates (US, Euro bloc countries, UK, Japan), exchange rates (US dollar versus euro, sterling, Swiss franc, yen), equity indexes (S&P 500, Nasdaq 100, FTSE 100, DAX, Nikkei) and select commodities (Brent and light sweet crude, gold). Indeed, activity in these contracts is extremely significant. Not surprisingly, the number of offerings on specific insurance-related risks is still small and activity modest, certainly when compared with the liquid benchmark contracts – meaning that the same price and volume advantages do not exist. However, various instruments have appeared in recent years, most centered on catastrophic P&C risk and non-catastrophic weather risk, in some cases giving end-users and intermediaries additional risk management opportunities.

9.3.1   Exchange-traded catastrophe derivatives

Exchange-traded catastrophe insurance derivatives – futures and options traded via an authorized exchange that reference a variety of catastrophe indexes – were the first of the listed insurance contracts to enter the market. The earliest attempts at introducing a cat risk contract date back to 1992, when the Chicago Board of Trade (CBOT), one of Chicago's three listed exchanges, developed catastrophe futures based on an index created by the Insurance Services Office (ISO). ISO collected data on cat risks from 100+ companies and used the data to track US cat losses based on loss ratios. In mid-1993 the exchange introduced options on futures to try to spur growth, but was unable to generate meaningful activity and was eventually forced to abandon both contracts. Not to be deterred, the CBOT introduced a cash-settled options contract in 1995 based on the more transparent, and widely recognized, PCS index. PCS tracked nine loss indexes for the exchange (including references for national and regional sectors and high-risk states, such as Florida, Texas, and California). In contrast to the ISO index, the PCS index was established to measure losses through a daily survey of 70 participants involved in catastrophe risk (adjusted for non-survey participants). The

CBOT offered two specific instruments: large cap options (covering exposures of $20–50bn), and small cap options (below $20bn). The contracts featured a loss development (or runoff) period of either two or four quarters (in contrast to the relatively short one-quarter period of the original ISO contract). By assembling particular PCS spreads insurers and reinsurers could, at least theoretically, create synthetic XOL reinsurance layers. However, the instrument was unable to attract the number of participants and level of activity needed to make it a truly competitive alternative to other traditional and ART instruments, and was ultimately abandoned in 2000. We can point to various reasons for delisting, including lack of natural hedgers on both sides of the market (a prerequisite, certainly over the medium term, in ensuring contract success), lack of a deep OTC cat derivative market to provide additional liquidity, hedges and pricing references, lack of transparency, excess of basis risk, and pricing challenges.

The CBOT is not the only exchange to have attempted to introduce catastrophe derivatives. In 1996 the Bermudan Parliament authorized the development of the Bermuda Commodities Exchange (BCOE) – a forum for listing and trading catastrophe derivatives. The BCOE was intended as a member-owned mutual exchange with a separate clearinghouse owned by a variety of highly rated industry players (to ensure a strong credit rating for the clearinghouse itself). The BCOE intended to list cat options based on the Guy Carpenter Catastrophe Index (GCCI), an index comprising data from 39 insurance companies. Unlike the PCS's total dollar loss metric at the state/regional level, the GCCI produced industry loss-to-value ratios at a granular (e.g., postal code) level. The BCOE options were also structurally different from the CBOT's, paying out on a digital or binary basis (e.g., 100% payout above the strike, 0% below the strike), rather than a standard intrinsic value basis. Although considerable planning and effort went into the development phase, the exchange was unable to gain sufficient support from the reinsurance industry, which saw flaws with the structure of the contracts (digital, 100% margin), the index (e.g., GCCI's homeowner loss focus), and fees. The BCOE project was ultimately abandoned.

No other global derivative exchanges offer listed catastrophe derivatives. Despite the fact that countries such as France, Germany, and Japan are exposed to various cat perils (e.g., floods, windstorm, earthquake), local exchanges have not noted enough demand for specific listed contracts on such risks. However, the New York-based Catastrophe Risk Exchange (CATEX), founded in 1995, has developed into a conduit for matching cedants and insurers/reinsurers for contracts covering various P&C exposures, including those associated with catastrophic risk. Although CATEX is not a formally regulated exchange and does not trade standardized contracts, it brings together multiple parties in a central forum so that they can execute cat risk covers in an organized fashion. In practice, participants (who must be subscribers) make use of CATEX's technology platform to post exposures they seek to cover or protect. Once posted and matched, the two parties conclude discussions in a private setting; CATEX might therefore be regarded as a hybrid listed/OTC transaction-matching conduit. During the first five years of operation, an estimated $5.5bn of insurance limits was negotiated.

9.3.2   Exchange-traded temperature derivatives

While listed catastrophe derivatives have failed to generate interest or a critical mass, **exchange-traded temperature derivatives** – listed futures and options contracts referencing temperature indexes in specific cities – have achieved a core following and continue to expand, with new contracts appearing at reasonably regular intervals.

The Chicago Mercantile Exchange (CME), another of Chicago's major listed forums, introduced cash-settled futures and futures options on temperature indexes on 10 US cities in 1999. Contracts are traded via the CME's electronic platform (Globex 2) and all parties face the CME Clearinghouse as their counterparty. The temperature indexes are based on the standard heating degree day (HDD) and cooling degree day (CDD) measures that are commonly used as a reference by energy companies and weather derivative dealers. HDDs are a reflection of heating usage (the colder the temperatures, the greater the heating usage, the higher the HDDs), while CDDs reflect cooling usage (the warmer the temperatures, the greater the cooling usage, the higher the CDDs). HDDs subtract from a baseline (typically $65°$ F or $18°$ C) the average daily temperature, while CDDs subtract the average daily temperature from the baseline. Thus,

$$\text{Daily HDD} = \max(0, \text{baseline} - (T_{\max} + T_{\min})/2))$$
$$\text{Daily CDD} = \max(0, (((T_{\max} + T_{\min})/2) - \text{baseline})$$

where $T_{\max}$ is the maximum daily temperature and $T_{\min}$ is the minimum daily temperature.

Thus, a $T_{\max}$ of $30°$ F and $T_{\min}$ of $25°$ F yields daily HDDs of 37.5. To compute the dollar value of the contract, daily CDDs or HDDs are accumulated each day during the life of the contract and multiplied by $100. For instance, HDDs of 30, 40, 40 and 45 yield a value of $15 500.

While the CME's contracts remained relatively inactive for the first two years of their existence, general interest in the weather risk management market and growing liquidity in OTC derivative contracts on temperature led to increased volumes starting in 2002. As evidence of growing interest, the CME supplemented its original monthly contracts with seasonal contracts (e.g., November–March heating season and May–September cooling season) in 2003; this is consistent with the trading convention followed in the OTC temperature derivative market, as noted below. The exchange also added to its list of reference cities, and announced plans for even more references in the future.

CASE STUDY

Using listed temperature derivatives to hedge risks

Excessive heat or cold can have a significant impact on the revenues or costs of companies in select industries, and lead to financial shortfalls or outright losses. For instance, energy companies have to supply more power to customers when temperatures are very high or very low; if they cannot produce sufficient power to meet demand they suffer loss of revenues. Gas distribution companies are very sensitive to warm winters; if temperatures are too high, demand for gas declines and revenues are negatively impacted. Agricultural producers are exposed to excessively hot conditions, when high temperatures might damage crops, lower per acre yields, and affect revenues. Beverage companies are exposed to cool summers, when demand for product can decline significantly and affect earnings. Seasonal hospitality and entertainment companies (e.g., theme parks, ski resorts, outdoor restaurants) are also exposed to overly hot or cold temperatures, and can experience revenue weakness. Some companies in these industries have become active users of temperature derivatives in recent years as they recognize that temperature fluctuations during a particular day, month, or season can have a negative impact on financial performance. Indeed, for these firms temperature is simply another dimension of risk that can be considered and managed in a loss-financing framework.

Consider the example of a local distribution company delivering gas during the winter season to residential customers. The firm favors very cold winters (i.e., those with a high number of HDDs) as demand for gas and gas-selling prices are both higher – meaning that revenues increase. The reverse scenario, of course, presents a risk: warm winters (i.e., those with a small number of HDDs) mean less demand, lower prices and less revenue. These relationships are depicted in Figure 9.8. Accordingly, the distribution company needs to protect its downside risk and can do so by selling an HDD future or buying an HDD futures put option. In either the case the city selected as the reference must be proximate enough to the distribution company's base of operations to have a strong correlation with local temperatures; if it is not, too much basis risk might arise, rendering the hedge ineffective. Although selling the futures contract does not require payment of upfront premium, it exposes the company to a bilateral payoff profile; this means that if temperatures decline and HDDs rise, the company will lose on its futures contract (although it will gain on its core operations, creating an offset). Buying the futures put option entails the payment of upfront premium but does not expose the company to a bilateral payment profile. Thus, if HDDs rise above the strike price the put expires worthless and the only amount lost is premium paid – but the premium represents a certain upfront cost, one that the futures contract does not impose.

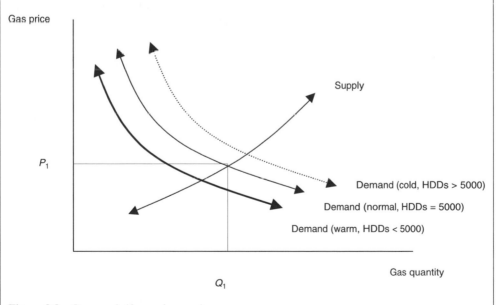

Figure 9.8   Gas supply/demand scenarios

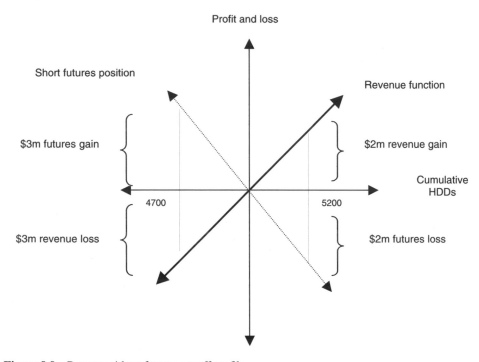

Figure 9.9   Revenues/short futures payoff profile

The gas company quantifies its exposure and determines that an up/down move of 100 HDDs translates into an up/down move in revenues of $1m. Thus, based on a budgeted level of 5000 HDDs, a season that generates 4700 HDDs leads to a $3m loss in revenues, while a season with 5200 HDDs leads to a $2m increase in revenues, and so on. This function is illustrated in Figure 9.9.

Assume that the company sells 100 futures contracts on the HDD index at a level of 5000. If weather during the heating season becomes very cold HDDs might rise to 5300, meaning that the company loses $3m on its futures position; however, it earns an incremental $3m in revenues as a result of stronger demand for heating. If the winter is warm HDDs might only amount to 4700, giving a $3m loss of revenue from core operations, but a gain of $3m on the futures position. These positions are summarized in Figure 9.10a and 9.10b. It is important to stress that the efficacy of the hedge in this, and any other, risk management structure, depends on precise quantification of a company's revenue sensitivity to market variables (such as HDDs); thorough analytical work is vital.

The gradual success of the CME's effort and the growing interest in the European temperature market led the London International Financial Futures Exchange (LIFFE, part of the Euronext exchange group) to introduce listed contracts of its own in 2001, tradable through the electronic LIFFE Connect platform with margins posted through the London Clearinghouse. LIFFE's contracts are conceptually similar to the CME's (i.e., cumulative temperature indexes), except that the indexes are based on average daily temperatures rather than HDDs or CDDs (e.g., the midpoint of T_{max} and T_{min} is combined with averages for the month to date). LIFFE contracts

Warm winter: HDDs fall to 4700

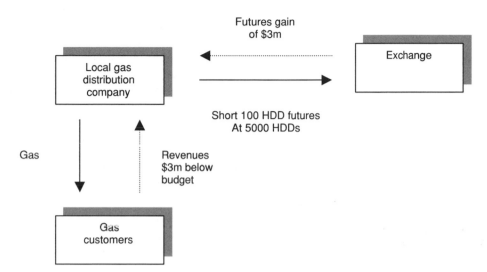

Figure 9.10a   Using HDD contracts to hedge temperature risks

Cold winter: HDDs rise to 5300

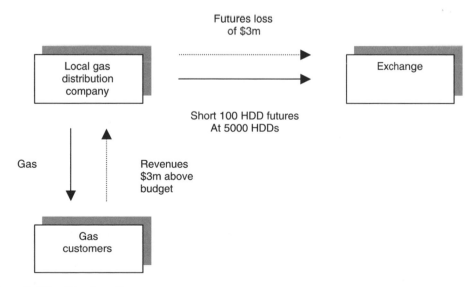

Figure 9.10b   (*Continued*)

were originally offered on three European cities, with plans for regular expansion thereafter. Further European efforts appeared in mid-2003 when the CME and the UK Meteorological Office announced the formation of the Weather Xchange joint venture – a platform to jointly develop global weather future and futures options. The venture commenced with monthly and seasonal contracts on HDDs and cumulative average temperatures on five European cities, tradable via the CME and the CME Clearinghouse. Further reference cities will be added over time. In addition to specific contracts traded via CME and LIFFE, various other electronic trading efforts have emerged in recent years in support of temperature derivatives. For instance, the Intercontinental Exchange (ICE, owned by a consortium of energy companies and financial institutions) offers certain standardized temperature/energy contracts through its platform.

Temperature derivatives have been successfully received because the weather market features natural hedgers on both sides (e.g., those benefiting from warmer or cooler temperatures, and vice versa), an active OTC market based on the same pricing indexes that supplies additional liquidity and price references, indexes that minimize (but do not eliminate) basis risk, and growing transparency. However, temperature derivatives (both listed and OTC) are heavily reliant on very robust historical data for accurate modeling, valuation, and risk management. In the absence of 30–50 years of high-quality daily temperature data, the pricing exercise becomes difficult and subjective, which can lead to erroneous risk management choices. Given this minimum requirement, most activity remains concentrated in locations that have good data records under the quality control of a national weather or meteorological agency (e.g., US, Canada, Europe, Japan, Australia). Expansion into other countries without this minimum requirement will be slow.

9.4 OTC INSURANCE DERIVATIVES

The hallmark of the OTC market is flexibility, so it is no surprise that the most innovative insurance derivatives are still developed, and traded, through the OTC sector rather than formal exchanges. In fact, the ability to customize deals has made the OTC market a more liquid forum for managing insurance risks (the same is generally true for mainstream financial risks). For instance, corporate risk managers wanting to protect non-cat weather risks still find better liquidity and tighter pricing in the OTC market than via the CME or LIFFE. Those requiring cat risk management via derivatives must use the OTC market; since the delisting of CBOT contracts and the abandonment of the BCOE initiative, firms cannot turn to the exchange markets. In this section we consider general characteristics of OTC catastrophe reinsurance swaps, pure catastrophe swaps, temperature derivatives, and other weather derivatives (although credit derivatives, as part of a financially traded sector, are out of the scope of our discussion, we include some general comments on the primary instruments in the notes to this chapter).

9.4.1 Catastrophe reinsurance swaps

Some insurers/reinsurers manage their cat risk portfolios using the **catastrophe reinsurance swap**, a synthetic financial transaction that exchanges a commitment fee for a contingent payment based on the onset of a catastrophic loss. By doing so they obtain many of the same benefits provided by reinsurance or securitization (e.g., portfolio diversification, increased capacity) but are able to avoid some of the structural complexities and costs associated with negotiated facultative or treaty agreements or full ILS issuance. Under a cat swap an insurer might pay a reinsurer Libor plus a spread over a multi-year period in exchange for a certain

Pre-cat event

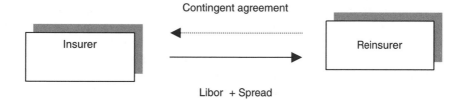

Post-cat event

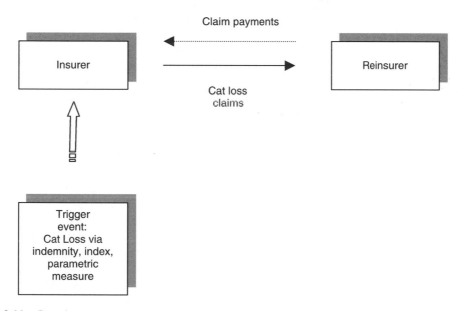

Figure 9.11   Cat reinsurance swap

amount of contingent exposure capacity (tied to a defined index, indemnity, or parametric event). If the named event occurs and creates a loss, the reinsurer provides the ceding swap party with compensation and assumes the claim rights through subrogation. If it does not, the transaction terminates with the insurer's portfolio remaining unchanged. For instance, Mitsui Marine and Swiss Re arranged a cat reinsurance swap where Mitsui paid Swiss Re Libor +375 bps and Swiss Re accepted $30m of contingent exposure to Tokyo earthquake, triggered on a parametric basis. Figure 9.11. summarizes a generic cat reinsurance swap.

9.4.2 Pure catastrophe swaps

In some instances reinsurers prefer to alter their portfolios through the **pure catastrophe swap**, a synthetic transaction that allows the exchange of uncorrelated cat exposures (and which may be documented through standard reinsurance agreements, thus appearing more as a swapping of reinsurance risks rather than a true derivative). Since risks being swapped are uncorrelated, participating insurers achieve greater portfolio diversification. For instance, a Japanese reinsurer with an excess of Japanese earthquake risk may swap a portion of its portfolio for other uncorrelated risks, such as North Atlantic hurricane. Since the analytics and risk parameters governing different types of cat risks are often quite similar, insurers with an existing book of business are not obliged to shift their methods of evaluating low-frequency/high-severity risks, which is a considerable advantage. In some cases a swap might involve the exchange of multiple, but still uncorrelated, perils, such as California earthquake for a combination of Monaco earthquake, Japanese typhoon, and European windstorm. For instance, Swiss Re and Tokio Marine entered into a 1-year, $450m swap where Swiss Re exchanged a portion of its California earthquake exposure for some of Tokio Marine's Florida hurricane and French windstorm exposure; simultaneously, Tokio Marine swapped a portion of its Japanese earthquake portfolio for Swiss Re's Japanese typhoon and cyclone risks. The end result of this series of exchanges was greater portfolio balance for the two insurers (arranged on a relatively quick and cost-effective basis). Tokio Marine later executed similar transactions with State Farm Insurance, where the two insurers swapped portions of their parametric earthquake exposures (e.g., New Madrid for Japan). Various other insurers have made similar use of pure cat swaps in recent years. Figure 9.12 summarizes a generic Tokyo/California catastrophe swap.

9.4.3 Temperature derivatives

Although conceptually similar to the CME contracts described above, activity in OTC **temperature derivatives** – customized contracts referencing one of several temperature indexes – pre-dated the exchange's efforts by approximately two years. In fact, the first HDD and CDD swaps and options were arranged between various energy companies in 1997. The market grew steadily from that point as more energy companies, then banks and insurers, and then specialized investment funds, began hedging or speculating on US-based temperature indexes. In recent years participants from other industries have joined the marketplace; however, where corporate by-laws or regulatory restrictions exist, some corporate end-users choose to obtain the temperature cover in the form of standard insurance contracts rather than OTC derivatives. After initial success in the US markets, activity began to appear in the European markets, primarily in contracts on average temperature indexes (rather than HDDs or CDDs) referencing major European cities.[5] Activity in the Asia–Pacific markets, apart from Japan and Australia, has remained extremely limited through the early part of the millennium, in part because of the data challenges mentioned earlier.

As more institutions have joined the market, certain standard dealing conventions have developed, including contract tick size ($5000 per HDD, CDD, or cumulative average temperature), limits ($2m), tenor (November–March and May–September) and reference cities

---

[5] The main reference cities for summer and winter include London, Paris, Amsterdam, and Berlin.

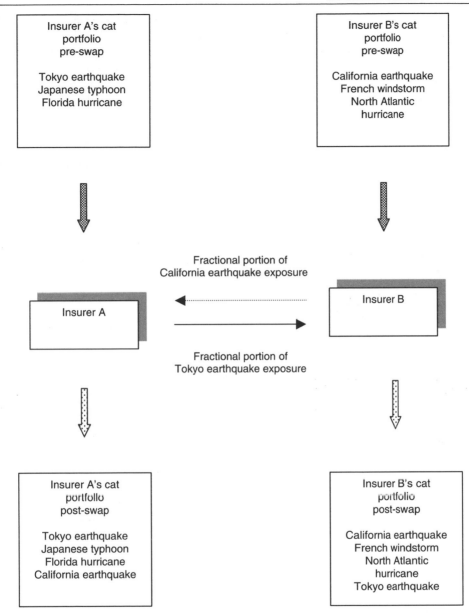

Figure 9.12   Pure catastrophe swap: Tokyo/California earthquake

(10 to 12 major US cities for each season, 4 to 6 in Europe).[6] Reasonable liquidity in such "standard" OTC structures has appeared. OTC temperature derivatives regularly occur in the form of forwards, swaps, call and put options, and multiple option strategies such as **collars**

---

[6] For instance, the primary reference cities for the winter HDD season include Atlanta, Boston, Chicago, Kansas City, Little Rock, Minneapolis, New York, Philadelphia, Pittsburgh, and Washington, DC; the primary summer CDD season cities include Atlanta, Chicago, Cincinnati, Dallas, Houston, Kansas City, Las Vegas, New York, Phoenix, Sacramento, and Tucson.

(a combination of a long call/short put or long put/short call), **straddles** (a call and a put with the same strike and maturity), and **strangles** (a call and a put with different strikes but the same maturity). Although single season deals remain the norm, multi-year transactions that reset each year are also arranged. In addition, single day T_{max} or T_{min} transactions are available, and this is particularly useful for risk cover of one-day events. Non-standard temperature contracts – including those on alternative temperature indexes, humidity, and heat indexes (temperature plus humidity) – can also be arranged. This occurs when an end-user has a particular revenue or cash flow sensitivity to specific temperature thresholds (and can often be found in agricultural applications). Liquidity in any of these "non-standard" structures (whether by tenor, index, or reference city) is much lower than in the core liquidity that has been built around single-season HDD, CDD, and average-temperature deals.

9.4.4   Other weather derivatives

Although temperature swaps and options are the mainstay of the OTC weather derivative market, other forms of weather risk protection are available, including swaps, forwards, and options on precipitation, humidity, wind, and stream flow. Since each represents a specific end-use application, volume is very limited; nevertheless, such derivatives are arranged on a fairly regular basis to meet corporate risk management requirements.

Precipitation derivatives are contracts that provide protection against, or exposure to, snowfall or rainfall based on the amount of liquid or solid precipitation falling in a given location over a set period of time (solid precipitation, including hail or snow, is usually converted to a rain-equivalent amount); US transactions are measured via the imperial standard, while Canadian, European, and Asian deals use the metric standard. Energy companies, while active in temperature, are not significant participants in the precipitation market as the impact of rain or snow on operations is minimal. Instead, the main end-users are those with revenues that are sensitive to the amount of water falling during a given season. Agricultural producers, for instance, are sensitive to the amount of precipitation as an excess (flood) or dearth (draught) can cause crop damage. The same is true for those in the winter tourism sector (e.g., ski resorts) and the transportation industry (e.g., airlines, airport authorities).

Stream flow derivatives are contracts that provide protection against, or exposure to, natural or regulated water discharge in a channel or surface stream. They are primarily of interest to electricity producers in regions that are heavily dependent on hydroelectric power, such as the Western US and Scandinavia. Stream flow is an index that measures the ability of a river to generate electricity or supply reservoirs for future generation. It is very sensitive to a number of hydrological variables, including the amount and timing of snow falling in the snow basin, the level and timing of temperatures that create snow melt and stream/river feeding, and so on. If any of these variables deviates sharply from the norm, stream flow may be impacted and the ability to generate power can be affected. This, of course, can lower an electricity producer's revenues.

Wind derivatives, the last of the non-temperature weather derivatives, are contracts that provide an economic payoff if a wind speed index is above or below some predefined level. Energy companies that invest in the creation of wind farms for power generation face considerable capital costs that they must recoup over time through variable revenues based on wind generation. If the wind index referencing the installation indicates that insufficient power is being produced, the company suffers a loss in revenues and has difficulty recovering its investment; a derivative contract based on the wind index at the specific location can provide downside protection.

Non-temperature weather derivatives are obviously a niche within a relatively small market. Although transactions occur (and are growing in size and frequency) they are, and will remain, very modest compared to other types of risk transfer/hedging arrangements. The main point we wish to highlight through this discussion is that the ART market makes possible the management of risks that might otherwise be considered too idiosyncratic or esoteric to warrant attention.

9.4.5   Credit derivatives

While the focus of ART-related derivative business is primarily on traditional insurance risks, such as non-catastrophic weather and catastrophic P&C, we note once again that insurers and reinsurers are also significant participants in the credit sector from both an asset and liability perspective; this is at least partly related to their desire to assume risks that are uncorrelated with standard P&C business. Not only do they provide specific credit risk coverage via surety bonds, credit insurance, CDO credit wraps, and credit guarantees, they are also very large investors in credit products, including balance sheet CDOs and synthetic CDOs, loans, and bonds. It is no surprise, then, that some have become active participants in the credit derivative market, the OTC forum for credit forwards default swaps, credit spread options, and total return swaps. Banks have welcomed the participation of the insurance sector as it provides another means of sourcing or hedging credit exposure. As the underlying credit derivative market becomes increasingly liquid, banks have a simpler, and more efficient, task in managing their portfolios, and at least part of this is due to the entry of insurers/reinsurers as significant credit derivative players. Thus, while credit risk is not strictly an insurance risk (i.e., it is generally considered a standard financial risk), insurers and reinsurers are active participants (often dealing with financial institutions through dedicated capital markets subsidiaries in order to adhere to regulatory requirements). The fact that these cross-sector institutions are increasingly active in dealing with one another in the credit sector is further evidence of market convergence. Although a complete discussion of credit derivatives is beyond the scope of this book, we provide some additional background on the essential components of the credit derivative market in the notes (portions of the material have been adapted from Banks (2004)).[7]

---

[7] The *credit spread option* compares the differential between a credit-risky instrument such as a corporate bond or loan, and a risk-free benchmark, such as a high-quality government bond. Credit spread puts are purchased by institutions that believe the credit quality of an issuer will deteriorate – as reflected in the widening of a company's bond credit spread against the risk-free benchmark. Sellers of credit puts believe an issuer's credit quality will remain stable/improve, and generate premium income if this view proves correct (alternatively, they may be selling puts as part of an overall credit portfolio risk management exercise). Institutions that believe that the credit quality of an issuer will improve, purchase credit spread calls. In order to buy or sell a credit option, the target credit must have a traded debt security that can be used as a reference; this should ideally be liquid enough to provide a fair assessment of market value. Credit spread options can be settled in cash or physical; an investor that is long a physical settlement credit put can deliver bonds or loans to the seller at a predetermined price/spread if the option is exercised. Options can be price- or spread-based (in spread-based options the final payoff must be adjusted for the price sensitivity of the spread through a duration factor, which is simply a reflection of the average maturity of the bond's cash flows.) A *credit forward* is a single period bilateral contract that references the appreciation or depreciation of an issuer's credit quality in either price or spread terms – up to, and including, the point of default. Through the forward a buyer contracts with a seller to purchase a given reference bond at an agreed forward date and forward price (or spread against a risk-free benchmark); if the underlying credit improves (e.g., the bond price rises or the credit spread narrows) the buyer realizes a gain and the seller a loss. If an institution believes a credit will deteriorate, it sells the reference bond at an agreed forward date and forward price (or spread); if the underlying credit deteriorates (e.g., the bond price falls or the credit spread widens), the seller realizes a gain and the buyer sustains a loss. The extreme event in this situation relates to counterparty default; if the reference credit defaults, the price of the obligation will fall (or spread widen) dramatically; the payoff to the seller will relate to the value assigned to the reference obligation in bankruptcy. In addition to using credit forwards to take a view on the direction of an issuer's credit quality, forwards can also be used to manage portfolios of credit exposures. Credit forwards (which can be settled in cash or physical) carry maturities ranging from several months to several years and can be structured to reference the target bond's price or spread; forwards which are structured in spread terms include a duration adjustment to account for the basis point price sensitivity of the underlying reference bond. The *default swap* – one of the original instruments of the credit derivative market – is a bilateral, multi-year derivative used to transfer credit risk between two parties. Default swaps can be used to take a specific speculative view on the probability of credit default or protect/hedge an underlying credit position. Under a standard default swap a counterparty with excess credit exposure on its book pays

9.5   BERMUDA TRANSFORMERS AND CAPITAL MARKETS SUBSIDIARIES

Historically, insurers/reinsurers have been unable to deal with commercial and investment banks in the full range of derivatives and structured products as a result of regulatory restrictions. Banks, for their part, have been eager to find more suppliers of investment capital/risk capacity, particularly those with an appetite for, and general expertise in, credit, weather, cat, and energy risks. However, they have not generally been able to deal directly with insurers/reinsurers since they are often not authorized to write primary insurance or reinsurance.

This barrier has led to the development of "transformer" companies, many of them domiciled in Bermuda. Some banks (e.g., Goldman Sachs, Lehman Brothers, Deutsche Bank, Société Generale, among others) have found it beneficial to establish **Bermuda transformers**, Class 3 Bermuda insurers that are authorized to write and purchase insurance/reinsurance. The transformer can covert insurance/reinsurance contracts into derivatives, and vice versa. Since a Bermuda transformer can buy/sell both classes of instruments and match obligations on each side, the process becomes transparent to the bank and insurer – each party can acquire or shed risk in the most efficient manner, while adhering to appropriate rules and accounting conventions (e.g., a bank marks-to-market its derivative risks but an insurance company does not mark its insurance risks; a bank can trade derivatives on a secondary basis but an insurer cannot do the same with its policies; and so on). Figure 9.13 illustrates generic credit insurance transactions originating from both a reinsurer and insurer and flowing through the transformer, which converts them into credit derivative form for use by a bank. The same technology can be applied to the transformation of weather risks, cat risks, and so on.

In practice a transformer sells a derivative to a bank and collects derivative premium for doing so. After covering its expenses and relevant profit margin, it then seeks identical cover from an insurer or reinsurer by paying a premium. The reverse transactions can also be arranged. Note that rather than create standalone Class 3 insurers, some financial institutions prefer to use individual cells of protected cell companies (as discussed in Chapter 5) to buy or sell insurance/reinsurance in support of their derivative activities. This can be a quick and efficient way of gaining access to a transformation conduit.

Various large insurance companies (e.g., AIG and Swiss Re, among others) have established **capital market subsidiaries**, dedicated units that are authorized to deal directly with banks in the financial markets. Some subsidiaries are established to write and buy insurance as well, and

---

a second counterparty a periodic fee (often a fixed number of basis points against a notional amount) in exchange for a lump sum if the underlying reference counterparty defaults. The default payment is typically based on the difference between the pre- and post-default price of the reference credit's publicly traded debt. The *total return swap* (TRS) has emerged as a popular derivative that can be used to synthetically replicate and transfer the price appreciation/depreciation of a reference asset. Though virtually any asset can serve as a reference, the instrument has been used widely in the credit markets. A standard credit-based TRS provides credit protection for one party (the buyer) and a synthetic off balance sheet position in a risky bond (or an entire portfolio of bonds) for a second party (the seller). Through the TRS a buyer transfers the economics, and hence credit exposure, of the risky bond, meaning it effectively purchases credit deterioration/default protection; the seller, in contrast, receives the economics of the risky bond, indicating that it has synthetically purchased the instrument. Under a standard TRS the buyer of the swap pays the seller a flow which reflects the coupon on a third-party reference bond; in exchange, the seller passes the buyer a smaller flow (often Libor-based). In addition, at maturity of the transaction the current price of the bond is compared to a predetermined starting price: if the price has declined (a possible sign of credit deterioration), the seller pays the buyer a lump sum payment reflecting the depreciation; if the price has risen, the buyer pays the seller a lump sum payment reflecting the appreciation. The seller thus has a synthetic long position in the bond without actually holding the security on its balance sheet – it receives appreciation and periodic interest payments reflecting the coupons from the bond and pays depreciation. The buyer, in turn, hedges its exposure to the issuer of the bond. If, for example, the bond issuer defaults, the buyer of the TRS loses on its own balance sheet inventory position (or related credit exposure) but receives a compensatory lump sum payment from the seller; if the bond issuer performs, the buyer of the TRS is repaid on the bond (or related credit exposure) by the issuer, but makes a lump sum payment to the seller of the TRS in an amount reflecting the appreciation. Note that most TRS maturities range from 6 to 24 months, though longer-term transactions can be negotiated. And, although interim payments are exchanged (e.g., bond coupons for a Libor payment) the main economic payoff generally relates to the capital gain/loss at the conclusion of the transaction. Variations on these structures also exist, including first-to-default swaps, basket swaps, basket options, and so on.

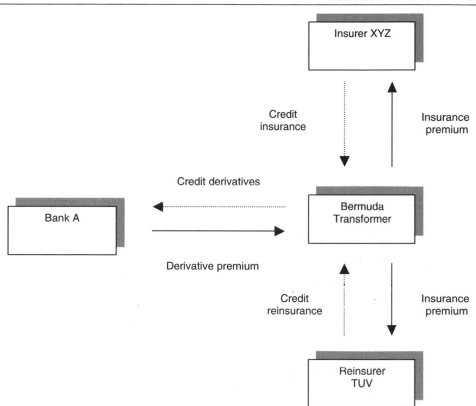

Figure 9.13 Bermuda transformer with credit transformation

thus take the form of multi-purpose transformers. Others cannot deal in insurance directly and must therefore have a mechanism with the parent company that permits risks to be written or acquired through the parent. Although the specific exposures are isolated from one another (and may receive different accounting treatment), the portfolio risk profile of the consolidated entity (i.e., at a holding company level) may look perfectly matched, as illustrated in Figure 9.14.

Transformers and capital markets subsidiaries fulfill an important role because they bridge two distinct, but related, markets. As long as regulatory and accounting differences exist, they are likely to remain in use; as distinctions are resolved through harmonization of rules or broadening of authorized business scope, the need for such vehicles may become less apparent. For instance, contractual differences still arise between the underlying documentation used by banks and insurance companies for transactions referencing the same risk. In the credit derivative market, for example, banks trade on the basis of market-driven events, while insurers are focused on proof of loss; this is a fundamental difference that becomes especially evident when a claim or payment must be made (e.g., on a credit default swap or credit insurance policy after an event of default).[8] Short of using a transformer to convert a liability under a credit derivative contract into an insurable loss falling within the scope of an insurer's activities,

---

[8] For example, a group of 10 monolines writing credit default insurance contested whether a debt restructuring by Xerox in 2002 should have triggered payment under credit default swaps. The monolines indicated to ISDA and the financial community that the debt restructuring should not have been seen as a credit event as the restructuring was not an outright default (although it was an act that created losses for Xerox debtholders).

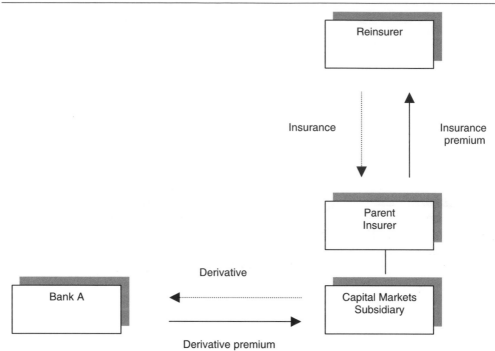

Figure 9.14   Parent Insurer and Capital Markets Subsidiary

some participants are pressing the insurance sector to deal through legal documents used by the derivative industry (e.g., the International Swap and Derivatives Association (ISDA) master agreement and its customized schedules), which standardizes terms, conditions, and events of importance.[9] In fact, some insurers have adopted this approach and are utilizing ISDA documentation in their dealings.

Bermuda transformers and capital markets subsidiaries have been an important evolutionary step in the convergence of the financial and insurance sectors because they permit institutions from different industries (with different approaches to risk management) to cede or assume risks as needed. As greater integration between the two sectors emerges through the specific dismantling of regulations or the uniform treatment of accounting and legal parameters, the need for dedicated transformers and subsidiaries may become less pressing (a process, it should be noted, that is likely to take many years to achieve). In fact, for some institutions the move towards combined bancassurance platforms may be the ultimate "end-game" in the merging of products and risks that perform similar functions but are currently handled separately.

---

[9] The ISDA master agreement, introduced in 1993, revised on various occasions, and reissued as a new agreement in 2002, contains important elements related to net payments, termination rights, automatic stay provision exclusions from US Bankruptcy law, etc.; for a more detailed discussion readers may wish to refer to Banks (2004).

Part IV
ART of the Future

10

Enterprise Risk Management

In the first three parts of this book we have focused on the theoretical underpinnings of the ART market and discussed a series of insurance and financial market mechanisms and conduits that comprise the "building blocks" of the ART market. In this chapter we consider how some of the building blocks can be assembled to create integrated, or holistic, risk management programs. Indeed, for many end-users an enterprise-wide approach to risk management is becoming both a priority and a reality. Below we review the concept of enterprise risk, general advantages and disadvantages of combining risks, the steps involved in developing an enterprise risk management program, and the perspective and experience of end-users. In the next chapter we build on this foundation by considering the dynamics of discrete and consolidated approaches to risk management and their possible impact on the ART market of the twenty-first century.

10.1 COMBINING RISKS

10.1.1 The enterprise risk management concept

The concept of **enterprise risk management** (ERM) – a risk management process that combines disparate financial and operating risks into a single, multi-year program of action – has captured the attention of end-users and intermediaries, as it offers advantages over the traditional transactional or "incremental" approach to risk management. The key of ERM is not only to develop a risk management plan that mitigates exposures, but also to synchronize and optimize perils, maturities and attachments, and even identify opportunities to assume incremental risks. Various surveys point to the fact that, through the early part of the millennium, major companies in North America and Europe followed, or intended to follow, a more integrated approach toward the management of risks (though only a minority had implemented consolidated programs)[1]; growth prospects appear strong because end-users have started focusing on the benefits consolidate risk management can provide.

The trend during the 1990s and into the millennium has been on expanding the scope of corporate risk management coverage: not just operating risks characterized by pure losses, but financial risks with their unique speculative traits, as well as risks once thought to be uninsurable, such as exposures to product liability, political events, terrorism, intellectual property theft, volumetric changes, and so on. This is consistent, too, with the trend toward consolidated

---

[1] For instance, in a survey of North American companies conducted by KPMG, 81% of respondents indicated that they followed a more integrated approach to risks, e.g., ensuring cross-unit communication on exposures, considering the management of risks jointly and/or transferring them to a centralized unit. However, by 2001 only 20% had contemplated implementation of a dedicated ERM program and only 10% had actually done so (KPMG, 2001); clearly, more work remains to be done. A survey conducted by the Economist Intelligence Unit (2001) suggests that 53% of European, 34% of North American, and 33% of Asian, companies followed some type of integrated approach to risk management in the early part of the millennium. By mid- to late decade, 73% of companies surveyed believed that they would implement an enterprise risk management program.

management of assets, liabilities, and off-balance-sheet contingencies. Companies have discovered that interdependencies exist not only in individual asset, liability, or contingent portfolios, but also across them. Furthermore, they have come to recognize that in some cases the act of consolidating the firmwide risk profile reveals opportunities to assume incremental risks at attractive returns. This is an important distinction that sets ERM apart from the multiple peril products discussed in Chapter 6, where the focus is on grouping "like" exposures in order to mitigate risks and lower costs. ERM can lead to the reduction and assumption of different risks and can thus be a much more flexible platform for achieving stated risk goals. In general, ERM should not be viewed solely as a platform for reducing or eliminating risks, but as one that allows broad management of risks: managing retentions more actively, structuring multiple post-loss financing facilities, embedding speculative risks into business strategies, assuming different exposures to introduce particular portfolio effects, etc. Actions must, of course, be consistent with a firm's stated risk philosophy and tolerance. The spectrum of risks, channels and horizons that can be considered through an enterprise-wide program is summarized in Figure 10.1.

The centerpiece of ERM is a migration from incremental, to joint, management of risks. Consider Figure 10.2, an adaptation of the diagram we presented in Chapter 6, which depicts a number of risk exposures facing a company and the discrete covers arranged to protect against losses. Each individual exposure is considered and managed separately, and the end result is a series of individual insurance policies, financial derivatives, and other loss-financing techniques that are meant to provide protection. As we have noted previously, this may be a very inefficient way of managing corporate affairs, leading to instance of excess cost, overinsurance/overhedging, and capital mismanagement – detracting from enterprise value maximization in the process. Figure 10.3 reflects the consolidated results obtained by uniting all of the exposures in a single platform; the individual vertical covers disappear and are replaced with one program that eliminates coverage gaps, lowers costs, and improves capital and administrative efficiencies. Fundamentally, the net risk of a portfolio of individual risks is smaller and less volatile than a simple summation of those risks, hence a key reason for managing them jointly. This approach lets a firm take advantage of the incremental portfolio diversification benefits that can be obtained with each new risk source, and moves thought and action away from the static and isolated risk/return view. It also allows incremental risks to be assumed when it makes sense to do so from a risk/return perspective – by again considering exposures in light of the entire corporate portfolio. The ultimate goal is enterprise value maximization.

The ERM platform does not require that all exposures be channeled through a "master" insurance policy. While this is one aspect of the market the platform, by definition, is highly customizable, and accommodates multiple features. For instance, the risk retained under a program can be channeled through a group captive or funded via liquid resources, catastrophe coverage can be based on a dual trigger and allow for the issuance of incremental equity, returns on an investment portfolio might be floored through the use of equity options, and so on. This "cross-product/channel" flexibility, as we noted in Chapter 3, is one of the strengths of the ERM concept. An example of this approach is provided in Figure 10.4.

From an analytic program design, and risk capacity perspective, aspects of global deregulation and market convergence make it simpler for intermediaries to act as "one-stop shops" in the provision of ERM solutions. Each sector brings its own expertise to bear in the analytical and market/product knowledge process, which helps to give clients the best possible

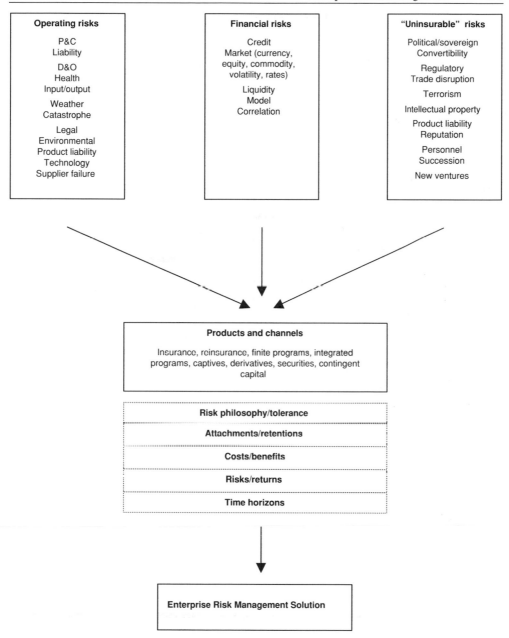

Figure 10.1   Universe of ERM risk coverage

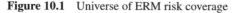

solution; it also helps to strengthen the convergence movement. Universal banks, commercial banks, and investment banks with Bermuda transformers or insurance subsidiaries can provide a full range of insurance and financial covers and services. Likewise, global insurance companies with capital markets capabilities are increasingly able to offer insurance cover as well as derivatives or ILSs (if such are economic under an ERM program).

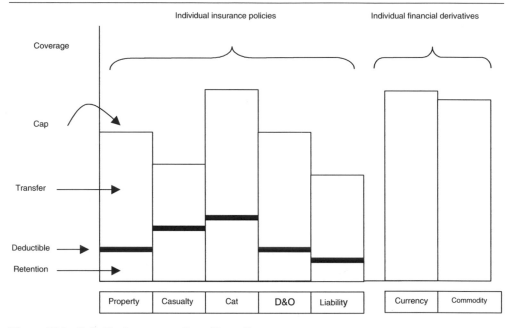

Figure 10.2   Individual coverage of specific perils

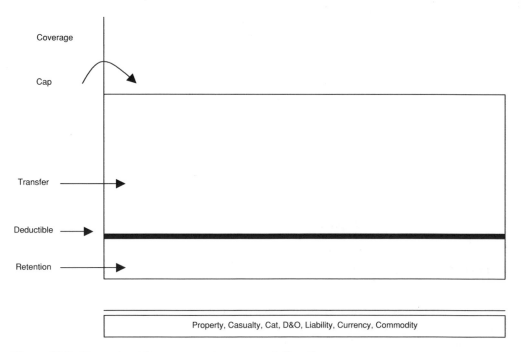

Figure 10.3   Enterprise risk management coverage of all perils

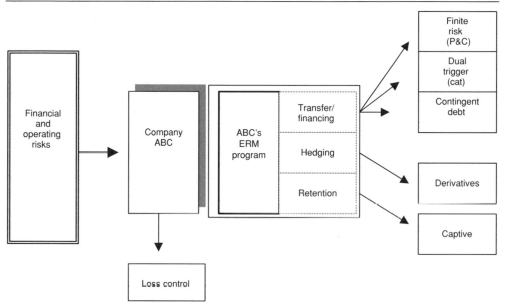

Figure 10.4   Example of a flexible ERM program

10.1.2   Costs and benefits

In our discussions on risk pooling and diversification in Chapter 1 and multiple peril products in Chapter 6, we indicated that combining uncorrelated risks conveys a variety of benefits.[2] Not surprisingly, these benefits, and several others, also extend to the ERM platform. In particular a firm gains:

- improved understanding of financial and operating risks;
- greater ability to balance a portfolio of risks;
- increased likelihood of covering uninsurable risks and reducing overinsurance and over-hedging;
- better ability to avoid earnings surprises/disasters and improve earnings stability;
- more opportunities to combine cross-products to take advantage of pricing and efficiency;
- greater ability to improve capital efficiencies and lower the costs of risk and capital;
- more incentives to reduce costs, increase administrative efficiencies, and implement loss control mechanisms for retained risks.

A process that allows a firm to unite its risks and consider them on a portfolio basis leads to greater insight into financial and operating exposures; since the exercise demands considerable rigor (e.g., identifying all sources of risk, dissecting their impact on the balance sheet, income statement, cash flows, and so on), the financial picture that ultimately emerges is more

---

[2] Many of these theoretical benefits are consistent with the actual benefits end-users expect to derive from implementing ERM programs. For instance, a Tillinghast survey conducted in 2000 indicates that 100% of survey respondents would expect an ERM program to deliver better capital management and earnings stability, 97% expect improved return on capital, 81% better management of assets and liabilities, 80% improved earnings growth, and 57% stronger cost control (Tillinghast-Towers Perrin, 2000).

transparent and readily understood by those inside the firm. The ERM process also provides more opportunities to balance an entire portfolio of exposures. Since many risks relate to one another in particular ways, then a combination of risks is bound to yield more opportunities to sensibly balance the portfolio. An ERM program takes advantage of portfolio risk effects that may reside, knowingly or unknowingly, within a firm's operations. In addition, we have seen earlier in the book that multiple risks, when considered jointly, can render once-uninsurable exposures insurable. The interaction of correlations and use of joint probabilities can lower the probability of loss from these unique risks to acceptable levels; the same is true, on an even broader scale, with an ERM consolidation of risks. Ultimately, covering the uninsurable means helping to avoid disasters. Managing risks on a joint basis also reduces the chance that horizontal or vertical layer "coverage gaps" will appear and create earnings surprises. The same techniques can lead to reductions in overinsurance, overhedging, and other forms of financial overcommitment that waste corporate resources. Certainty of coverage, particularly over a multi-year time horizon, can create greater earnings stability and has been empirically shown to have a significant positive impact on market valuations. Ultimately, less capital needs to be allocated to the overall risk management effort. Of course, any mechanism that can cover uninsurable risks, eliminate coverage gaps, and inject earnings stability can lead to improved valuation and lower cost of capital. Furthermore, a process that brings together the active management of both capital and risk can generate incremental benefits. While capital management, the responsibility of the CFO in most companies, is focused on ways of optimizing the use of balance sheet, leverage, and liquidity to lower the cost of capital, it is often isolated from risk management. Since risk management is concerned with the proper use of capital resources to protect the firm, there should be a close relationship between the two – a relationship that an ERM program can help to strengthen. From a theoretical perspective the consolidation exercise, based as heavily as it is on correlations and joint probabilities, must lead to a cost savings; the sum of risk cover expense for a portfolio of risks is theoretically lower than the sum of the individual risk cover expenses. The inefficiencies that characterize the incremental "silo" approach to risk coverage can be reduced or eliminated, particularly if all (or significant) portions of a program are centered with a single capacity provider (coverage centered with a single provider also eliminates the need to share sensitive corporate information with a larger number of institutions, though it raises potential credit concentration issues). From a competitive perspective a firm that can thoroughly identify, and actively manage, its risks in a consolidated fashion may achieve a comparative advantage over one that is not as keenly aware of its exposures.

A company considering an ERM program must determine whether realizable benefits and gains actually exist (or are merely theoretical), and whether any significant disadvantages can arise, including[3]:

- some uncertainty regarding actual cost reductions;
- greater structural and organizational hurdles;
- greater difficulties in measuring risk on an aggregate basis;
- increased likelihood of concentrated counterparty credit risk.

---

[3] Again, the actual hurdles involved in creating an ERM program mirror, in some instances, the theoretical ones. For instance, the Tillinghast survey cites lack of measurement tools as a significant barrier for 50% of respondents, organizational structure 47%, and process challenges 41%. While most participants were satisfied with their ability to mitigate or transfer "standard" risks, including those related to interest rate, credit, reinvestment, and asset value, some were concerned about an inability to protect effectively against risks arising from intellectual capital, distribution channels, and reputation (Tillinghast-Towers Perrin, 2000).

For instance, while theory suggests that the cost of protecting two uncorrelated exposures must be cheaper than the cost of protecting each one individually, market realities driven by supply/demand factors in any particular sector may occasionally make cost savings impossible to achieve – rendering one of the key ERM drivers invalid. In addition, companies often face significant organizational barriers in trying to combine their risk management functions (and the risk functions embedded in individual business units). Those that have traditionally managed financial risks via a central treasury unit, insurance risks via a dedicated insurance risk unit, and operating risks through individual business units, may find it difficult to consolidate risk management activities. To be useful and valid, a program must be properly supported by risk infrastructure and data, which is likely to lead to increased one-time costs. Indeed, for some firms the political, financial, and technical costs of combining risk units may outweigh any cost savings and administrative efficiencies. Measuring disparate risks on a consolidated basis can be a complicated task, and may expose the firm to an excess of mathematical or statistical assumptions. Developing proper metrics to consider risks in unison is complex because individual risk factors can behave in very unique ways, and correlations between them can be unstable. The quantification and subsequent aggregation task is likely to require a variety of metrics based on tools such as sensitivity analysis, risk equivalent exposures, cash flow variability, enterprise value-added analysis, risk adjusted returns on capital, internal and industry benchmark performance, value-at-risk, earnings-at-risk, and so on; decisions about how to quantify intangibles such as goodwill, intellectual property, and reputation, must also be made. The quantification process can therefore be challenging.[4] In addition, the number of intermediaries that can structure and underwrite a combined program is still very limited. Perhaps a dozen financial conglomerates are capable of protecting a broad spectrum of financial and insurance risks and, while most of them have good credit ratings, an end-user engaging such an intermediary faces concentrated credit risk. Risk essentially migrates from financial/insurance/operating exposure to credit exposure; for some, this many run contrary to standard diversification preferences. It should be clear, then, that before a company can consider developing an enterprise risk management program, it must carefully review and analyze all advantages and disadvantages and associated costs/benefits.

10.2 DEVELOPING AN ENTERPRISE RISK MANAGEMENT PROGRAM

It is increasingly true that the modern corporation no longer decides whether or not to protect its risk exposures, but which exposures to protect against, and in what specific form. Indeed, the importance of corporate risk management in protecting capital and enhancing shareholder value has been widely recognized and accepted. This means that a significant mindset "barrier" has already been overcome, and the typical company can begin to consider a broader enterprise program. This does not mean, of course, that an ERM program is a necessary or desirable risk solution for all firms, but simply that there is greater willingness to consider the

---

[4] Companies involved in the EIU survey cite this as a major challenge. For instance, 46% of companies aggregated exposures within operating risks, 55% within financial risks, but only 15% across operating and financial risks. Even within the broad class of financial risks, aggregation must be handled with caution, as it is prone to error in times of extreme market stress. For instance, the widely used value-at-risk measure, which aggregates portfolios of market risks, depends heavily on a series of statistical assumptions such as correlation, volatility, and the shape of the statistical distribution – any, or all, of which may become unstable in the event of a financial dislocation.

relative costs and benefits associated with such programs when developing a risk management strategy.

10.2.1 Strategic and governance considerations

Before creating an ERM program, a company must develop a risk strategy based on its philosophy of risk and risk tolerance. It must determine how risk relates to its business goals, including financial targets (e.g., leverage, economic capital, and probability of insolvency), revenues, market share, and geographic and industry presence and how much of its financial resources it is willing to put at risk. A firm cannot develop a risk strategy and, by extension, an ERM strategy in a vacuum. The actions it takes must be tied to the realities of corporate business goals. Most companies pursue a general goal of enterprise value maximization. The delineation of a corporate risk strategy can determine the impediments that stand in the way of achieving this goal, and help to create a stronger link between goals and implementation. Also, a focus on resources is obviously vital as these are the financial assets that permit a firm to operate. Economic capital must be sufficient to support the financial and operating strategies of the firm and reduce the probability of ruin to the level defined by the firm's executives and directors; it places boundaries around a firm's risk tolerance, or the maximum loss that can be sustained in particular circumstances. It is important to stress that risk-taking, unlike other forms of industrial production, is not a zero-loss game. A firm is always exposed to periodic loss, must accept losses but limit them. Ultimately, economic capital serves as a tolerance guide and should be allocated on a risk-related basis to individual business units; this permits ongoing measurement of risk-adjusted performance and helps to determine whether the firm is truly maximizing earnings for the level of risk it is taking (e.g., the efficient frontier portfolio we described in Chapter 1). If risk diversification benefits arise from the implementation of an ERM program, then individual business units can share in the benefit on a prorata basis through lower capital allocations.

Once a risk strategy is defined and agreed by the board of directors and executives, a firm can proceed with the development of a hypothetical ERM program. The firm can consider an ERM strategy based on company, industry, and competitive factors (e.g., how such a program will impact its standing in the marketplace, what competitive advantages/disadvantages will arise, how others in the industry cope with similar issues, what constrains or flexibilities it adds to business operations, what can go wrong, who is responsible, etc.). As noted, a firm must also weigh the program in light of financial targets, including capital attributions (by business unit and in total), target leverage and liquidity, credit-rating sensitivities, revenue goals, and asset/liability mix. By developing a strategy a firm crystallizes its practical risk tolerance levels, which are an essential element of corporate governance and a main way of relating to equity investors. While the theoretical ERM strategy must be consistent with overarching business goals, it can also serve to drive aspects of corporate strategy. Indeed, the ERM planning must be viewed as a platform not only for managing risks effectively, but also for making decisions that can ultimately improve the firm's profitability. This, again, signals a move away from the traditional approaches to risk management that focus primarily on risk mitigation or neutralization. The ultimate goal should be to migrate from controls that limit problems, to optimization routines that allow risks to be eliminated or assumed, depending on the relative risk-adjusted returns that are available.

Assuming that a company develops an ERM approach that is consistent with its strategy and finds that the relative benefits outweigh potential costs, it must then align its structure, operations, and operating mindset. A firm embarking on an ERM program should not manage its businesses in strict product/geographic "silos". It must migrate away from the mentality of examining and addressing, on a discrete or incremental basis, a single risk over a short time horizon (e.g., the standard one-year insurance time frame). It must be willing to examine, on a portfolio basis, the loss control, loss-financing, and risk reduction options available over a multi-year period, with a view toward managing exposures through joint retentions, covers, caps, vehicles, and instruments deemed most efficient. Consolidating a risk management function can be a significant help in unifying firmwide risk goals. Creation of a single team, responsible for all aspects of financial/operating risk (as defined via the firm's risk strategy), can be a wise course of action. Integration must also extend to the business units. In some companies business units are given specific goals of maximizing value for the firm. They may take actions that are consistent with that goal when considered in isolation, but inconsistent when considered more broadly. For instance, a business unit with a currency exposure might be advised to hedge that risk, but in doing so it might be overhedging the firm, as another unit may already have the opposite exposure in place; enterprise value will not be maximized in such cases. Coordination across business units is vital, and proper integration of activities should be the final goal. Proper governance demands that the responsibilities of an integrated team – as well as business managers and executives – be clearly defined. There must be transparency regarding the responsibilities and authorities of parties that can shape the firm's risk profile.

ERM programs often follow an evolutionary process. Indeed, it is unusual for a company with no prior experience in active risk management to simply decide to create an integrated platform. It is more common for a firm to gain comfort with specific aspects of financial and operating risk management and then use its experience to design a program with a broader scope. For instance, the process might start with managing risks on a discrete basis, coping with new exposures incrementally as they arise. Although this is not necessarily efficient or cost-effective, it is the reality of corporate risk management in a dynamic business environment. Once this process is well entrenched, a company is likely to realize that it has opportunities to view and manage its risks holistically. It may then enter a second phase by taking account of all risks generated by the asset side of its balance sheet. The firm may then realize the correlations that exist between these asset-based risks and implement certain risk management techniques that take advantage of asset diversification. In a final phase it might examine the entirety of its assets, liabilities, and contingencies, engaging in a thorough analysis of risk interdependencies in order to create the most efficient integrated risk program possible.

ERM implementation can, of course, take different forms and is likely to depend on the structure and characteristics of the organization and the nature of the risks being managed. For example, some companies might favor central identification and coordination, but local implementation. This might be beneficial when a company is large and operates through branches and subsidiaries in many countries. Knowledge of local regulations, customs, and access – which might all impact the nature of the program – can often be handled best at a local level. Alternatively, a company might prefer centralized identification, coordination, and implementation. This might be beneficial when the majority of a company's operations are centered in a single country or marketplace, or it needs to keep tighter control of subsidiary risk management operations. There is no single correct approach to this matter, but it is generally true that the identification and coordination aspects of an ERM program must be managed in a consolidated fashion in order to ensure consistency and take advantage of the benefits that can accrue. Some companies are making use of the role of the chief risk officer (CRO) as the focal point of risk activities. A CRO can serve as the link between the CEO and directors, business managers, and independent risk managers: helping to guide risk strategy in a unified fashion, knowing which aspects of the process must be centralized, which can be decentralized to individual business units, etc.

A company must monitor the impact of a program over time. This involves reviewing the specific outcomes/results through metrics that are agreed *ex-ante* (e.g., revenues, investment profits, net income, return on equity, risk-adjusted return on equity, cash flow, leverage, expected/unexpected risk losses). It also involves monitoring the firm's risk management performance against external events and benchmarks. In general, internal monitoring should include a review of specific costs for integrated coverage compared to the ongoing costs of discrete coverage, the implicit financial benefits derived from administrative efficiencies, claims-time turnaround, gains from organizational consolidation, returns from incremental risks, and the explicit savings from the reduced use of capital. If an ERM program is to be successful, it should help a firm to achieve better balance in the management of capital resources. If the firm's actual capital is near its required capital (as defined by a combination of regulatory requirements and internal prudency analysis related to the level of risks being carried and the nature/magnitude of business being undertaken) then it is minimizing its use of capital and cost of capital. Conversely, if monitoring reveals that the firm's capital is still greater than needed, it is overcapitalized (to the detriment of investors, who are no longer earning the returns they require) and capital levels must be reduced. If monitoring suggests that the firm's capital is less than needed, it is undercapitalized and may incur additional costs related to the specter of financial distress. Again, the joint consideration of capital and risk is of paramount importance. Ultimately, monitoring permits adjustments to be made during renewal periods, e.g., adding new covers, changing strike prices, deductibles, caps, contingent capital terms, and so on. It might also suggest that aspects of the integrated program are no longer needed or that greater advantages exist in pursuing separate coverage for particular risk variables.

10.2.2 Program blueprint

Integrated risk programs are generally developed by corporate end-users in conjunction with specialists from the insurance and/or banking worlds; insurance brokers often assist in the process, which can be analytically demanding. Although many approaches exist, we consider one ERM blueprint in this section. The description is sufficiently generic to be applied across a range of companies, industries, and risks. It is important to note that this approach focuses on tactical corporate actions rather than longer-term strategic actions such as those that might be recommended by a firm's executives and board directors. While strategic activities – including acquisitions, divestitures, new product/market expansion, and so on – can impact overall risk exposures, they cover much longer time horizons (in fact, changes in the risk profile in such instances may be a by-product, rather than a driver). We therefore concentrate on tactical operations (which can, of course, cover a multi-year commitment period) as a representation of the deliberate steps a firm takes to reshape its risk profile.

- *Identification of risks*   The program begins with an identification of all sources of risk that might impact a firm. This reverts to our discussion in Chapter 1 on the risk management process. According to proper governance, a company should feature a team of skilled professionals that can accurately identify all sources of risk – financial and operating, pure and speculative, insurable and uninsurable. Identification should focus on causes, consequences, and timing. While conventional risks can be readily identified, a firm must not overlook "new" risks, or those that change over time (e.g., exposures related to reputation, market share, information, technology, strategy, cybercrime, intellectual property theft, etc). During this assessment stage it is also important for a firm to prioritize any exposures it identifies. A company is bound to have dozens, perhaps even hundreds, of sources of risk, and not all of them can be given the same level of attention; some will invariably have a much larger significance on the volatility of earnings or the structure of the balance sheet, and must therefore be given proper priority.
- *Disaggregation of risks*   Every risk identified must be isolated and decomposed so that it can be analyzed and understood. In many instances this is quite easy to do, particularly if the risk is transparent; in other cases it is more difficult, as the risk might be embedded with others.
- *Quantification of disaggregated risks*   The economic impact of each disaggregated risk must be estimated in order to determine its contribution to the total risk profile of the firm and its effect on cash flows and the balance sheet. Quantification can take a variety of forms, including financial analytics, simulation, actuarial techniques, regression/factor analysis, scoring, and so on, and must take account of potential time frames during which losses might occur. Quantification measures for exogenous financial risks are quite well established, but the same is not necessarily true of operating risks. Since some operating risks are endogenous than exogenous to a firm, measurement depends heavily on how a firm manages its internal processes. A company may thus attempt to quantify operating risks through a proprietary historical loss database reflecting its experience related to event risk, business execution risk, and so on. Alternatively, it may use causal models with input from business managers, and attempt to simulate the dynamics of cause/effect relationships in a hypothetical environment.
- *Mapping of risks*   Once disaggregated, risks must be analyzed through a correlation process to enable the firm to determine how each source of risk interacts with others (if at all). The end result is often a correlated map of risks that reveals how specific sources of risk impact the totality of a firm's operations (e.g., whether they are reduced or amplified when particular events occur); this leads to a summary of interdependencies.
- *Analysis of risk interdependencies*   With mapping information on interdependencies, a firm can identify natural hedges within its existing portfolio and consider diversification techniques to reduce its overall cost of risk. This typically centers on using uncorrelated or negatively correlated risks to produce mini-risk portfolios (consistent with our discussion of diversification and pooling). The analysis stage should include testing of "what if" scenarios under stressed market conditions, and inclusion/exclusion of risk variables from the portfolio; these actions can help to reveal weak points or possible changes in portfolio dynamics as risk exposure correlations change and losses (or gains) mount. It is important for a company to consider the impact of loss from low-frequency/high-severity events that it may never have experienced previously. Since these may be new and unique, the apparent cost of risk transfer may well outweigh any supposed gains; accordingly, a simulation process, which

can clearly demonstrate how the cost/benefit tradeoff can change under different scenarios, is an important part of the process.

- *Creation of an integrated program* The end goal of the process should be the creation of a program with a lower cost of risk than can be obtained through incremental management. If this cannot be achieved, then no increase in enterprise value is possible through the integrated program. Assuming that savings can be achieved, a firm finalizes the process by working with a broker or adviser on specific implementation, e.g., establishing a captive to retain certain core operating risks, creating an integrated policy that covers P&C, interest rate, credit, and environmental liability risks to particular cap levels, using derivative contracts to completely hedge out currency risks, establishing a contingent capital facility to secure post-loss financing, etc. The ERM platform is so flexible that few boundaries exist when designing a program. This represents the practical "culmination" of the process of analysis and negotiation.
- *Implementation of the program* Once developed, the program must be implemented within the firm's operating structure; this, as noted, may involve restructuring of the risk management and business unit functions and the flow of information, responsibilities, and authorities. It may also require enhancement of the technology base. Successful implementation is critical; the best ERM program will fail in practice if it is not implemented carefully.
- *Monitoring of results* The ERM process does not end once a program has been implemented. Risk management is dynamic, and impacted by internal and external events, meaning the review of an ERM program must be just as dynamic. Again, good governance requires that appropriate tools/metrics and regular audits/reviews be put in place to gauge the efficacy of the program. If necessary, a firm must be prepared to adjust the program as shortcomings are discovered, new risks are added, market variables shift, the firm's operating strategies change, and so on.

The steps of the program blueprint are summarized in Figure 10.5.

The nature of a company's risks and operations, and the time and resources it is able to devote to closely analyzing its profile, will dictate the complexity and sophistication of the platform. Even when intricate work cannot be performed, an ERM program can still be developed. For instance, rather than using in-depth simulation or analytic techniques, some firms opt for a relatively straightforward scoring system to "quantify" exposures and list them in rank order. These can then be packaged into various combinations to determine relative strategies and cost savings. A firm, for instance, can determine the probability that firmwide losses from all sources of risk will exceed a specified threshold in particular years, and how much it will lose in an average year. Applying different risk management techniques with different costs and coverage levels over the long term provides an indication of long term costs of an ERM program and the variability of performance. The company can then answer important questions, such as its ability to handle the average (annual) loss, the 1 in 100 loss, and so on.

We stress once again that the essential aspect of any integrated program is the identification of risk interdependencies during the mapping stage. This reveals whether corporate efficiencies and financial savings can be obtained by managing risks jointly. Consider, for instance, a company that is exposed to both the risk of catastrophe (e.g., a hurricane striking its factories and warehouses and creating physical damage, business interruption, and so on) and the risk of equity market losses (e.g., an investment portfolio heavily weighted toward global equities).

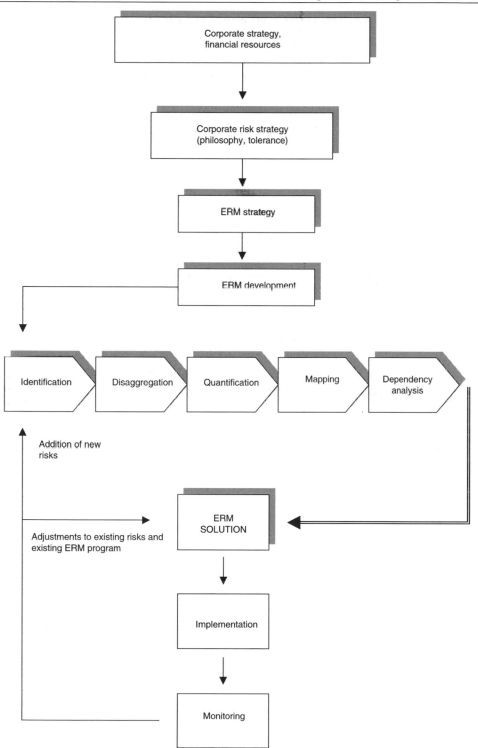

Figure 10.5 Development of an ERM program

We term these RC and RE, respectively. If the mapping process reveals that RC and RE are uncorrelated – that the onset of a hurricane will not cause any direct decline in the equity markets – the cost of risk incurred through joint risk coverage of RC and RE should be lower than separate coverage of RC and RE. Accordingly, the company has an opportunity to increase enterprise value and stabilize cash flows. Thus, if covariance (RC, RE) is ≤ 0 then cost(RC + RE) $\leq$ cost(RC) + cost(RE); in addition, σ(cost(RC + RE)) $\leq \sigma$(cost(RC)) + σ(cost(RE)), which stabilizes cash flows (and can ultimately help to boost enterprise value). The key is that the aggregate volatility of risk transferred is lower than the sum of the two, so the resulting risk solution should be cheaper.

10.2.3 Program costs

The cost/benefit tradeoff is an important element of the ERM decision-making process, particularly since customized programs carry costs on two fronts: upfront development costs and ongoing risk management costs. While ERM programs help firms to manage their risks in a specific manner, the very fact that they are firm-specific means that they cannot usually be standardized or commoditized (although some insurers provide a broad template for consideration of specific risks, and then customize from that point on).[5] Accordingly, the cost savings that normally come from constant duplication of a standard product or program are largely absent. A customized risk program created by an insurer for a cedant, or a reinsurer for a ceding insurer, typically cannot be re-used for others and must therefore draw some incremental upfront cost. The tradeoff that exists in other bespoke programs exists with integrated risk programs: the customization that is essential in creating a program that adds most value to a firm costs more than any general program. The analysis and design process is generally quite intricate, particularly for a firm that has many risks and a complex organizational, product, and market structure. In addition, acquiring data for the identification and quantification process is generally a non-trivial exercise.

The upfront development costs may be quite justified in the face of ongoing cost savings and is, for many, a worthwhile 'investment'. Ultimately, the holistic view of risk interdependencies means less risk, less overinsurance/overhedging, and lower capital allocation. These translate into lower capital costs and savings on both administration and transaction fees – which can offset the higher development costs, certainly when considered over a multi-year time frame (which is a key reason that companies opting for an ERM solution must remain committed for several years; abandonment means that upfront investment costs will not be recouped). Another benefit, as mentioned earlier, arises from stability of costs. By creating a program that stabilizes cash flows and earnings a firm reduces cash flow uncertainty and helps to boost enterprise value. Further cost savings can come from internal realignment of risk management functions. Companies that previously managed risks through decentralized units (e.g., a treasury function for financial risks, an insurance unit for insurance risks, business units for operating risks) may be able to reduce expenses by consolidating functions with duplicative personnel, technologies, and so on. We consider one such approach in the Iscor case study.

---

[5] For instance, AIG's COIN program provides cover for P&C, workers' compensation, general/auto/product liability, environmental liability, currencies, and primary commodities. Further refinement, including amounts, retentions, deductible, maturities, references, and so on, must then be tailored to the customer's precise requirements, meaning that the same type of identification/analysis/ interdependency work must be carried out.

CASE STUDY

Iscor's organizational changes

One of the beneficial by-products of the ERM process can be the structural integration of a firm's risk management function. The South African resource company, Iscor, serves as a good example of a company that has used an ERM program to streamline its risk management process and organizational structure. In the late 1990s, Iscor's executives determined that the company's risk operations were too diffuse and informal to ensure proper coverage and protection of exposures. Accordingly it investigated the possibility of developing an integrated program that would not only consolidate risk exposures, but also add structure and formal responsibility to the risk decision-making process. The intent was not to remove responsibilities for particular units or executives, but to formalize the chain of communication and command. Senior Iscor officials felt that the best way of doing so was under the umbrella of a new ERM program.

After months of work analyzing its risk management process, identifying exposures, and seeking the best opportunities to cover the firm's insurance and commodity risks, the executive team developed a new organizational structure for its risk operations. In particular, it delegated responsibility for overall risk control to a new Executive Risk Committee (ERC), chaired by the CFO, which meets quarterly to:

- determine Iscor's risk goals and strategies;
- coordinate risk activities;
- evaluate exposures and reporting;
- ensure policy compliance;
- approve insurance/retention/hedging limits and renewals.

Once every year the ERC focuses on adjustments to the company's overall risk tolerance and the risk capital allocations for each business. The development of a tolerance is based on the firm's key financial ratios, which are weighted by relative importance.

From a practical operating perspective, the ERC delegates to 40+ subcommittees (at the Executive, Business Unit and Department levels) certain other responsibilities, including identification of risks, prioritization of risks that have been identified, implementation of solutions consistent with the ERC's risk goals and strategies (and within the financial boundaries established by the ERC), and ongoing benchmarking of performance. These committees meet formally every quarter (and informally as required) to focus on:

- risk identification, assessment and prioritization;
- evaluation of the potential frequency and severity of losses impacting each Business Unit and Department;
- establishment of risk ratings for cross-unit comparison purposes;
- examination of actual quarterly loss experience against expectations;
- design and implementation of loss controls consistent with the risk prioritization scheme;
- design and tracking of risk benchmarks;
- preparation of risk management reports for the ERC and executive management.

The assessment and benchmarking phases are outsourced to third parties in the interest of efficiency. Iscor's end-goal through the integrated program promulgated via the consolidated

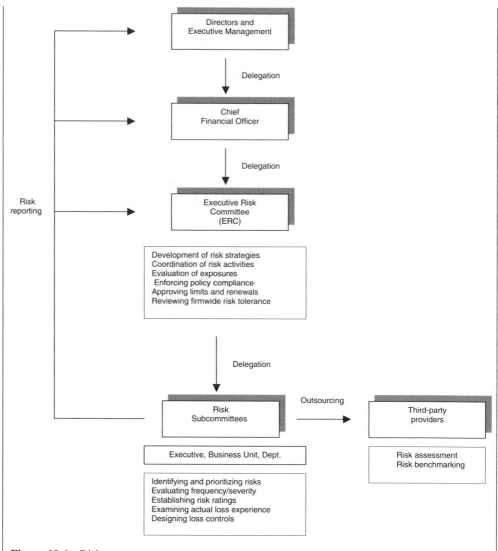

Figure 10.6 Risk process structure

risk management structure is to reduce estimated maximum losses. Figure 10.6 summarizes the company's approach and process. This is, of course, just one of many ways to structure a consolidated function but it demonstrates how a firm can use an integrated risk program to realign its management of risk exposures.

10.3   END-USER DEMAND

As we have already noted, one of the most important advantages of the ERM process is the ability for end-users to bring disparate risks together under one umbrella to consider and manage them jointly. As end-users from different industries often have unique risk exposures that they need to protect (or take advantage of), customization is vital. Also, while the market for standard financial and operating risk covers is well established (i.e., ready availability during most market cycles), the ability to address the broad group of uninsurable risks is a considerable advance. For instance, a firm can now combine P&C risks, credit risk, and market risk with volumetric risks, political risks,[6] or new venture risks.[7] Such combined coverage was simply not possible several years ago.

Based on industry surveys and actual corporate experience, demand for ERM programs by corporate end-users appears to be strong and growing. Many of those that have explored the matter and enacted programs appear convinced of the benefits. Some of those that are still exploring the issue appear willing to test the matter on a trial basis. In fact, for end-users who believe the ERM process can yield benefits, a logical approach involves implementation of trial programs within specific departments or units (e.g., a targeted trial before broader implementation across the entire firm). Not only is this approach cheaper and more efficient, it can reveal possible pitfalls (e.g., organizational stumbling-blocks, measurement/aggregation problems, and so forth) at any early stage. This type of approach is particularly suitable for companies that lack centralized risk functions.

Companies that feature integrated risk departments responsible for all dimensions of financial and operating risk may move directly toward broader test programs. In fact, firms such as Danone, Dell Computer, United Grain Growers, Honeywell (prior to its acquisition by Allied Signal), Mobil Oil, and others, have followed just such an approach. For example, Honeywell (which we consider in the case study below) was an ERM pioneer, introducing its consolidated risk program in 1997. United Grain Growers of Winnipeg was another early adopter, working with insurance broker Wills in the late 1990s to identify, analyze, and manage dozens of operating/financial risks impacting its business. It eventually prioritized several of the most important (e.g., credit, weather, environment, inventory, and grain price/volume), considered a variety of solutions (including those involving separate weather derivatives and vertical insurance covers), and settled on a 3-year integrated program from Swiss Re (incorporating risk coverage of credit, weather, inventory, grain, and standard P&C exposures).

CASE STUDY

Honeywell's integrated program

In July 1997 the board of directors of Honeywell, a global developer and manufacturer of space avionics systems and controls for heating/air-conditioning systems, gave executive management permission to proceed with a new ERM program, one of the first of its kind in the corporate world. Honeywell's ERM program was the end result of more than two years of intensive analytical work and internal corporate restructuring, and was based on a stated goal of managing corporate risks more cost-efficiently. The underlying analytical work and program structuring was performed by Honeywell's newly consolidated treasury risk management team, insurance broker Marsh, accounting firm Deloitte and Touche, and insurer AIG (who also provided the relevant covers).

---

[6] The range of potential political risk coverage is considerable, and can include protection against loss from sovereign confiscation or expropriation, license cancellation, embargo, forced abandonment, contract abrogation (unilateral termination, non-performance), war, discriminatory actions, currency inconvertibility, repatriation/capital controls, and so on.

[7] This might include protection against losses arising from failure to obtain new venture-licensing agreements or government/regulatory approvals.

At the time Honeywell started to draw up plans for the program, the organization featured 50 000 workers in 95 countries and generated costs and revenues in various currencies. Its general approach to risk management was extremely decentralized, with responsibilities divided among the groups noted in Table 10.1. In fact, one of the company's secondary goals in implementing an ERM program was to consolidate its risk function in order to reduce duplication and eliminate communication problems.

Table 10.1   Risk management responsibilities at Honeywell prior to the ERM program

Risk/peril	Responsible unit
P&C/insurance hazard	Treasury/Insurance Risk Management Group
Currency	Treasury/Financial Risk Management Group
Interest rates	Treasury/Financial Risk Management Group, Capital Markets Group
Credit	Treasury/Financial Risk Management Group, Capital Markets Group
Operating	Business Units
Environmental	Health, Safety and Environment Unit
Technology	Technology Department
Legal	Office of General Counsel
Regulatory	Office of Government Affairs

Pre-ERM program risk strategy

The Treasury Group had two units responsible for insurance and financial risks. Traditional insurance risks (P&C, liability, environmental) were covered by separate, annual policies (one for each major insurable risk exposure). Each policy featured its own deductible, up to $6m in size, and each loss was subject to separate retention, implying new deductibles for each occurrence. Much of the company's financial risk management was focused on currency exposure. Since Honeywell operated in many countries, it was exposed to foreign exchange transaction and translation losses. Transaction risk arises from individual corporate deals that generate a spot or future currency exposure and can be managed (as Honeywell did) with spot and forward currency hedges. Translation risk arises from the conversion of reported earnings from an offshore subsidiary back into a home currency (in Honeywell's case, dollars). The company had traditionally managed this risk by estimating future earnings in different offshore operations and then hedging a percentage of that amount through at-the-money currency options. In fact, the centerpiece of the program was an OTC basket option comprising 20 currencies that accounted for 85% of the company's revenues. Based on 3-year forecasts supplied by each business unit, the financial risk management group regularly hedged up to 90% of an upcoming year's estimate through the basket option. For instance, units in the UK, Germany, and Canada – responsible for 40% of group revenues – featured similar weightings in the basket structure. Honeywell paid an average of $5m per year in currency option premiums from the early- to the mid-1990s.

The ERM strategy

With a desire to manage risks more efficiently, reduce costs, and restructure its overall risk management unit, Honeywell's senior risk and finance personnel began an analysis focused on earnings volatility and the cost of risk (which it defined much as we have in Chapter 2, i.e., retained loss costs plus expenses plus insurance premium plus option premium), with an initial emphasis on savings that could be achieved by combining all of the individual insurance risks into a single platform. In fact, this had been Honeywell's experience with the basket option, where it received favorable pricing on the package of 20 currencies. The company also reviewed its approach to retentions, where the firm had traditionally used historical loss records to estimate one-year expected losses for each risk. By using simulation techniques to estimate expected losses and losses net of protection payments under different deductibles and caps, the firm generated a wider range of potential alternatives. (Honeywell's managers favored setting retention levels so that the firm faced a 45% probability of having a loss greater than the retention level.) The next step was to determine the effects of combining the insurance risks and the currency translation risk over a multi-year horizon (rather than the one-year horizon it had been using). The company constructed a probability distribution of aggregate portfolio risks and parameters (e.g., μ and σ), assuming no correlation between currencies and insurance exposures. During the initial stages of the process, Marsh helped the company with the mechanics of the currency translation and insurance hazards, while Honeywell managers began consolidating the risk function – starting with joint meetings and communication, and heading eventually toward a full cross-function integration.

After working for more than a year, the team created a new "Integrated Risk Management" program that replaced the previous "piecemeal" approach. Honeywell's risk management team viewed this as the foundation of an ERM program that would grow over time, with risks such as commodity prices, weather, and so on, to be added as needed. The final ERM program included:

- multi-year cover of insurance risks and currency translation risk under a master insurance policy underwritten by AIG;
- single annual deductible of $30m (approximately equal to the firm's expected losses on the portfolio);
- specific coverage under the master policy for general liability, global product liability, global property and business interruption, global fidelity, global employee crime, D&O, global political risk, global ocean marine, US auto liability, US workers compensation, and currency translation;
- a currency translation basket based on specific strike prices weighted by currency contribution, with strikes reset every year based on the weighted average of the preceding year's monthly spot rate;
- maximum payout cap of $100m over 2 $\frac{1}{2}$ years;
- excess annual cover of $200m for select covers.

The annual savings through the consolidation of risks was estimated at 15–20% per year. In particular, the company's cost of risk declined from $38.7m prior to the program to $34.6m under the new program, as summarized in Table 10.2.

Table 10.2 Honeywell's cost of risk

	Before ERM program ($ m)	With ERM program ($ m)
Expected retained loss	27.5	26.1
Combined premium (insurance and currency)	11.2	8.5
Total cost of risk	38.7	34.6

Honeywell retained the ERM program for a number of years, believing that it provided the requisite cost savings and efficiencies; a full integration of the once-disparate risk management functions into a single core team was a beneficial by-product. However, in 1999 Honeywell was acquired by defense company Allied Signal, which eventually dismantled the firm's pioneering ERM program in order to manage exposures within its own established framework. Nevertheless, the work performed by Honeywell, Marsh and AIG, and the company's willingness to discuss its approach publicly, has undoubtedly been of help in promoting similar programs at other firms.

As noted, an end-use company must monitor the progress of its ERM program over time to ensure that it is delivering the required coverage benefits, costs savings, and efficiencies; when it is not, adjustments have to be made. In more extreme cases, the entire program may have to be abandoned, which can occur if the firm can no longer obtain desired cost reductions, exposures become uninsurable, suppliers cut back on capacity, or the firm goes through a radical change. In fact, some former ERM users have abandoned their programs in the face of corporate restructuring (e.g., acquisition by, or merger with, another company).[8] Others, of course, continue to operate (and even expand) their ERM programs as a result of the financial and efficiency benefits they obtain (Union Carbide, Mead, Sun Microsystems, and others have renewed their programs repeatedly). Again, the main point to stress is that performance monitoring is an essential element of the ERM process; integrated management of risks does not end when a specific program is created – the process actually commences.

---

[8] In addition to the cancellation of Honeywell's program after the Allied Signal acquisition, Mobil Oil abandoned its program after merging with Exxon.

11

Prospects for Growth

Throughout this book we have discussed general aspects of the ART market, and focused on specific mechanisms that can be used to manage traditional financial and operating risks, as well as "new" risks and those that have previously been regarded as uninsurable. In this chapter we summarize our material by considering the market's growth prospects. In particular, we focus on drivers of future growth, such as need for companies to access cost-effective risk solutions and alternative channels of capacity, to diversify exposures, and to cope with changing regulatory schema. We also consider barriers that might slow or impede growth, such as organizational complexities, educational difficulties, pricing challenges, capacity/supply problems, and contractual issues. We then summarize the outlook for the individual products and channels we have discussed in Parts II and III, and consider how different classes of end-users might impact demand. We conclude with some thoughts on future convergence.

11.1 DRIVERS OF GROWTH

Growth in the ART market in future years is likely to be fuelled by many of the same elements that brought the market to its state of development in the early part of the millennium. These, as we have discussed in Chapter 2, center on creating instruments, conduits, and overall solutions that help firms to:

- maximize enterprise value;
- cope with market cycles;
- access new sources of risk capacity;
- diversify exposures;
- cope with forces of regulation and deregulation.

We re-emphasize that *all* of the factors that led to the development and expansion of the ART market between the 1960s and the millennium will remain important to future expansion. However, the overarching driver of growth over the next few years is likely to come from stronger demand for risk capacity. As companies in other nations join the mainstream of industrialization and become more sophisticated in the management of their risks, they will require more risk transfer than ever before. The same is true for companies operating in industrialized nations that have not yet taken an active stance toward corporate risk management. Demand may also be driven by the incidence of one or more major catastrophes. While damaging cat events have occurred at regular intervals in recent decades, the "mega" catastrophe – a hurricane or earthquake costing $50bn to $100bn – has, fortunately, not occurred (the clash losses of 9/11, resulting in direct/indirect losses of $30–50bn, remain the closest to testing this scenario). However, should such a disastrous eventuality occur, the pool of available risk capacity would be placed under extreme stress, and would require mobilization of capacity from multiple sources/vehicles. Future demand will also come from the growing need to manage exposures that are becoming part of the "mainstream". For instance, risks associated with technological exposures (technological business interruption, cybercrime), intellectual property rights exposures (copyright infringement, fraud), and so on, may play a more important role in the risk management market of the future, absorbing some amount of available capacity. The combined forces of demand will, at any point in time, render traditional risk solutions, such as full insurance, insufficient. Reverting to our discussion of supply/demand, we know that an excess of demand drives up prices – meaning that the use of alternative mechanisms to fill a risk capacity shortfall at an economically viable price should expand. In fact, the market cycles that have previously characterized the insurance industry may begin to shorten as a result of lower barriers to entry (e.g., ability to quickly mobilize capital and establish a reinsurance company) and growing availability of risk substitutes such as those we have considered in the book. It should be clear that future demand for risk capacity to cover non-cat and cat events will have to be met through traditional insurance and financial risk management instruments, and also through current and as-yet undeveloped mechanisms of the ART market.

11.2   BARRIERS TO GROWTH

Although the drivers of future growth are strong, they will not go unchallenged. In fact, the sector faces considerable hurdles that will have to be overcome if truly efficient risk transfer and financing is to occur. Some of the most notable barriers to growth, which will impact both intermediaries and end-users, include:

- organizational complexities;
- educational difficulties;
- pricing challenges;
- capacity/supply problems;
- contractual differences.

We have noted on several occasions that companies have greater opportunities for cost savings and efficiencies when they can integrate aspects of their risk management functions. The creation of logical risk management processes requires some degree of internal unity. Indeed, any framework that operates on the basis of "silos" and incremental decision-making is unlikely to lead to the most optimal or comprehensive solution, such as those that can be accessed through the ART market. But reorganizing risk functions is a complicated task. For many, it is difficult to undo years of corporate practice. As the change in mindset and the costs associated with restructuring may be politically and financially unpalatable, continuation of the status quo is an easy solution. If internal barriers preventing consolidation of risk management function/process cannot be overcome, the turn toward efficient ART market solutions will be slowed. An associated hurdle comes from the educational difficulties associated with the marketplace. The risk management sector in general, and the ART market in particular, demands knowledge of firmwide risks (identification, decomposition, interdependencies, quantification) and knowledge of instruments, channels, and solutions that can serve to address firmwide risks. Educating corporate end-users on both fronts is a challenging task that often falls to insurance brokers, banking specialists, financial advisors, and so forth. It is also a continuous process, as end-users must be kept abreast of changing regulations, market conditions, pricing issues, and solutions. The time and expenses associated with educational efforts can therefore slow advances and activity in ART-based risk management (e.g., an ERM program might take one or two years to investigate, analyze, discuss, and develop; the analysis and issuance of an ILS, 6 to 12 months, and so forth).

Pricing challenges present another barrier, on at least two fronts: absolute levels and complexity. We have already indicated that ART-based solutions often feature cost advantages that can give corporate risk managers the economic justification needed to participate. In some instances, however, absolute pricing advantages are not apparent. Depending on the type of cover and the specific market cycle, an end-use client may not be able to achieve the desired cost savings, forcing a return to traditional methods of risk management, including incremental retention or insurance; this, in turn, can lead to additional managerial and administrative inefficiencies. Pricing complexity is another challenge. While the behavior of many types of operating and financial risks is by now well understood (and manageable through standard actuarial statistics or financial mathematics) the same is not necessarily true for complex, multidimensional risks and new/uninsurable risks, which often have unique properties. Terrorist risk serves as one example of this; prior to the events of 9/11, the process for valuing such exposures was based largely on conventional insurance techniques. In the aftermath of the tragic event new approaches to valuing and pricing such risks have been sought; no wholly satisfactory approach yet exists, but some have turned to the use of cat models to attempt to value such exposures. While new pricing techniques are developed and tested for the cadre of new and unique risks, growth necessarily slows.

Capacity and supply problems are continual issues in the risk management markets. While demand for risk capacity is an important driver of ART growth, the growth can be stifled by supply bottlenecks or contraction, due to factors such as regulatory action, onset of catastrophic losses, poor underwriting or financial performance by providers, superior investment alternatives, and so on. One of the main functions of the ART market is, of course, to supply additional risk capacity when traditional mechanisms cannot do so. However, since many of the players in the ART market are also involved in conventional insurance and financial dealings, there may be instances where a downturn affects the traditional and ART sectors simultaneously. Regulatory, legal, or accounting barriers can also impeded delivery of capacity. Finally, we note that contractual differences between participants can prevent, or at least slow, growth. Since the ART market bridges different sectors, many with unique accounting rules and legal/regulatory treatment, there may be occasions where distinct requirements lead to extra costs and a slowdown in activity. To reiterate one simple example, we noted that differences exist between swap and insurance documentation and definitions of default and insurable events. While these gaps can help to promote arbitrage activities and generate growth opportunities, they can also slow the risk management process (and may even dissuade participation). In general, even though ART risk-financing solutions and OTC derivatives can often be used to create similar risk management solutions, they are governed by different regimes and are thus subject to additional barriers.

There are clearly various forces at work in both promoting and constraining growth in the ART market; these are summarized in Figure 11.1. Ultimately, however, it is our belief that a combination of increasingly dynamic corporate risk management processes, deregulation, and end-user sophistication will lead to greater demand for risk management solutions generally, and ART market solutions specifically. Accessing/providing capacity through any means possible in order to give all participants the benefits they seek would appear to be the overriding driver of the coming years.

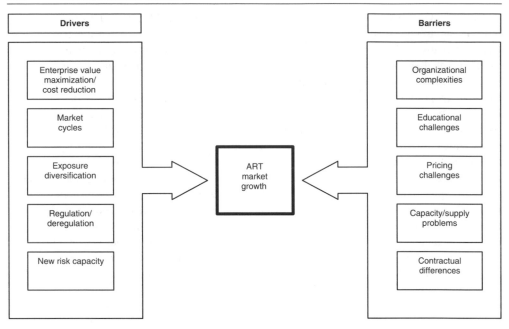

Figure 11.1   ART Market Drivers and Barriers

11.3   MARKET SEGMENTS

To consider the growth prospects of the ART market in more specific terms we divide our discussion into the broad categories of instruments, channels, and solutions that we have discussed earlier in the book, including finite structures, captives, multi-risk products, capital markets issues, derivatives, and ERM programs.

11.3.1   Finite structures

Finite structures – such as loss portfolio transfers, adverse development cover, retrospective aggregate development covers, financial reinsurance – are an important part of corporate risk management and promise to remain so in coming years. The very characteristics and advances that have popularized the structures over the past two decades – including specification of optimum levels of financing versus transfer, reduction of costs through larger retentions, sharing of returns via the experience account, stabilization of cash flows, and lengthening of transfer/ financing terms – are tangible benefits that are likely to attract further participants. Indeed, we have already seen that many companies prefer to finance, rather than transfer, portions of their exposures, and any holistic approach to risk management must feature an option that permits efficient financing.

Although there has been concern in some sectors that finite growth might be stifled by changes in accounting rules or negative perception regarding the active "smoothing" by companies of their cash flows and earnings, such fears appear to be misplaced. Even after the extensive corporate scandals of the early millennium (some involving accounting deception, fraudulent earnings manipulation, and so forth), no permanent fallout or gravitation away from finite policies occurred – primarily because the instruments themselves are seen as a legitimate way of coping with volatile cash flows and injecting certainty into corporate operations rather than a tool to fabricate a misleading financial picture.

Growth prospects for finite structures must be regarded as strong, both in the corporate sector (as finite insurance) and the insurance sector (as finite reinsurance).

11.3.2 Captives

The growth record of the captive market, which spans more than 40 years, provides ample evidence that the vehicles have become an important and accepted element of the ART market and corporate risk management. Again, there is every indication that the expansion will continue; the turn toward a greater amount of self-insurance and retention is increasingly a feature of the corporate risk management sector. The very fact that new offshore centers have passed captive legislation to allow development of local or regional operations hints at even stronger growth in the future (particularly as new companies in emerging nations begin to participate more actively in the risk management process). Within the general group of captives, the prospects for protected cell companies and rent-a-captives must be regarded as very strong. Many companies have demonstrated that they prefer to pay a fee for the use of a vehicle that allows them to reap many of the same benefits as full ownership, without the costs or administrative burdens. In addition, securitization and derivative-based activity, which often flow through offshore entities, continues to grow rapidly, meaning that PCCs and RACs remain attractive alternatives. Further growth may be spurred by clarification of tax issues. Although some countries have done a good job in delineating applicable tax treatment, certain "gray areas" continue to exist (particularly for pure captives); greater clarity will undoubtedly help the matter and possibly lead to additional usage.

Growth prospects for captives generally, and PCCs/RACs specifically, are very strong; growth in captives outside the traditional centers (e.g., Bermuda, Guernsey) also appears to be promising.

11.3.3 Multi-risk products

The outlook for multi-risk products, including multiple peril policies and multiple trigger instruments, can be divided by sector. Integrated multiple peril contracts, which have existed for decades, are likely to expand in future years, but perhaps only gradually. In fact, although they are an accepted mechanism for managing portfolios of similar risks (e.g., P&C or liability), they may lose ground to more comprehensive ERM programs, which group disparate risks and use the most efficient vehicles/instruments. Integrated policies are much more limited in scope, meaning that companies seeking to manage a portfolio of corporate risks (and spending the time and money to do so) may find it more beneficial to move directly to an ERM program.

Multiple trigger contracts, in contrast, should feature strong end-user demand. The relative pricing efficiencies that can be obtained have already been well demonstrated in the marketplace and many transactions have been arranged (particularly in the energy sector). Recognition of the savings that can be achieved by basing risk protection on multiple contingencies has become more widely broadcast and insurance brokers and financial intermediaries actively market such instruments to a growing base of constituents; more work needs to be done, of course, to expand demand outside of the energy sector.

Growth prospects for multiple peril policies might therefore be seen as moderate, while prospects for multiple triggers appear stronger.

11.3.4   Capital markets issues

We have noted earlier that insurance-based securitization efforts, particularly in the catastrophic risk sector, feature growing momentum. The large number of issues successfully launched in the market over the past few years suggests that issuers and investors have become comfortable with the risk mitigation and investment opportunities that are available and realize the value in being able to turn to another mechanism for managing risk exposures and investment portfolios. The establishment of a core base of dedicated ILS investors that is prepared to absorb available supply lends further support to this notion. Further growth will also come from continued improvements in the risk analytics developed by third-party vendors (which are essential for issuers, investors, and rating agencies seeking to understand risk/return tradeoff scenarios).

While the bulk of activity in the medium term is likely to remain focused on the traditional cat sector, there are no specific barriers that should impede growth in the non-cat risk sector. Activity in weather bonds, residual value securitizations, trade credit securitization, and so forth, appears ready to expand as corporate end-users seek alternative mechanisms to shed their risks, and as investors attempt to find new, uncorrelated investment opportunities with attractive yields. Although it seems unlikely that non-cat securitizations will challenge the dominance of the cat ILS market, more meaningful, and steady, issuance should appear. The effort, however, will demand considerable work by brokers, financial intermediaries, and third-party specialists regarding education and analytics. There is also no particular reason why more corporate issuers cannot access the market directly. While the majority of deals coming to market since the 1990s have been floated by insurance companies (as a substitute for reinsurance cover), the corporate sector can do the same (as a replacement for insurance cover); several new direct corporate issues have appeared in recent years and more should be expected.

In general terms, the ILS market should begin to feature deals with more lower-rated and multi-peril tranches, larger equity tranches (in order to adhere to SPE non-consolidation rules) and longer terms. There is also likely to be greater issuance of single tranche, multiple peril deals (which, as we have noted, can be complex to value and will demand greater education efforts), and continued migration from indemnity triggers to index/parametric triggers.

The growth prospects for cat-based ILS over the medium term are strong; non-cat ILS issuance will expand but seems likely to remain modest for some years.

11.3.5   Contingent capital

Contingent capital, like insurance, has the advantage of removing funding uncertainties that might otherwise cause a company to experience financial distress. Despite the fact that they offer greater *ex-ante* certainty, they are also impeded by structural constraints, including the timing and conditions under which drawdown or issuance can occur, and the amount of credit risk assumed with the capital provider. These factors, together with potential costs, mean that contingent capital facilities have failed to attract the largest possible number of end-users. Actual usage has been relatively modest in the past years, although some mechanisms, such as contingent lines of credit and contingent surplus notes, appear to have drawn a steady base of users. Flexibility regarding drawdown/issuance, and syndication of credit exposure among a larger number of intermediaries could help to spur additional activity in the market.

Growth prospects for the broad group of contingent capital structures are likely to remain moderate over the medium-term.

11.3.6 Insurance derivatives

The general class of insurance derivatives can be considered along two dimensions: exchange versus OTC and non-cat versus cat. The greatest successes have come in the OTC and exchange-traded non-cat weather market. Since the derivative markets operate, to some degree, on the basis of a "self-fulfilling cycle" (i.e., liquidity generates more liquidity) the non-cat weather market is likely to continue growing in coming years. A broader base of end-users, recognizing the need to actively manage weather risks just as any other operating exposure, has started taking advantage of the benefits offered by the instruments. As more players enter the market, volume increases, spreads tighten, and cost advantages become clearer. The fact that transactional temperature data is becoming more readily available around the world, and new reference cities are being used for both exchange and OTC contracts, provides further proof that the market is attracting a much wider base of interest. Furthermore, the sector features a natural base of end-use clients on both sides of the market, an essential ingredient for sustained growth.

The other end of the spectrum – cat contracts in the OTC and exchange markets – faces far greater challenges. Cat derivatives have not gathered a meaningful following and organized efforts to mobilize trading have not yet succeeded. Contracts and planned exchanges have been abandoned for a number of reasons, for example, poor contract construction (including difficulties creating appropriate indexes without an excess of basis risk), high trading costs, and one-sided participation. Exchange-based cat contracts have been unable to offer end-users any compelling financial reasons for participation – indeed, excellent coverage exists through insurance, reinsurance, ILSs and contingent capital – and it seems unlikely that they will be reintroduced in the near future. The prospects are somewhat more positive in the OTC cat market, though activity is based primarily on matching up insurers with the exposures they wish to exchange in order to rebalance their portfolios; this business is not totally comparable to a standard OTC financial derivative market, which features two-sided business flowing through intermediaries, and a general balance of speculative and hedge activity. The non-cat and cat derivative marketplaces are analytically intensive, meaning that advances in analytics, data, and technology will influence future growth. The markets will also depend on the active participation of brokers and financial intermediaries, who will have to educate potential end-users about the advantages and prospects of insurance derivatives.

Growth prospects for insurance derivatives are decidedly mixed: the non-cat weather derivative market looks bright, and should continue to reflect growth in volume, expansion of reference cities, and a deepening of liquidity. Cat-based efforts are likely to remain illiquid and underdeveloped for some time and are unlikely to provide a viable alternative in managing cat exposures.

11.3.7 Enterprise risk management

The ERM movement has advanced at a relatively steady pace since the late 1990s. The "active" (though transactional/incremental) approach to risk management, which is increasingly evident across companies, industries, and countries, is virtually a requirement in the corporate and financial world of the twenty-first century: prudent behavior and regulations help focus on the need for risk management, and there appear to be very few firms, certainly in industrialized nations, that are not engaged in some basic form of risk control. This, as we have mentioned, is an essential step toward more ERM activity. Once company executives and directors recognize

Table 11.1   Growth prospects for ART mechanisms/solutions

ART mechanism/solution	Medium-term growth prospects
Finite risk policies	Strong
Captives	Strong, particularly for protected cell companies and rent-a-captives
Multi-risk products	Moderate for multiple peril policies; strong for multiple trigger products
Capital markets issues	Strong for the cat-based ILS sector; moderate for the non-cat ILS sector
Contingent capital	Moderately strong
Insurance derivatives	Strong for the listed/OTC temperature sector; weak to moderate for other sectors
Enterprise risk management	Strong, particularly for larger companies

the need for active risk management and define a risk strategy and tolerance, it becomes simpler to move toward a firmwide consideration of risks.

Some companies with complex risk profiles have started managing their risks in an integrated manner, but the trend is far from uniform. Various surveys seem to indicate that many corporate executives in North America, Europe, and Asia embrace the idea of integrated risk management, but most remain rooted in the theoretical/conceptual, rather than practical, stage. Many appear to believe that ERM is logical and potentially quite beneficial, but have not yet taken steps toward implementation. Indeed, it is not difficult to understand their hesitation. The pre-implementation steps of the ERM process are complicated and rigorous, and demand investment, resources, analysis, and even structural change. For some this is daunting (potential benefits notwithstanding), so the process can remain stalled at the conceptual level.

This may remain true for several years, although further growth might be fuelled by stronger participation from insurance brokers and other corporate risk management advisers – teams that can provide the tools and expertise to help a company to move through the required stages. (While some brokers already provide such services and have witnessed an upturn in business in recent years, additional work remains to be done in this area.) The corporate sector requires more education on ERM, and greater assistance in identifying and decomposing risks, quantifying alternative solutions, and creating sensible and flexible platforms; it may also require specific help in restructuring internal risk management functions.

Growth prospects for ERM must be regarded as strong over the medium term, as costs and operating efficiencies undoubtedly exist for many potential end-users. However, such growth is likely to remain centered with larger companies with more complicated portfolios of risk for the foreseeable future.

Table 11.1 summarizes the medium term (3–7 year) prospects for major classes of ART mechanisms/solutions.

The use of any of these instruments/channels/solutions will, as we have noted, depend on the specific goals of end-users and the relative advantages, disadvantages, costs, and benefits that are offered. Drawing on our discussion from previous chapters we summarize various characteristics of major ART mechanisms in Table 11.2, including the ability for each mechanism to reduce moral hazard, increase the level of insurability, substitute risk transfer with risk financing, and reduce dependency on hard/soft market cycles.

Table 11.2   Summary features of ART market mechanisms

	Ability to reduce moral hazard	Ability to expand insurability	Ability to substitute transfer for financing	Ability to reduce dependence on insurance cycles
Captives	Yes	Yes	Yes	Some
Finite programs	Yes	Yes	Yes	Yes
Multiple peril policies	Yes	Yes	No	Yes
Multiple trigger structures	Yes	Yes	No	Yes
Contingent capital	Yes	Yes	Yes	Some
Capital markets issues	Yes	Yes	Yes	Some
Insurance derivatives	Yes	Yes	Yes	Yes

11.4   END-USER PROFILES

Growth in the ART market over the medium term will be driven by demand from industrial and financial companies seeking tools and solutions to manage their risk exposures. Obviously, not every company has the same risk management needs or goals, so demand will vary. Accordingly, we can segment end-users into broad categories – basic, intermediate, advanced – and consider how each might influence demand for ART over the medium term.

- *Basic* corporate risk managers are those that require only fundamental coverage of risks. They are focused primarily on simple risk management tools and need (or want) very little complexity in their strategies. While they have recognized the need to identify and manage their risks, they prefer to do so in the most elemental way possible. This group might include small or middle-market companies that are still limited in operating scope and balance sheet size; their risk exposures are likely to be relatively narrow, and quite predictable. Their primary goal is likely to center on protecting against financial distress, and their demand for risk management services will be based on mechanisms that permit greater retention, including policies with higher deductibles and a captive (or a cell in a PCC/RAC), as well as those that provide excess layer protection against catastrophe.
- *Intermediate* corporate risk managers are likely to be medium-sized or large companies that are exposed to a much broader range of perils, thus requiring greater access to innovative solutions. They are almost certain to be active risk managers interested in a more comprehensive approach to exposure management – but one focused on transfer and hedging with only a small amount of financing. Their primary goals are likely to relate to avoiding financial distress and lowering the cost of risk. They might therefore use captives or cells, multiple peril policies, basic finite structures (e.g., paid loss retrospective policies), financial derivatives and possibly contingent capital or excess layer coverage for low-frequency/high-severity events. In addition, since their operations are larger than those of the basic group, their absolute dollar demand for coverage will be commensurately higher.
- *Advanced* corporate risk managers are obviously the most sophisticated of the three groups (and may, in fact, be more sophisticated than many providers – i.e., their solutions are likely

to be arranged/executed with one of a small number of leading-edge intermediaries). This group is apt to include medium to large multinational companies that have actively managed risks for many years; they are almost certainly exposed to a broad array of risks and may be very interested in managing earnings and cash flows through a combination of retention, transfer, and financing. They will make use of the broadest array of ART instruments and solutions, including captives, finite policies, financial derivatives, multiple trigger products, contingent capital structures, and ILSs. They may also consolidate and coordinate aspects of their program through comprehensive ERM platforms. Given their size, their dollar demand for risk cover is likely to be quite significant.

In all three cases there is likely to be a greater focus on loss control/loss prevention. Many firms have discovered the wisdom of implementing all necessary precautions in order to minimize hazards; and in many cases the upfront investment is easily justified in the NPV framework. Also, as noted, all three are likely to be heavily attuned to retentions and use of captives. It is by now well known that small, frequently occurring risks can be managed most cost-effectively through a retention program. There is also a good chance that end-users will be less "exclusive" in their choice of intermediaries/counterparties. While financial relationships are obviously critical for many end-users, so, too, are the cost efficiencies, premium services, and credit risk diversification benefits that a firm obtains by using multiple providers. Those that are able to provide solutions on a creative and competitive basis – whether they come from the insurance or banking sector – are likely to be the most successful.

Although each of these groups has – and will continue to have – distinct needs, all are important for growth within the risk management markets generally, and the ART market specifically. For instance, because small companies prefer to use simpler solutions and require lower absolute dollar coverage levels, it does not mean they should not be considered an integral part of the marketplace and an essential component of market demand. To be sure, as small firms increase in both size and sophistication, they may migrate toward larger, and more intricate, ART market solutions.

11.5   FUTURE CONVERGENCE

The ART market exists, in part, because of the convergence forces we mentioned at the beginning of the book. In the search to create the best possible risk solutions for end-users and attractive investment alternatives for investors, intermediaries from different sectors create products/mechanisms that play to their strengths. As they offer solutions in their own unique ways, they draw once-distinct markets closer together, and permit risk exposures and risk solutions to become more fungible – the XOL layer versus the ILS, the full insurance policy versus the contingent capital facility, the SPE versus the PCC cell, and so forth. When convergence reaches its final state, the end-user becomes indifferent to the nature of the capacity provider/intermediary or, indeed, to the source of the risk solution. In the end game a client should simply be able to contact a broker or intermediary and request a risk management solution to address a defined corporate strategy. The end-user's primary interests will be that (a) the solution is effective in allowing it to fulfill its risk strategy and (b) it is the most efficient and cost-effective method available. Apart from these factors, the firm should be indifferent to the nature of the solution or the characteristics of the provider (except for possible credit risk issues).

If deregulation continues across industry sectors and countries in future years, there is little doubt that the convergence movement will deepen. Although regulatory barriers certainly exist, deregulation in most sectors of the financial and insurance markets is by now an accepted fact. Indeed, the move toward deregulation – which we consider to be any act that allows institutions to participate, directly or indirectly, in another industry – is sufficiently well established, and has enough political and industry support that institutions from insurance, banking, and securities are virtually certain to encroach on one another's territory. Each of these groups may offer products outside their traditional boundaries, or operate subsidiaries that do so. Deregulation-based convergence does not, of course, mean that intermediaries need to be financial monoliths based on the "bancassurance" or "financial supermarket" model. This is certainly one structure, but is not the only one. Convergence can exist equally through banking, insurance, or specialist institutions that shun the broader approach in favor of more targeted implementation. Thus, an investment bank that is an active issuer of capital markets instruments in the financial sector may apply the same techniques, pricing, and distribution to the issuance of ILS; or, a bank that actively grants short-term credit and long-term loans across sectors may grant contingent lines of credit that can only be accessed in the event of an insurable loss; or, a monoline insurer that insures single obligor credit risk may offer basket credit protection to a bank through an insurance policy that resembles a financial credit derivative. In each of these examples convergence forces are at work, but are confined to the expertise and organizational structure of the institutions.

The political, regulatory, and industrial commitment to the harmonization of rules, which we consider to be distinct from deregulation, is not as clear. Thus, an institution might be allowed to participate in a new market (deregulation), but on terms that are specific to the institution or industry (harmonization). Harmonization of rules and regulations, so that institutions from different industries face the same financial, operating, and legal requirements, is not especially advanced across sectors or countries. Despite efforts by regulatory authorities and industry groups to promote some degree of uniformity, considerable cross-industry differences exist in the treatment of accounting, capital, funding, revenue recognition, legal documentation, and so forth. Indeed, complete harmonization may actually remove some of the growth drivers that have helped to expand the ART market. Regulatory tax and accounting arbitrage, which fuels opportunities for different institutions to participate and generate profits, exists as a result of differences in rules (i.e., lack of harmonization). For instance, banks and insurers have different approaches to pricing credit risk as a result of different capital rules; this lack of standardization means that there is an opportunity for banks to buy credit protection from insurers – both can participate, but must follow different rules. If the capital and accounting treatment of credit risk is identical for banks and insurance companies, and both choose to price exposures in a similar manner, the arbitrage incentives that act as market drivers are removed. A purely level "playing field" can remove incentives to participate and can actually slow growth.

Ultimately, of course, deregulation and harmonization are related. Greater deregulation is bound to lead to greater harmonization, and regulators must be aware of this fact. A fully deregulated market that features different rules and regulations for institutions that are essentially performing the same function can lead to inefficiencies. When deregulation and harmonization are complete, arbitrage opportunities disappear and products, services, and capacity are then provided on a purely competitive basis (e.g., the lowest price/best service wins the business). When the final stage is reached the end-user becomes relatively indifferent to the nature of the service provider; it can source its finite policy, ERM program, insurance derivative, or ILS issue from any institution equipped to handle the business. Of course, competitive advantages will remain in force for years to come, and traditional pockets of expertise should continue to feature in the marketplace. Thus, the investment bank is still the institution most capable of distributing ILS, the insurance company is the best equipped to write finite risk policies, and so on. Over time, however, complete convergence should lead to the efficient delivery of all financial and risk services by any institution that is so qualified.

In concluding this work it only remains to stress that the ART market is dynamic and flexible, and is capable of providing risk solutions in a manner that helps to contain exposure and maximize value. It is, nevertheless, a constantly changing market, and is subject to continuous revisions and enhancements, which means that the ART market of the twenty-first century should continue to adapt to reflect the new requirements and realities of the global financial and economic systems.

Glossary

Since the ART market contains a reasonable amount of technical language and jargon, we have included a glossary as a general reference for readers.

Adverse development cover   a finite insurance contract where the cedant shifts the timing of losses that have already occurred, as well as those that have been incurred but not yet reported. Through the policy the cedant pays a premium for the transfer of losses exceeding an established reserve and receives financing on existing liabilities in excess of that reserve level.

Adverse selection   mispricing of risk as a result of information asymmetries. This occurs when a protection provider cannot clearly distinguish between different classes of risks, and leads to too little or too much supply of risk coverage at a given price.

Agency captive   a captive owned by one or more insurance agents that is used to write cover for a large number of third-party clients.

Aggregate excess of loss   A reinsurance agreement providing the primary insurer with cover for a large number of small losses arising from multiple policies (all occurring in the same year).

Alternative risk transfer (ART)   a product, channel or solution that transfers risk exposures between the insurance and capital markets to achieve specific risk management goals.

Alternative risk transfer (ART) market   the combined risk management marketplace for innovative insurance and capital market solutions.

Attachment method   a process of combining several monoline policies (e.g. separate covers for P&C, general liability, and so on) under a new master agreement.

Attachment point   the level at which an insurer's (or reinsurer's) liability comes into effect under a policy; the liability covers an amount extending from the attachment point to the policy cap.

Balance sheet collateralized debt obligation   a CDO based on assets physically held in an investment or loan portfolio that are sold into a conduit for tranching.

Basis risk   the risk of loss arising from an imperfect match between a loss-making exposure and a compensatory payment, or an underlying exposure and a hedge.

Bermuda transformer   a Class 3 Bermuda insurance company that is authorized to write and purchase insurance/reinsurance; often used by banks to convert derivative instruments into insurance/reinsurance contracts.

Capital market subsidiary   a dedicated unit owned by an insurer/reinsurer that is authorized to deal directly with banks in the derivatives market.

Captive   a risk channel that is used to facilitate a company's own insurance/reinsurance, risk financing or risk transfer strategies; a captive is generally formed as a licensed insurance/reinsurance company and can be controlled by a single owner or multiple owners (or sponsor(s)).

Catastrophe bond   a tradable instrument that securitizes any catastrophic exposure, including earthquake, hurricane, and windstorm.

Catastrophe per occurrence excess of loss   a reinsurance agreement providing the primary insurer with cover for adverse loss experience from an accumulation of catastrophic events; such agreements often have an incremental deductible and coinsurance.

Catastrophe reinsurance swap   a synthetic financial transaction that exchanges a commitment fee for a contingent sum payable in the event of a catastrophic loss.

Cedant   a party that transfers, or cedes, risk to another party; also known as an insured or beneficiary.

Central Limit Theorem   a statistical rule that indicates that the distribution of the average outcome approaches the normal distribution as the number of observations gets very large.

Clash loss   a scenario where various insurance lines are impacted by claims simultaneously (e.g. P&C, business interruption, life, and health).

Coinsurance   a 'shared loss' component between cedant and insurer.

Collar   a derivative strategy involving a long call/short put or long put/short call, providing upside or downside protection/exposure (through the long option) at a cheaper price (through premium from the short option).

Collateralized debt obligation (CDO)   a securitized structure that repackages credit-sensitive instruments (such as loans or bonds) into tranches with a variety of risk and payoff profiles; by creating a CDO a bank shifts default risk in its credit portfolio to investors.

Combined ratio   the ratio of paid losses, loss adjustment expenses and underwriting expenses to premiums; if the ratio is greater than 100, insurance business is unprofitable, if it is less than 100 it is profitable.

Commercial general liability (CGL) policy   a multiple peril insurance policy used by firms seeking to cover exposure to various liabilities simultaneously, such as those arising from premises, products, contracts, contingencies, environmental damage, director and officer fiduciary breaches, and so forth.

Commercial umbrella policy   an insurance policy that provides protection for very large exposure amounts (e.g. well in excess of those that might be obtained through a standard P&C policy or a commercial general liability policy); the umbrella policy covers a broad range of insurable risks (i.e. it is multiple peril), but serves as an excess layer facility rather than a first loss cover.

Committed capital facility   funded capital that is arranged in advance of a loss, and typically accessed when two trigger events are breached (i.e., a loss event and lack of cheaper funding alternatives).

Contingency loan   a bank of line of credit that is arranged in advance of a loss and invoked when one or more trigger events occur; unlike a traditional line of credit, the contingency loan is only available for drawdown to cover losses arising from a defined event.

Contingent capital   contractually agreed financing facilities that are made available to a company in the aftermath of a loss event.

Contingent debt   post-loss debt financing triggered by one or more specific events; the class includes committed capital facilities, contingent surplus notes, contingency loans, and guarantees.

Contingent equity   post-loss equity financing triggered by one or more specific events; the class includes loss equity puts and put protected equity.

Contingent surplus notes   a form of contingent securities financing arranged in advance of a loss; securities are issued by an insurer/reinsurer to outside investors via a trust if a predefined loss event occurs.

Convergence   a cross-sector fusion of business activities; insurers and financial institutions participate in each other's markets by creating mechanisms to assume and transfer a variety of insurance and financial risks.

Cost of risk   the implicit or explicit price paid to manage risk exposures, typically comprised of the expected costs of direct and indirect losses arising from retained risks, loss control activities, loss financing activities and risk reduction activities.

Credit risk   the risk of loss should a counterparty fail to perform on its contractual obligations.

Declarations   specific insurance contract terms and attestations contained in a policy.

Deductible   a 'first loss' amount paid by the cedant before the insurer makes a payment; the deductible can also be regarded as a retained risk.

Derivatives   financial agreements – including futures, forwards, options and swaps – that derive their value from a market reference; derivatives can be used to hedge or speculate.

Diversifiable risk   risk that is company-specific, meaning that it can be reduced by holding a portfolio with a large number of obligations/exposures; also known as idiosyncratic risk.

Diversification   a spreading or diffusion of risk exposures, commonly used to lower risk by combining exposures are not related to one another.

Dual trigger   a contract that requires the onset of two events before payout occurs.

Efficient frontier   a boundary defined by portfolios that provide the maximum possible return for a given level of risk.

Enterprise risk management   a risk management process that combines disparate risks, time horizons and instruments into a single, multi-year program of action.

Enterprise value   the sum of a firm's expected future net cash flows, discounted back to the present at an appropriate discount rate (e.g. risk free rate plus relevant risk premium).

Excess of loss (XOL) agreement   a reinsurance arrangement where a reinsurer assumes risks and returns in specific horizontal or vertical layers; depending on the magnitude of losses and the sequence and level of attachment, a reinsurer may or may not face some cession and allocation of losses on each loss event.

Exchange-traded catastrophe insurance derivatives   listed futures and options traded via a formal exchange that reference a variety of catastrophe indexes; early attempts by exchanges such as the Chicago Board of Trade and the Bermuda Exchange to introduce cat futures and options failed to generate sufficient interest.

Exchange-traded temperature derivatives   listed futures and options contracts referencing temperature indexes in specific cities, available on exchanges such as the Chicago Mercantile Exchange and London International Financial Futures Exchange/Euronext.

Exchange-traded derivatives   standardized derivative contracts, traded through an authorized exchange and its clearinghouse, that are subject to standard margin requirements and clearing rules; futures, options and futures options comprise the primary types of exchange-traded contracts.

Expected loss   the expected value of the loss distribution function.

Expected utility   the weighted average utility value (defined as satisfaction from income or wealth) derived from a particular activity.

Expected value   the value that is obtained given certain probabilities of occurrence. Expected value (EV) is determined by multiplying the probability of occurrence times the outcome of an event; in risk management terms this is often summarized as frequency (probability) times severity (outcome), or, $EV = (Probability \times Outcome) + ((1 - Probability) \times Outcome)$.

Experience rated policy   a loss sensitive insurance contract where the insurer charges a premium that is directly related to the cedant's past loss experience: the greater the past losses, the higher the premium.

Experience rating   an insurance premium rate modified by past loss experience.

Facultative reinsurance   any reinsurance transaction that involves a case-by-case review and acceptance of underwriting risks by the reinsurer; the arrangement is often used for large or unique risks.

Fair premium   an insurance premium that covers expected claims and operating and administrative costs, and provides a fair return to suppliers of risk capital; also known as gross rate.

Financial distress   a state of financial weakness that might include a higher cost of capital, poorer supplier terms, lower liquidity, and departure of key personnel.

Financial guarantee   a risk transfer mechanism that also functions as a form of contingent financing by giving the guaranteed party access to funds from the guarantor in the event a loss trigger is breached.

Financial risk   the risk of loss arising from the financial activities of a firm, including credit risk, market risk, and liquidity risk.

Finite quota share   a finite reinsurance agreement where the reinsurer agrees to pays on behalf of the ceding insurer a fixed or variable proportion of claims and expenses as they occur; ceding commissions and investment income from reserves typically cover actual claims but if they are insufficient, the reinsurer funds the shortfall and recoups the difference from the insurer over the life of the contract.

Finite reinsurance   a reinsurance contract with limited risk transfer that a reinsurer makes available to an insurer; the insurer pays premiums into an experience account (upfront or over time) and the reinsurer covers losses under the policy once they exceed the funded amount (up to certain predetermined maximum limits). Finite reinsurance can be written in the form of spread loss, financial quota share, loss portfolio transfers, adverse development covers, funded excess of loss, and aggregate stop loss; also know as financial reinsurance.

Finite risk programs   minimal risk transfer insurance contracts that are generally used to finance, rather than transfer, exposures; they can be structured as retrospective finite programs (encompassing loss portfolio transfers, adverse development cover and retrospective aggregate loss cover) and prospective finite programs.

Fixed trigger   a trigger in an insurance contract that is simply a barrier determining whether or not an event occurs; fixed triggers do not usually impact the value of the contract, they simply indicate whether a contract will pay out.

Fortuitous event   any unforeseen, unexpected, or accidental event.

Forwards   customized off-exchange contracts that permit participants to buy or sell an underlying asset at a predetermined forward price.

Full insurance   an insurance contract providing complete coverage of a risk exposure in exchange for a higher risk premium; it can be considered a maximum risk transfer contract, and is characterized by small deductibles, large policy caps, limited (or no) copay/coinsurance and limited exclusions.

Futures   standardized exchange-traded contracts that enable participants to buy or sell an underlying asset at a predetermined forward price.

Group captive   a captive that is owned by a number of companies and writes insurance cover for all of them; also known as an associate captive or a multi-parent captive.

Hard market   an insurance market cycle where insurers reduce the amount of coverage they are willing to write, causing supply to contract and premiums to rise.

Hazard   an event that creates or increases peril.

Hedging   a process generally associated with risks that are uninsurable through a standard contractual insurance framework, and which typically result in the transfer, rather than reduction, of exposure.

Horizontal layering   an excess of loss agreement where different reinsurers take percentage portions of the same loss layer.

Incurred loss retrospective policy   a loss sensitive insurance contract where the cedant pays an incremental premium during the year based on the insurer's best estimate of losses (e.g., actual losses plus an estimate of future losses).

Indemnity   a central principle of insurance that indicates that the cedant cannot profit from insurance activities; that is, insurance exists to cover a loss, not to generate a speculative profit.

Indemnity contract   an insurance contract that covers actual losses sustained by cedant.

Indemnity trigger   a trigger on an insurance-linked security where the suspension of interest and/or principal occurs when actual losses sustained by the issuer in a pre-defined segment of business reach a certain level.

Index trigger   a trigger on an insurance-linked security where the suspension of interest and/or principal occurs when the value of a recognized third-party index reaches a certain threshold.

Insurable interest   proof that the cedant has suffered an economic loss once a defined loss event occurs; an essential element for a valid insurance contract.

Insurance contract   an agreement between two parties (the insurer as protection provider and the cedant as protection purchaser) that exchanges an *ex-ante* premium for an *ex-post* claim, with no ability to readjust the claim amount once it has been agreed.

Insurance-linked securities (ILS)   securities referencing insurance risks, issued in order to transfer exposures and create additional risk capacity. An insurance or reinsurance company issues securities through a special purpose reinsurer and bases repayment of interest and/or principal on losses arising from defined insurance events; if losses exceed a pre-determined threshold, the insurer/reinsurer is no longer required to pay investors interests; if structured with a non-principal protected tranche all, or a portion, of the principal can be deferred or eliminated as well.

Investment credit program   a tax-advantaged loss sensitive insurance program that contains elements of financing and transfer.

Large deductible policy   a loss sensitive insurance contract that features a deductible that is typically much greater than one that might be found on a fixed premium, full insurance contract; the cedant retains, and thus finances, a much larger amount of risk and pays a smaller premium to the insurer.

Large line capacity   the ability to write a large loss exposure on a single policy.

Law of Large Numbers   a statistical rule that indicates that as the number of participants gets very large, the average outcome approaches the expected value.

Life acquisition cost securitization   an insurance-linked security that transfers to the capital markets the upfront costs associated with writing life policies to the securities markets.

Loss control   a risk management technique where a firm takes necessary precautions to reduce the threat of a particular risk (also known as loss prevention).

Loss equity put   a contingent capital structure that results in the issuance of new shares in the event a pre-defined trigger is breached.

Loss financing   a broad category of risk management techniques – including transfer, retention, and hedging – that is primarily concerned with ensuring the availability of funds in the event of a loss.

Loss portfolio transfer   a finite insurance policy where the cedant transfers unclaimed losses from previous liabilities in the form of an entire portfolio. The cedant pays the insurer a fee, premium and the present value of net reserves to cover existing portfolio liabilities; the insurer assumes responsibility for those losses. The LPT thus transforms uncertain 'lump sum' liabilities into certain liabilities, with a present value that is equal to the net present value of unrealized losses.

Loss reserves   reserve accounts established by insurers and reinsurers that include an estimated amount for claims reported and adjusted but not yet paid, claims reported and filed but not yet adjusted, and claims incurred but not year reported.

Loss sensitive contracts   partial insurance contracts with premiums that depend on loss experience.

Manuscript policy   a customized insurance policy where terms are tailored to a cedant's specific needs.

Moral hazard   a change in behavior arising from the presence of insurance or other forms of risk protection.

Mortgage default securitization   an insurance-linked security that permits mortgage purchasers to obtain default insurance through securities rather than the purchase of a standard insurance policy.

Multi-risk products   insurance policies that combine multiple risks in a single structure, delivering the client a consolidated, and often cheaper and more efficient, risk solution.

Multiline policy   an insurance policy used by companies seeking to cover multiple perils; the standard multiline policy contains common policy declarations and conditions, and specific coverages (with their own declarations, coverage forms and causes of loss forms). If a loss occurs in any of the mentioned perils, the ceding company is covered to a net amount that reflects an overarching deductible and cap.

Multiple peril products   insurance contracts that provide coverage for multiple classes of related or unrelated perils.

Multiple trigger products   insurance contracts that provide coverage only if multiple events occur.

Non-diversifiable risk   risk that is common to all companies and cannot therefore be eliminated; also known as systematic risk.

Operating risk   the risk of loss arising from the daily physical operating activities of a firm.

Options   standardized exchange or customized off-exchange derivative contracts that grant the buyer the right, but not the obligation, to buy or sell an underlying asset at a predetermined strike price.

Over the counter (OTC) derivatives   bespoke derivative contracts that are traded directly between two parties rather than via a formal exchange; popular OTC derivatives including swaps, forwards and options.

Overhedging   an excess of derivative hedge protection that might not be required when broader portfolio exposures with "beneficial" correlations that produce natural offsets are taken into account.

Overinsurance   an excess of insurance protection that might not be required when broader portfolio exposures with "beneficial" correlations that produce natural offsets are taken into account.

Paid loss retrospective policy   a loss sensitive insurance contract where the cedant's incremental premium is due when the insurer makes actual payments (a period that might span several years, suggesting a multi-year risk financing).

Parametric trigger   a trigger on an insurance-linked security where interest and/or principal are suspended when a specific damage metric reaches a certain value.

Partial insurance   an insurance contract providing fractional coverage of risk for a lower risk premium; fractional coverage is achieved through deductibles, exclusions and policy caps.

Peril   a cause of loss.

Policy cap   a maximum payout amount by an insurer to a cedant, or a reinsurer to a ceding insurer, under an insurance/reinsurance contract.

Post-loss financing   financing arranged in response to a loss event (e.g., via cash/reserves, retained earnings, debt or equity).

Post-loss management   a process that ensures a firm operates as a "going concern" in the aftermath of a loss, with stable earnings and minimal possibility of financial distress.

Precipitation derivative   a customized contract (forward, swap, option) that provides protection against, or exposure to, snowfall or rainfall based on the amount of liquid or solid precipitation falling in a given location over a set period of time.

Pre-loss financing   anticipatory financing that is arranged in advance of a loss situation (e.g., via insurance, derivatives, contingent capital).

Pre-loss management   a process that prepares a firm for possible losses in a manner that maximizes corporate value (and which covers legal and contractual obligations).

Premium capacity   the ability for an insurer/reinsurer to write a large volume of policies on the same line of cover.

Premium loading   the amount needed to cover insurance overhead expenses and produce an appropriate profit margin; a component of fair premium.

Probability of ruin   the probability that the distribution of average loss exceeds a solvency benchmark value (e.g., some minimum surplus or tangible net worth amount).

Property per risk excess of loss   a reinsurance agreement providing the primary insurer with cover for any loss in excess of the specified retention on each type of risk.

Proportional agreement   a quota share or surplus share reinsurance arrangement that calls for the insurer and reinsurer to share premiums, exposures, losses and loss adjustment expenses on the basis of a pre-defined formula, such as a fixed or variable percentage of policy limits.

Prospective finite policy   an insurance policy that seeks primarily to shift the timing risk of losses that are expected to occur in the future.

Protected cell company   a captive insurance company similar to a rent-a-captive, but with legal protections designed to provide more robust protection of customer accounts (cells); cells are separated by statute, rather than a shareholders' agreement, meaning commingling of assets is not possible.

Pure captive   a licensed insurer/reinsurer that is wholly owned by a single sponsor and writes insurance cover solely or primarily for that firm; also known as a single parent captive.

Pure catastrophe swap   an OTC transaction that allows insurers/reinsurers to exchange uncorrelated catastrophic exposures.

Pure premium   the amount an insurer needs to charge to cover losses and loss adjustment expenses; a component of fair premium.

Pure risk   risk that only has the prospect of downside, e.g., loss.

Put protected equity   a contingent equity facility where a company buys a put on its own stock from an intermediary; the position generates an economic gain as the value of the stock declines (such as in the aftermath of a large loss).

Quota share   a proportional reinsurance agreement where the insurer and reinsurer agree to split premiums, risk, losses and loss adjustment expenses as a fixed percentage of the policy limit, rather than in specific dollar terms.

Random variable   a variable with an uncertain outcome; it may be discrete (appearing at specified time intervals) or continuous (appearing at any time), and it may be limited to a defined value or carry any value at all.

Rate on line   a measure of gross insurance profitability, calculated as the insurance premium divided by the amount of coverage (or limit).

Reinsurance contract   an insurance contract taken out by an insurer to cover specific risk exposures; the contract may be arranged on a facultative or treaty basis.

Reinsurance pool a group of reinsurers who agree to underwrite risks on a joint basis; under a typical pool each pool member agrees to pay a set percentage of each loss (or a percentage of each loss above some retention level).

Rent-a-captive a form of captive that makes available an account to a firm that wishes to self-insure but does not want to administer its own captive program; a rent-a-captive segregates assets, liabilities and exposures in individual accounts through a shareholder's agreement.

Residual value guarantee a contingent financial guarantee that provides protection against the residual value inherent in leased assets by providing a capital infusion in the event of a shortfall.

Residual value securitization an insurance-linked security that protects an insurer against the residual value risks embedded in a variety of hard asset leases by shifting exposure to the capital markets.

Retrocedant a reinsurer acquiring insurance from (ceding risks to) another insurer.

Retrocession contract an insurance contract taken out by a reinsurer to cover specific risk exposures.

Retrospective aggregate loss cover a finite insurance contract where the cedant finances existing losses and losses incurred but not yet reported through a premium payment equal to the value of reserves, and cedes liabilities to the insurer; however, the cedant must pay for losses above a specified amount when they are incurred, and thus retains some timing risk.

Retrospective finite policy a finite insurance contract that allows the cedant to manage the timing risks of liabilities that already exist and losses that have already occurred. Popular structures include loss portfolio transfers, adverse development cover and retrospective aggregate loss cover; also known as a post-funded policy.

Retrospectively rated policy a loss sensitive insurance contract requiring the cedant to pay an initial premium and, at some future time, make an additional premium payment (i.e., a retrospective premium) or receive a refund (i.e., a retrospective refund), depending on the size of any losses that occur.

Reverse convertible bond a hybrid security that grants the issuer, rather than the investor, the right to convert bonds into shares at a specified strike price.

Risk uncertainty associated with a future outcome or event.

Risk aversion a characteristic of a company that prefers less, rather than more, risk, and is willing to pay a price for protection/mitigation (e.g. through insurance).

Risk capacity risk coverage that allows exposures to be transferred from one party to another.

Risk identification defining all of a firm's actual, perceived or anticipated risks.

Risk management   the core of active risk decision-making, where a firm elects to control, retain, eliminate, or expand its exposures.

Risk management process   a four-stage process centered on identifying, quantifying, managing and monitoring financial and operating risks.

Risk management techniques   the broad group of methods, including loss control, loss financing and risk reduction, that are often used to manage risks.

Risk monitoring   tracking and reporting risks and communicating them internally and externally.

Risk philosophy   a statement that reflects the firm's objectives related to the management of risk.

Risk pooling   a practical implementation of risk diversification, and a fundamental mechanism of the risk management markets, based on the idea that independent (e.g., uncorrelated) risks can be combined to reduce overall risks.

Risk premium   a payment made by a risk averse firm to secure coverage of risk protection.

Risk quantification   a process to determine the financial impact that risk can have on corporate operations.

Risk reduction   risk management techniques that include withdrawal from a business with particular risk characteristics or the diversification of exposures through a pooling or portfolio technique.

Risk retention group   a retention vehicle, conceptually similar to the group captive, where a group assumes and spreads the liability risks of its members via pooling.

Risk transfer   a loss financing technique where one party shifts an exposure to another one, paying a small, certain cost (e.g., a risk premium) in exchange for coverage of uncertain losses.

Schedule rating   an insurance premium rate modified by physical characteristics of cover.

Securitization   the process of removing assets, liabilities or cash flows from the balance sheet and conveying them to third parties through tradable securities.

Senior captive   a form of pure captive that writes a greater amount of third party business and receives greater tax benefits.

Single text method   a process where existing disparate insurance covers are redrafted into a new policy so that all named perils are included under a single agreement.

Sister captive   a vehicle that acts as an extension of the pure captive, writing cover for other companies forming part of the same 'economic family,' i.e., subsidiaries or affiliates of the parent or holding company sponsor.

Soft market   an insurance market cycle where excess supply of risk capacity from the insurance sector leads to lower insurance pricing.

Speculative risk   risk that has the possibility of upside or downside, e.g., gain or loss.

Spread loss   a form of finite reinsurance where the cedant pays a premium into an 'experience account' every year of a multi-year contract period; the experience account generates an agreed rate and is used to pay any losses that occur. If a deficit arises in the account at the end of any year, the cedant covers the shortfall through an additional contribution; if a surplus results, the excess is returned. If the spread loss account is in surplus at the end of the contract tenor, the cedant and reinsurer share profits on a pre-agreed basis.

Stop loss excess of loss   a reinsurance agreement designed to protect overall underwriting results after accounting for other forms of reinsurance by providing indemnification for losses incurred in excess of a specified loss ratio or dollar amount.

Straddle   a call and a put with the same strike and maturity; a long straddle seeks to capitalize on high market volatility, a short straddle on low market volatility.

Strangle   a call and a put with different strikes but the same maturity; a long strangle seeks to capitalize on high market volatility, a short strangle on low market volatility.

Stream flow derivative   a customized derivative contract (forward, swap, option) that provides protection against, or exposure to, natural or regulated water discharge in a channel or surface stream.

Subrogation   transfer of rights of loss recovery from cedant to insurer.

Surplus notes   subordinated securities that function as contingent surplus notes, except that they are issued directly by the company rather than a trust; surplus notes typically have maturities of 10 to 30 years and must be approved by relevant insurance regulators.

Surplus share   a proportional reinsurance arrangement where the reinsurer agrees to accept risk on a variable percentage basis above the insurer's retention limit, up to a defined maximum; the amount the ceding insurer retains is referred to as a 'line' and is expressed in dollar terms.

Swaps   customized off-exchange derivative contracts that enable participants to exchange periodic flows based on an underlying reference.

Switching trigger   a trigger in an insurance contract that varies based on how individual risk exposures in the cedant's portfolio are performing, i.e., if one part of the firm is doing well it can bear more risk on one trigger, and vice-versa.

Synthetic cat bond   an option on a cat bond that permits, but does not obligate, the bond issuer to launch a specific bond transaction when, and if, needed.

Synthetic collateralized debt obligation   a CDO based on assets that an investment portfolio manager purchases and actively manages in order to achieve desired results. Funded synthetic CDOs involve the actual purchase of assets in the portfolio through proceeds raised from note issuance, while unfunded synthetic CDOs involve the use of credit derivatives, including total return swaps, basket options or basket swaps.

Temperature derivative   a customized derivative contract (forward, swap, option) referencing one of a number of temperature indexes (such as cumulative average temperatures, heating degree days, cooling degree days).

Temperature-linked bond   an insurance-linked security with principal/interest redemption that is contingent on the level of cumulative temperatures in a particular city, group of cities, or region.

Total return swaps   over-the-counter derivatives that synthetically replicate the timing and magnitude of an underlying cash flow position (e.g., a credit-risky bond).

Trade credit securitization   an insurance-linked security that provides for the transfer of trade credit insurance to the securities markets.

Treaty reinsurance   a reinsurance contract where risks are automatically ceded and accepted; the primary insurer agrees, *ex-ante*, to cede a portion of all risks conforming to pre-agreed guidelines, which the reinsurer is bound to accept.

Triple trigger   an insurance contract that requires the onset of three events before payout occurs.

Underinvestment   a phenomenon where capital is directed towards projects with lower returns and risks in order to benefit creditors rather than equity investors.

Unearned premium reserve   liabilities representing the unearned portion of premiums on insurance policies that remain outstanding.

Valued contract   an insurance contract that provides the cedant with a stated payout amount (agreed *ex-ante*) in the event of a loss.

Variable trigger   a trigger in an insurance contract where the value of the payout is determined by the level of the trigger in relation to some defined event or value.

Variance   a common measure of risk, which indicates the magnitude by which an outcome will differ from the expected value. This is given as $Var = Probability \times (Outcome - Expected\ value)^2$; risk may also measured as the standard deviation, or the square root of the variance.

Vertical layering   a process where several reinsurers, participating in an excess of loss reinsurance agreement, each take a preferred layer of exposure.

Volumetric risk   risk of loss from volume imbalances, due either to pure demand forces or a supply constraint.

Wind derivative   a customized derivative contract (forward, swap, option) that provides an economic payoff if a wind speed index is above or below some pre-defined level.

Selected References

SELECTED BOOKS AND ARTICLE

Auer, M. and Berke, J. (2000) Risk management: Insuring the deal. *DailyDeal.com*.

Banham, R. (1994) Shopping the market for finite risk products. *Risk Management*, September, pp. 34–43.

Banks, E. (2004) *The Credit Risk of Complex Derivatives* (3rd edn). London: Palgrave Macmillan.

Banks, E. (2003) *Exchange-Traded Derivatives*. Chichester: John Wiley & Sons.

Banks, E. (2002) *The Simple Rules of Risk*. Chichester: John Wiley & Sons.

Banks, E. (Ed.) (2001) *Weather Risk Management*. London: Palgrave.

Banks, E. and Dunn, R. (2003) *Practical Risk Management*. Chichester: John Wiley & Sons.

Brealey, M. and Myers, S. (1981) *Principles of Corporate Finance*. New York: McGraw-Hill.

Buck, G. and Riches, P. (1999) *Risk Management: New Challenges and Solutions*. London: Reuters.

Carter, R., Lucas, L. and Ralph, N. (2000) *Reinsurance* (4th edn). London: Reactions.

Culp, C. (2001) *The ART of Risk Management*. New York: John Wiley & Sons.

Cummins, J.D., Harrington, S. and Klein, R. (1991) Cycles and crises in property/casualty insurance. *Journal of Insurance Regulation*, **10**, 50–93.

Das, S. (2000) *Credit Derivatives and Credit Linked Notes* (2nd edn). New York: John Wiley & Sons.

Doherty, N. (1985) *Corporate Risk Management: A Financial Exposition*. New York: McGraw-Hill.

Doherty, N. (1997) *Financial innovation in the management of catastrophe risk*. University of Pennsylvania Working Paper.

Doherty, N. (2000) *Integrated Risk Management*. New York: McGraw-Hill.

Economist Intelligence Unit (2001) *Enterprise Risk Management: Implementing New Solutions*. Washington, DC: EIU.

Flitner, A. and Trupin, J. (2001) *Commercial Liability Insurance and Risk Management* (4th edn). Malvern, PA: American Institute for CPCU.

Froot, K. (1999) *The Financing of Catastrophic Risk*. Chicago: University of Chicago Press.

Froot, K., Scharfstein, D. and Stein, J. (1994) Risk management: Coordinating investment and financing policies. *Journal of Finance*, **48**(5).

Hameed, O. (2000) ART: A legal view. *Global Reinsurance*, pp. 70–72.

Harrington, S. and Niehaus, G. (1999) *Risk Management and Insurance*. Boston: Irwin McGraw-Hill.

Hartwig, R. (2002) *The Long Shadow of September 11: Terrorism and its Impacts on Insurance and Reinsurance Markets*. New York: Insurance Information Institute.

Hoffmann, W. (1998) *Multiline Multiyear Agreements*. Zurich: Swiss Re.

Kiln, R. (1991) *Reinsurance in Practice*. London: Witherby & Co.

Kloman, M. and Rosenbaum, D. (1982) The captive insurance phenomenon: A cautionary tale. *Geneva Papers in Risk and Insurance*, **7**, 129–151.

KPMG (2001) ERM advice for pioneers. *Risk Management*, p. 64.

Lane, M. and Beckwith, R. (2001) Current trends in risk-linked securitizations. *Risk Management*, August, pp. 17–28.

Matten, C. (2000) *Managing Bank Capital* (2nd edn). Chichester: John Wiley & Sons.

Mayers, D. and Smith, C. (1982) On the corporate demand for insurance. *Journal of Business*, **22**, 281–296.

McDonald, R. (2003) *Derivatives Markets*. Boston: Addison Wesley.

Mehr, R. and Cammack, E. (1980) *Principles of Insurance* (7th edn). Homewood, Illinois: Irwin.

Monti, R. and Barile, A. (1995) *A Practical Guide to Finite Risk Insurance and Reinsurance*. New York: John Wiley & Sons.

Muller, A. (1999) Integrated risk management. Munich Re Working Paper, Munich.

Outreville, J.F. (1998) *Theory and Practice of Insurance*. Boston: Kluwer.

Phifer, R. (1996) *Reinsurance Fundamentals: Treaty and Facultative*. New York: John Wiley & Sons.

Pincott, A. (2001) *Transferring Risk: Insurance and its Alternatives*. London: Elborne Mitchell Publication.

Rejda, G. (2003) *Principles of Risk Management and Insurance* (8th edn). Boston: Addison Wesley.

Rosenbloom, J.S. (1972) *A Case Study in Risk Management*. New York: Meredith Corp.

Schon, E., Bochicchio, V. and Wolfram, E. (1998) *Integrated Risk Management Solutions*. Zurich: Swiss Re.

Shimpi, P. (2001) *Integrating Corporate Risk Management*. New York: Texere.

Shimpi, P. (2001) The insurative model. *Risk Management*, August, pp. 10–15.

Smithson, C. (1999) *Managing Financial Risk* (3rd edn). Boston: Irwin McGraw-Hill.

Sullivan, L. (2001) Building a risk management program from the ground up. *Risk Management*, pp. 25–29.

Swiss Re (1999) *ART For Corporations: A Passing Fashion or Risk Management for the 21st Century?* Zurich: Swiss Re Sigma Research.

Swiss Re (2003) *The Picture of ART*. Zurich: Swiss Re Sigma Research.

Tavakoli, J. (1998) *Credit Derivatives*, New York: John Wiley.

Tillinghast-Towers Perrin (2000) *ERM in the Insurance Industry 2000 Survey*, New York: Tillinghast.

Tillinghast-Towers Perrin (2001) *The September 11 Terrorist Attack: Analysis of the Impact on The Insurance Industry*. New York: Tillinghast.

Vaughan, E. and Vaughan, T. (2002) *Essentials of Risk Management and Insurance,* (2nd edn), New York: John Wiley & Sons.

Vaughan, E. and Vaughan. T. (2003) *Fundamentals of Risk and Insurance* (9th edn). New York: John Wiley & Sons.

Weinberg, E. (2002) *Foundations of Risk Management and Insurance*. Malvern, PA: American Institute for CPCU.

SELECTED INTERNET RESOURCES

Alternative Risk Transfer Portal: www.artemis.bm
American Insurance Association: www.aiadc.org
American Risk and Insurance Association: www.aria.org
Captive Insurance Companies Association: www.captive.com
Insurance Information Institute: www.iii.org
Insurance Services Office: www.iso.org
Risk and Insurance Management Society: www.rims.org

Index